Bridging Paradigms

BRIDGING PARADIGMS

Positive Development in
Adulthood and
Cognitive Aging

EDITED BY
Jan D. Sinnott
and
John C. Cavanaugh

New York
Westport, Connecticut
London

Library of Congress Cataloging-in-Publication Data

Bridging paradigms : positive development in adulthood and cognitive
   aging / edited by Jan D. Sinnott and John C. Cavanaugh.
      p. cm.
    Includes bibliographical references and indexes.
    ISBN 0–275–93617–1 (alk. paper)
     1. Adulthood—Psychological aspects. 2. Cognition—Age factors.
   3. Aging—Psychological aspects. 4. Adulthood—Social aspects.
   5. Aging—Social aspects. I. Sinnott, Jan D. II. Cavanaugh, John
   C.
   BF724.55.C63B75   1991
   155.6—dc20   90–49073

British Library Cataloguing in Publication Data is available.

Library of Congress Catalog Card Number: 90–49073
ISBN: 0–275–93617–1

First published in 1991

Praeger Publishers, One Madison Avenue, New York, NY 10010
An imprint of Greenwood Publishing Group, Inc.

Printed in the United States of America

The paper used in this book complies with the
Permanent Paper Standard issued by the National
Information Standards Organization (Z39.48–1984).

10 9 8 7 6 5 4 3 2 1

Contents

Bridging Paradigms

1

On Building Bridges, Developing Positively, and Postformal Thinking Coming of Age: Confessions of a Nonconformist

JOHN C. CAVANAUGH

The successful publication of any book depends largely on its timing. Authors who accurately anticipate what topics will be hot, which methods will be in, and what new statistical alchemy will spin the best gold from straw data will carry the day. This volume is no exception. We hope we are on the crest of the wave in the study of adult development. We trust that our topics will light fires in the reader, that the novel methods reported here will create a whole new way of asking questions, and that the gold thus produced will have come not so much from computer wizardry as from good old-fashioned thought from both sides of the brain.

Accomplishing these goals would make most authors happy, but not us. This would be as fulfilling for us as discovering a bunch of dead bugs. If all we do is get people to read these chapters as if they were reading any empirical study or literature review, then we will have failed. As is apparent from the title, we wish to focus on the work of a different group of researchers and theorists—paradigm bridgers—who find missing links, want to shake others' beliefs and challenge their thinking, and go where no one has gone before. Paradigm bridgers are people who take Ralph Waldo Emerson's dictum in *Self-Reliance* to heart: "Whoso would be a man [or woman] must be a nonconformist." All the chapters in this book are written by nonconformists who challenge the status quo, who seek to push back the envelope, who believe that adult development is a very complex and dynamic process. Thus, our criterion for the success of this book is the degree to which the chapters provoke strong emotional reactions (positive or negative), question the most deeply held assumptions about people and research, and kindle the desire to extend or refute what is said. If we manage to accomplish these goals, then we will have a successful publication.

It is only fitting, then, to present some of these challenges in this introductory chapter. Because the avowed intent of this volume on bridging patterns is to examine positive development across adulthood, with particular emphasis on what has come to be called postformal thought, I will address four questions: What do we mean by bridging paradigms? What do we mean by positive development? What do we know (or think we know) about postformal thought? What do we not know (but really should know) about postformal thought? Following these explorations, I will briefly describe the rest of the book.

BRIDGING PARADIGMS OR BRIDGING *PARADIGMS?*

As one who has made a career of trying to make connections among what appear to be disparate fields (such as cognitive aging and sexual abuse; see Cavanaugh & Morton, 1989), I am constantly vexed by the foggy concept of integration or bridging. Exactly what it means to bridge or to be a bridge person has never been clear to me, nor have these issues been discussed clearly in the literature on adult development. I think my confusion is based on the fact that one can read "bridging paradigms" in two different ways: *bridging* paradigms, or bridging *paradigms*. Taking the first reading, one may ask some additional questions: Does bridging occur anytime one points out commonalities between two research literatures or theories? or does it mean that one has to go farther than that and integrate and blend (whatever that means) two different areas in order to create new ideas? or does it mean that one not only has to integrate, but also to put into practice, this integration? Taking the second reading, one may ask related questions: What do we mean by paradigms? Are we referring only to Kuhnian scientific paradigms, or are we taking a more restricted view and focusing on particular sets of research methods? If we mean Kuhnian paradigms, then how do we go about *bridging* disparate paradigms that may be mutually exclusive (in a strict Pepperian sense)? If we mean research methods, or perhaps even worldviews in a looser sense (see Cavanaugh, in press), then are we not back to the first reading (i.e., the emphasis is placed back on how the bridging occurs)?

The point of these queries is not to run around in strange loops. Rather, it is to point out that considerable space in the literature on adult development has been devoted to arguing about paradigms (e.g., laboratory versus real-world; mechanism versus organicism versus contextualism) and about how such arguments should be settled. What has *not* occurred is questioning whether, in a strict Kuhnian sense, we have a paradigm about which to argue. I think we do not. At best, what the literature on adult cognitive development contains is pockets of method-confounded-with-world view quasi-paradigms, which have been reified as if they were the real thing. I do not believe we have the kind of consensus in our field that Kuhn (1970) required for a paradigm. To be sure, a majority of researchers ascribe to a Piagetian model, and many of these also adopt a quasi-structuralist metatheory. However, there is insufficient agreement even within this group to qualify for a true paradigm.

I believe the pockets of consensus that we have reflect paradigms in a methodological sense. It is fair to say that the majority of researchers in postformal thought implicitly assume a Piagetian approach, and adopt methods aimed at uncovering evidence of qualitative change. Unfortunately, this often results in serious problems because Piaget's own assumption (and *his* particular worldview) are not explicitly adopted. Their zeal to show qualitative change across adulthood has blinded many investigators to the inherent contradictions between their method and their metatheory (madness?). A second group of people, those primarily approaching molar cognitive development from an experimental psychology background, implicitly adopt a Newtonian predict-and-control model grounded in mechanism. This group argues that such an approach is the only legitimate way to operationalize the science of psychology (see, for example, Kimble, 1990), and represents the only way to discover Truth (general laws). The problem, of course, is that Newtonian models are extremely limited in their applicability, as has been realized in other sciences since the end of the nineteenth century. Finally, a growing group of people desire to have it all; they argue that everything is interconnected, and should be studied that way. Viewed as radical in some circles, this contextualist perspective has much in common with the worldviews underlying the mythologies of so-called primitive societies (e.g., Campbell, 1948) and with creation spirituality (e.g., Fox, 1988). With such a dubious lineage (from a Newtonian or organismic perspective), it is not surprising that contextualism is viewed by some (e.g., Kramer, 1987) as not lending itself to traditional notions of scientific rigor.

Given the lack of a true Kuhnian paradigm, and the existence of several loosely defined groups instead, I will approach the issue of what it means to bridge paradigms from this latter perspective, and will therefore address the following question: What should bridging paradigms mean that it does not mean now?

GETTING DOWN TO BASICS: THERE'S MORE THAN MEETS THE EYE

Given three loose coalitions, each with its own party line, how do we go about building bridges? We can bridge only after giving serious thought to what *underlies* these party lines—only after serious consideration is given to four questions: *What* do we want to know? *How* should we find it? *Where* should we look? *Why* do we want to know, need to use this approach, look in this place, and so forth? Because these questions strike at the heart of any scientific inquiry, they are not unique to the study of adults' cognitive development. Because they are generally applicable, we typically ignore them in this context. Thorough answers to all these questions are well beyond the scope of this chapter; hence, in this section I will address the *how* or method question as an example. Aspects of the others will be addressed later.

Consider the following scenario:

Dr. Org Anismic is a strong believer in Piagetian theory and in the notion that qualitative change continues across adulthood. Dr. Anismic believes that there may be several levels of thinking that develop during adulthood, and decides to show that this development is age-related. Furthermore, Dr. Anismic believes that the amount of formal education a person has strongly influences the developmental process. To test these ideas, Dr. Anismic sets up the following study. First, a scale is developed asking people to rate their degree of agreement with different statements that supposedly reflect the different modes of thinking. Then, two groups of people (those with lots of formal education and those with little) at each of three age periods (young adulthood, middle age, and old age) are given the scale. Scores reflecting each of the styles of thinking are compared across age and education.

I believe this scenario is fairly typical of research on adults' cognitive development, at least in the postformal literature. Typically, such studies reveal different patterns of age differences in the various styles of thinking, and sometimes reveal interesting patterns of differences on the adjunct independent variable (e.g., formal education). Many people would consider a carefully executed study like this to be a good example of bridging the gap between the Piagetian tradition (read organicism) and experimental psychology. However, there is something fundamentally wrong with this picture. What it really represents is the way *not* to bridge paradigms. Why is this so?

The problem lies in not fully appreciating what particular methods assume. In the factorial design just described, it is assumed that formal education is an isolable influence on the development of thought. However, is this a reasonable assumption for an organicist? Moreover, the design also assumes that what is most important are differences in group means. Is this what truly interests an organicist the most? Finally, the use of rating scales implies that what is most important is the *outcome* of thinking, not the process of thinking. Is this what an organicist wants to know?

My point is that bridging methodological paradigms does not mean the wholesale (mis)appropriation of specific research designs from other perspectives. In the present case, I would argue that the design described is inappropriate if Dr. Anismic is interested in cognitive development from a true organismic perspective. However, if the question of interest is posed in a different way, such as mechanistically, then the approach would indeed be the one of choice. True paradigm bridging occurs at the level of concepts, not at the level of concepts-in-action. That is, the concept of science as the careful systematic observation of phenomena, a concept strongly espoused by experimental psychologists, *can* and *should* be incorporated into research irrespective of one's party affiliation. However, the translation of *systematic observation* into the action of tightly controlled factorial designs with a random assignment of participants does not lend itself to bridging. It is paradigm-bound and inappropriate for general application.

Having said this, I admit that the world is not an ideal place. Breaking the chains that bind us (i.e., the dictum that controlled experimentation is the sine qua non of science) is extremely difficult. Psychology as a discipline largely rejects Einsteinian science. Nonetheless, it is not impossible. A quick survey of the chapters in this book (especially Armstrong, Irwin, Johnson, Meacham, and Sinnott) reveals that progress toward liberation is being made. Methodological (or, forgive me, metamethodological) paradigm bridging in this tradition *is* possible, overdue, and sorely needed.

At the beginning of this section, I posed two interpretive readings of the phrase *bridging paradigms*, along with several questions with each. For now, the important issue is in the *how* of bridging. As I have tried to argue, bridging (methodological) paradigms is no easy matter. It clearly goes beyond the mere juxtaposition of ideas, but it is more complicated than simple integration. The secret lies in knowing at what level the integration needs to occur. Knowing that, the transition to action—the actual building of a rude bridge to arch the flood—becomes easy.

POSITIVE DEVELOPMENT, BUT ACCORDING TO WHOM?

The issue of what constitutes positive development is simultaneously trivial and intractable. It is trivial in the sense that everyone would agree that positive development in adulthood is *not* Alzheimer's disease, stroke, crippling arthritis, and the like. Although Elias, Elias, and Elias remind us in their chapter that we need to consider age-related psychological changes in the study of aging, they, or anyone else, never suggest that such conditions are normative. Thus, it is fair to say that we have a broad consensus on the extreme examples of what does not constitute positive development.

Beyond that, the going gets extremely rough. There is little consensus as to what positive development *is*. Does it mean finding pockets of evidence indicating either no age differences between young and old or perhaps even the superiority of the elderly? One certainly gets this impression from the postformal and discourse processing literatures, both of which have been quite vocal in pointing out that older adults "hold their own" with younger adults. Rankin and Allen, Sebby and Papini, and Wingfield and Stine adopt variants of this stance in their research on postformal thought and language processing. One can fault adherents of this approach for being guilty of deficit hunting in reverse; whereas previous researchers may have been biased to look for age-related decrements, these researchers may be biased to look for age-related compensatory processes and increased expertise. Pleading guilty to such charges is no crime. Indeed, such research is essential if scientists are to undo the damage that has resulted from the stereotypes produced by deficit hunting. The situation in the research on adults' cognitive development is parallel to research during the 1960s and 1970s on cognitive development in mentally retarded or developmentally disabled individuals. The work aimed at documenting competence flowing from the pioneering efforts of Jensen and Rohwer (1963) and others resulted in a complete reconceptualization not only of education and institutionalization policies, but of the mentally retarded and developmentally disabled people themselves. Researchers looking for competencies in older adults need to be applauded, and the rest of us need to work for a continued rethinking of what older adults are really capable of doing.

This brings us to the nearly intractable aspect of positive development. The danger in competency-based research is that optimal (cf. Fozard & Popkin, 1978) or positive development becomes defined from the *researcher's* perspective rather than from the *individual's* perspective. Memory research is a good example of this. Considerable effort has been exerted by some (e.g., Yesavage, 1983) to provide training in mnemonic systems (e.g., imagery) as a "treatment" for normative secondary memory decrements. Doing this implies several things: (a) Older adults have a problem that needs to be cured, (b) researchers doing memory training know the most appropriate cure, and (c) the same cure should be used for everyone. The problem is that all these assumptions are probably bad: (a) There is evidence (e.g., Cavanaugh & Morton, 1988; Cutler & Grams, 1988) that many older adults are not always bothered by secondary memory decrements; (b) research (e.g., Cavanaugh, Grady, & Perlmutter, 1983; Harris, 1980; West, 1984) indicates that most adults of all ages and many prominent international memory researchers (Park, Smith, & Cavanaugh, 1990) prefer external memory aids to classical mnemonics; and (c) careful inspection of all training research reveals enormous individual differences.

What we need to do is to keep the focus on the individuals in our research. What constitutes optimal or positive development needs to be defined from their perspective, not ours. Although not explicitly stated, all the authors in this book have adopted this perspective implicitly. After all, if a person is aware of some loss of functioning, and that loss is not significantly interfering with his or her daily life and he or she does not view it as a problem, why should we?

THE COMING OF AGE OF POSTFORMAL THOUGHT

As pointed out earlier, the timing of books is everything. Perhaps this is why I note that individuals born during the genesis of Perry's (1970) research on postformal thought in the mid-1960s are entering the period when we would expect them to begin acquiring postformal thought. What can we tell them to expect?

Certainly, we know that *something* is going on across adulthood, and that this something appears to take different forms. This developmental process appears to move from the recognition of situationally defined alternatives to the recognition of inherent contradictions and the need to make committed choices. We know that this movement is not universal across either content domains or people, and that such thinking is more likely to occur in social-cognitive domains than in other realms. In short, we have a substantial body of descriptive evidence about the styles of thinking used by some people under some conditions during their trek across adulthood.

What we cannot tell the cohort coming of age with a high degree of certainty is the following (see also Cavanaugh & Stafford, 1989): whether the styles reflect true qualitative changes (irrespective of whether that really matters); how these styles develop; whether there are necessary precursors (e.g., formal operations); why there is content-specificity; whether there is any relationship with physiological or neurological development; whether adults can deliberately control postformal thought; how postformal thought develops in different cultures; what key developmental experiences, if any, are needed for postformal thought to develop; and what postformal thought means in a practical sense.

Fortunately, these are the foci of the research and theory developed throughout this book. The authors reflect a diversity of backgrounds, assumptions, disciplines, and methods. Postformal thought and its correlates are described from physiological, psychological, sociological, anthropological, and clinical perspectives. Unlike other books, which group chapters together around themes, this volume makes no assumption about how this grouping should (or could) be done. Because the chapters largely defy clean categorization due to their interdisciplinary nature and our commitment to the sacredness of individuals' rights to their own relativistic and dialectical thoughts, we chose to sequence the chapters alphabetically.

Armstrong's opening chapter provides an intriguing look at the role of postformal thought in understanding and dealing clinically with multiple personality disorder. She argues convincingly that effective therapists are those who are able to use their postformal abilities to assist clients in dealing with the many aspects of themselves. Brannan and Camp review the major age-related changes in visual processing and place special emphasis on the distinction between transient and sustained channels. They speculate that the different types of information processed by the two channels may be implicated in differences in thinking style across adulthood. Elias, Elias, and Elias provide a thought-provoking discussion on the distinction between normal aging and disease. They call for a reconsideration of cognitive developmental research such that poor health or disease states, as well as known universal physiological changes, will be included as component factors in an index of cognitive vulnerability. This approach would provide considerable insight into what constitutes normal cognitive aging, as well as providing a better understanding of the role of disease in that process. Irwin calls for the explicit incorporation of affectively mediated social experiences in models of adult cognitive development. He draws attention to several aspects of current theories based on Piagetian models that are inadequate, and advocates the inclusion of ideas from Vygotsky, the sociology of knowledge, and affective information-processing models. Johnson describes a cross-cultural study conducted in Honduras that incorporated postformal thought in a development project involving cooperative groups. Her research indicates that when a teacher-facilitator uses postformal thought, the learning process is facilitated and long-term changes in participants' behavior are more likely to occur. Lee also describes a study of postformal thought in the context of teaching. She used Sinnott's framework to analyze a professor's problem solving while conducting a graduate class in education. The use of postformal thought is quite evident, and Lee makes the point that this may be what separates the truly excellent instructors from the average. Meacham's two contributions both involve interpersonal relations. In the first, he outlines the reasons why postformal thought is inherently interpersonal; this social-mind perspective provides a better explanation of adult cognitive development. In the second chapter, Meacham describes how conflict and cooperation are two operationalizations of the social-mind perspective. He argues that there is a difference between true and false cooperation, and that discourse is the way to express true interests.

Puckett, Reese, Cohen, and Pollina review everyday or practical cognition in the broader context of cognitive aging. After discussing several alternative theories and research outcomes, they argue that the distinction between everyday and academic cognition cannot be supported at this time. Rankin and Allen report results from an investigation of the relationships among postformal thought, stereotyping, and attributions. They found complex linkages; older adults were somewhat more inclined to process information in line with their expectancies, but this was moderated by cognitive developmental level. In a related study, Sebby and Papini investigated the connection between postformal thought and problem relevancy. Their results indicate that to the degree people perceive problems as more relevant, they are more likely to engage in postformal thinking. In two chapters, Sinnott presents evidence from laboratory and clinical settings that support her model of adult cognition. In her laboratory efforts, she manipulated several key variables and demonstrated how each mediates or moderates cognitive performance. Her chapter on a family in crisis provides clear clinical support not only for her own model, but for Meacham's social-mind approach as well. It is clear that inter-family communication would be greatly improved through the use of postformal thought. Tanon provides another fascinating glimpse of postformal thought in a cross-cultural setting. Her work, conducted with weavers in the Ivory Coast, demonstrates that the relationship between formal schooling and cognitive performance may be task-specific. Wingfield and Stine's concluding chapter describes how adults process spoken language. They show how reduced richness from sensory, bottom-up processing can be supplemented by top-down processes derived from the linguistic context. Such compensatory processes have important implications for understanding why age-related differences are observed in some verbal tasks and not in others.

The mix of topics, perspectives, and methods in this book is exactly what the field needs. Healthy debate and good-spirited conflict (among the present authors and with the reader) will produce just enough turbulence to push us further in our understanding of adults' cognitive development. This nonconformist book (where else would you find this particular mix of authors?), written by nonconformist researchers and theorists asking nonconformist questions, sets the stage for discovering the kinds of things we would like to tell the cohort that is coming of age. The field is maturing and acquiring its own brand of postformal thought (and the tolerance for ambiguity it brings). You may not agree with everything the present authors say, but that is not our goal. We just want you to think, react, go forth, and do.

REFERENCES

Campbell, J. (1948). *The hero with a thousand faces*. New York: Pantheon.

Cavanaugh, J. C. (in press). On the concept of development: Contextualism, relative time, and the role of dialectics. In P. van Geert & L. Mohs (Eds.), *Annals of theoretical psychology: Vol. 6. Developmental psychology*. New York: Plenum.

Cavanaugh, J. C., Grady, J., & Perlmutter, M. (1983). Forgetting and use of memory aids in 20- and 70-year olds' everyday life. *International Journal of Aging and Human Development, 17*, 113–122.

Cavanaugh, J. C., & Morton, K. R. (1988). Older adults' attributions about everyday memory. In M. M. Gruneberg & P. Morris (Eds.), *Practical aspects of memory: Current research and issues* (Vol. 1, pp. 209–214). Chichester, Engl.: Wiley.

Cavanaugh, J. C., & Morton, K. R. (1989). Contextualism, naturalistic inquiry, and the need for new science: A rethinking of childhood sexual abuse and everyday memory aging. In D. A. Kramer & M. Bopp (Eds.), *Transformation in clinical and developmental psychology* (pp. 89–114). New York: Springer-Verlag.

Cavanaugh, J. C., & Stafford, H. (1989). Being aware of issues and biases: Directions for research on post-formal thought. In M. L. Commons, J. D. Sinnott, F. A. Richards, & C. Armon (Eds.), *Adult development: Vol. 1. Comparisons and applications of adolescent and adult developmental models* (pp. 272–292). New York: Praeger.

Cutler, S. J., & Grams, A. E. (1988). Correlates of self-reported everyday memory problems. *Journals of Gerontology: Social Sciences, 43*, S82–90.

Fox, M. (1988). *The coming of the cosmic Christ*. New York: Harper & Row.

Fozard, J. L., & Popkin, S. J. (1978). Optimizing adult development: Ends and means of an applied psychology of aging. *American Psychologist, 33*, 975–989.

Harris, J. E. (1980). Memory aids people use: Two interview studies. *Memory and Cognition, 8*, 31–38.

Jensen, A. R., & Rohwer, W. D., Jr. (1983). The effect of verbal mediation on the learning and retention of paired associates by retarded adults. *American Journal of Mental Deficiency, 68*, 80–84.

Kimble, G. A. (1990). A search for principles in *Principles of Psychology*. *Psychological Science, 1*, 151–156.

Kramer, D. A. (1987, May). *Toward an organismic conception of the lifespan*. Paper presented at the annual meeting of the Jean Piaget Society, Philadelphia.

Kuhn, T. S. (1970). *The structure of scientific revolutions* (2nd ed). Chicago: University of Chicago Press.

Park, D. C., Smith, A. D., & Cavanaugh, J. C. (1990). The memories of memory researchers. *Memory and Cognition, 18*, 321–327.

Perry, W. I. (1970). *Forms of intellectual and ethical development in the college years*.
    New York: Holt, Rinehart & Winston.
West, R. L. (1984, August). *An analysis of prospective everyday memory*. Paper presented
    at the annual meeting of the American Psychological Association, Toronto.
Yesavage, J. A. (1983). Imagery pretraining and memory training in the elderly. *Ger-
    ontology, 29*, 271–275.

2

Keeping One's Balance in a Moving System: The Effects of the Multiple Personality Disordered Patient on the Cognitive Development of the Therapist

JUDITH ARMSTRONG

This chapter is written from the perspective of a practicing clinician who is using developmental theory to inform her work. Much of the education of psychotherapists concerns itself with developing a certain comfort in traversing disparate levels of thinking—the unconscious, affective dimension must somehow consciously connect with the concrete method, which in turn must be informed by the theory that gives meaning and direction to the therapeutic procedure. With one foot in the phenomenological world of the patient and the other in one's own cognitive realm, it is easy to lose equilibrium. But there are moments when we balance on these varied points of concentration. Then we can smoothly shift among paradigms without losing our grasp on meaning at a variety of levels.

It is the general thesis of this chapter that therapists cannot effectively bridge and coordinate multiple cognitive levels within themselves and within the patient unless they can think postformally. The cognitive tasks of therapy illustrate many of the basic characteristics of postformal thought: an ability to coordinate multiple, emotion-laden viewpoints (Sinnott, ch. 14, this volume) and an open-ended, relativistic vantage point, which enables one to shift priorities and beliefs (Commons, Richards, & Armon, 1984) and to link the pragmatic with the theoretical through recognition of the influence of the whole on its parts and the parts on the whole (Basseches, 1984). In addition, in my discussion of the necessity of postformal reasoning for psychotherapists, I am connecting the fields of cognitive development and clinical practice. It is hoped that this chapter will also stimulate some new ways of bridging these two paradigms in psychology.

There is no client who requires us to leap with ease between cognitive levels more than the multiple personality disordered (MPD) patient and therefore, none who better illustrates the importance of postformal thinking to treatment. I will not give a detailed description of the present clinical understanding of MPD here. This disorder has been of interest to cognitive theorists for some time as a paradigm of dissociation (Fischer & Elmendorf, 1986). In brief, the prevailing view is that MPD is a complex and creative response to severe, lifetime abuse (Putnam, 1985). It is neither implausible nor fascinating, but simply an ingenious method of bearing the unbearable by breaking up one's field of concentration. The divided states of consciousness that arise from long-term pain and overstimulation become reinforced over time by the defensive need to keep the full knowledge of trauma out of awareness (Horowitz, 1986; Spiegel, 1986). Traumas are parceled out among self-states in small, manageable packets—a feeling here, a thought there, a piece of a situation elsewhere. This compartmentalization allows the individual to retain a degree of developmental flexibility (Braun & Sachs, 1985; Ludwig, 1983). While certain self-elements incorporate painful memories or perform dangerous, humiliating, or avoidant activities necessary for survival in a murderous environment, other self-elements are relatively free of these burdens, and can play, contemplate, and otherwise learn about the world.

Since communication between self-aspects is disrupted, the individual with MPD feels as if she consists of discrete personalities (heretofore termed *alters*). Nonetheless, a number of major symptoms make it clear that an organizing self-system is not absent, but rather develops in an unusual form. Overlap and interference among alters is common (Putnam, 1989). Phenomena such as having one's speech, feelings, thoughts, and movements controlled, prevented, replaced, and facilitated; or hearing various internal voices offering advice, suggestion, and criticism; or suddenly losing or retrieving memories and abilities, give us a picture of a buzzing, bustling internal congestion that is not completely locked into dissociative compartments. Moreover, the sophistication with which MPD patients switch and combine alters in order to handle external demands (they are masters of controlling one's attention and of doing many things at once) also suggests the presence of an organizing method to this particular form of madness. Their belief is in independent selves, and ours is in a unitary self-system. It is absolutely essential that the therapist be able to think in both cognitive realms.

Unless we understand the alters' concrete frames of reference, we cannot begin to work with them. For example, the externally slit wrists that occur because one alter is trying to internally murder another cannot be dealt with by formal operational discussions! Perhaps the therapist will decide that everyone needs to voice a contract not to harm the body. Perhaps an uncontrollably aggressive alter must be placed in an internal prison by the others, or go to sleep, or find a safe place in the mind in which to hide. In any case, the type of thinking involved in such creative problem solving requires an empathetic comfort with playing with the extravagantly preoperational and concrete operational qualities of the MPD world.

However, unless we concurrently understand MPD as an interactive system, we are at risk of destroying an adaptive construction without providing a useful replacement. We can lift the barriers to internal communication by hypnosis in order to retrieve encapsulated memories. We then flood the patient with a past she has well understood to be excruciating (Loewenstein, 1988). If, on the other hand, we understand how the MPD system works in its variety of levels, we can use the organization to support orderly change (Kluft, 1985). For example, communication among alters on mundane matters can build skills to deal with affectively loaded issues. If a patient knows how to ideationally leave her body and fly to the ceiling when danger comes, she can learn to harness this ability to view traumatic memories from a safe distance.

Maintaining an equality of concentration among such conceptual levels is not an easy task. In this brief chapter I would like to explore with you some of the developmental challenges that therapists face as they attempt to share the complex and divergent mental space of their MPD patients. If our level of cognitive functioning is greatly influenced by interpersonal context (Meacham, ch. 9, this volume; Rankin & Allen, this volume), then how much more powerful the effect when we are dealing with multiple levels, all within the context of the over-powering affect of remembered trauma. No wonder we often forget how to think!

The data that underlie my ideas about complex cognitive functioning in MPD come from the more than 50 such patients I have assessed as part of a research project on MPD at the Sheppard Pratt Hospital (Armstrong & Loewenstein, 1990). Because I invite the patients' full self-system to enter into the assessment process, I have been able to observe the multi-leveled quality of their cognitive experience. Two examples from the WAIS-R IQ vocabulary subtest will illustrate the variety of MPD thinking (as well as the pitfalls that await anyone attempting to score such test protocols). In the first illustration, one sees the complete encapsulation of verbal from sensorimotor levels. An MPD patient is asked to define the word "perimeter." She asserts that she has never heard of it. During this denial her right hand moves to the side and reaches out to me, and a finger repetitively inscribes a circle in the air. When I ask the patient to look at that finger, her forward glance remains locked in place. Another patient shows a leakage of abstraction into her remarkably concrete verbal expression. When asked to define the word "ponder," she replies: "A small piece of water, a pond . . . er . . . to think . . . now where'd *that* come from . . . well, *I* still think it's a bunch of water!" A third patient manages to connect with a variety of modes of knowing. When asked to define the word "compassion," she elo-quently describes the sense of having empathy for the suffering of another person. As she speaks, she rocks back and forth with a distracted expression. When she is later asked to describe her thought process, she explains that while she was defining compassion, she was rocking a child alter who had memories of abuse and was internally humming a Chopin melody that gave comfort to other alters.

In the social-intellectual process of sharing such test results with the patients and their creative and harried therapists, we have raised some new questions and have sometimes found new understandings. These understandings have not only come about through abstract, objective, formal operational reasoning, but even more, have resulted from a postformal emphasis on open-ended, relativistic thinking. The therapist of the MPD patient must think in both more and less advanced ways, in subjective and objective ways, in logical and intuitive ways, and must somehow coordinate these levels of understanding. If the patient is constantly undergoing metatheory shifts, so too is the therapist. In this process, therapists are developmentally challenged to reexamine a number of their basic assumptions. Time, space and my own imperfect understanding allow me to only briefly outline three such issues and suggest how they stimulate the therapist's postformal thinking.

SOME COGNITIVE CONCERNS FOR THE MPD THERAPIST

What Is Truth and Reality?

This is a major question for the patient, who struggles between her needs to affirm and defensively deny her pain and dividedness. It is a central problem for the clinical field, which has engaged in a heated controversy over the credibility of MPD as a "real" diagnosis versus a disorder that is malingered, accepted without scientific skepticism, or even created by overzealous therapists (e.g., Dell, 1988; Fahy, 1988; Hilgard, 1988; Spiegel, 1988). It is very much an issue for the therapist who has been plunged into the contradictory and imaginative world of the MPD alter system and is struggling to determine what is going on (Putnam, 1989). The therapist is faced with the basic dilemma in what Sinnott (1984; ch. 14, this volume) has termed "postformal self-referential thought"—that as much as we may attempt to investigate external reality, it is not possible to escape one's subjectivity. Nonetheless, decisions about reality must be made in order for therapy to proceed. In deciding what has "really" happened concerning an experience the patient recounts, the therapist must coordinate cognitive elements (e.g., the intellectual level and state of awareness of the patient when the experience occurred, the therapist's careful inspection of external data), emotional factors (e.g., the effects of the patient's and therapist's anxiety levels on belief), social factors (e.g., the system implications and interpersonal meaning of the communication), and moral issues (e.g., whether the determination of reality is of significance). Moreover, this coordination must have a postformal fluidity—one's determination of truth and reality needs to be subject to change depending on new information, logical strains, intuitive and theoretical shifts, and so forth. An absolutist judgment on such matters leads to an uncritical acceptance or rejection of the patient's reality which is inimical to scientific and therapeutic work.

Who Is the Patient?

From the alters' points of view, the focus of the therapy is on them. From a clinical perspective, the focus of the treatment is the personality system. Practically speaking, the working therapist must simultaneously accept both views (and a third as well). With a postformal vantage point, one need not make a choice between the concrete (the individual alters) and the abstract (the system) since both lend meaning to the other. Moreover, a basic characteristic of systems is that they are programmed for interference (Miller, 1978). Therefore, the concrete parts of the patient are never totally divided off from each other or separated from the larger system. So the "patient" that one works with is not just a combination of particular, discrete alters and system functions, but an ever-reconfigurating constellation of alter-system presentations that change as they interact and are observed. The postformal therapist can never afford to rest on her previous solutions to the above question.

WHERE ARE WE GOING?

It is evident that the goal of treatment is to adaptively change the parts, the system, and the part-system interaction. I will briefly mention three approaches currently used in the field that illustrate a postformal treatment focus on part-whole and bridging relationships. The first is the distinction made by Braun (1986) and Kluft (1990) between personality integration as a process and personality fusion as one product of that process. Fusion, which refers to the merging of alters, is a specific goal of MPD therapy. Integration refers to the connecting of thought and affect within alters and the facilitation of communication and cooperation within the alter system. As such, integration is a general element of a variety of therapeutic interventions throughout treatment. It provides the means by which the patient attains and solidifies a feeling of wholeness while retaining a sense of differentiation. The following two techniques provide therapeutic tools for bridging the cognitive levels of the MPD system. The first is the metaphor (Kluft, 1989; Putnam, 1989). Because the metaphor has abstract, concrete, iconic, and affective qualities, it can be understood and used by alters at a variety of levels. The therapist of the MPD patient is challenged to become creative and playful at expressing ideas, goals, and solutions to problems in metaphorical terms. Humor is also used extensively in treatment. Jokes connect developmentally early and advanced meanings of an experience by affectively distancing their threatening components. (I am reminded of a colleague's patient who dealt with memories of her bizarre and frightening eating experiences by concluding, "I never eat anything that has a history!")

CONCLUSIONS

This discussion moves us in an educational direction to the usefulness of educating therapists in postformal thinking. Training, supervision, and consultation ought not only to focus on imparting concrete information, specific techniques, and abstract theory, but also on presenting therapeutic dilemmas in ways that encourage postformal problem solving. Therapeutic errors in treatment can also be understood in cognitive developmental terms. They may represent difficulties in entertaining the idea of alternative reality systems, or problems in bridging these systems, or the experience of becoming cognitively overwhelmed in a relativism that has many alternatives and no priorities. The MPD patient, because she presents with a complex, enigmatic, multileveled, and shifting self-system, can be a catalyst for cognitive change in a therapist who is willing to engage in the process of understanding and changing this complex person.

REFERENCES

Armstrong, J., & Loewenstein, R. J. (1990). Characteristics of patients with multiple personality and dissociative disorders on psychological testing. *Journal of Nervous and Mental Disease, 178,* 448–454.

Basseches, M. (1984). *Dialectical thinking and adult development.* Norwood, NJ: Ablex.

Braun, B. G. (1986). Issues in the psychotherapy of multiple personality disorder. In B. G. Braun (Ed.), *Treatment of multiple personality disorder* (pp.3–28). Washington, DC: American Psychiatric Press.

Braun, B. G., & Sachs, R. G. (1985). The development of multiple personality disorder: Predisposing, precipitating and perpetuating factors. In R. P. Kluft (Ed.), *The childhood antecedents of multiple personality disorder* (pp. 38–64). Washington, DC: American Psychiatric Press.

Commons, M. L., Richards, F., & Armon, C. (1984). *Beyond formal operations: Late adolescent and adult cognitive development.* New York: Praeger.

Dell, P. F. (1988). Professional skepticism about multiple personality. *Journal of Nervous and Mental Disease, 176,* 528–531.

Fahy, T. A. (1988). The diagnosis of multiple personality disorder: A critical review. *British Journal of Psychiatry, 153,* 597–606.

Fischer, K. W., & Elmendorf, D. M. (1986). Becoming a different person: Transformation in personality and social behavior. In M. Perlmutter (Ed.), *Cognitive perspectives on children's social and behavioral development* (The Minnesota symposia on child psychology, Vol. 18, pp. 137–176). Hillsdale, NJ: Erlbaum.

Hilgard, E. R. (1988). Commentary: Professional skepticism about multiple personality. *Journal of Nervous and Mental Disease, 176,* 532.

Horowitz, M. J. (1986). *Stress response syndromes.* New York: Aronson.

Kluft, R. P. (1985). The treatment of multiple personality disorder (MPD): Current concepts. In F. F. Flack (Ed.), *Directions in psychiatry* (pp. 1–9). New York: Hatherleigh.

Kluft, R. P. (1989). Playing for time: Temporizing techniques in the treatment of multiple personality disorder. *American Journal of Clinical Hypnosis, 32,* 90–98.

Kluft, R. P. (1990). Fusion, integration and unification of the MPD patient. In R. Loewenstein (Chair), *The treatment of multiple personality disorder* (Symposium of the Sheppard Pratt National Center for Human Development). Baltimore, MD: Sheppard Pratt Media Center.

Loewenstein, R. J. (1988). The spectrum of phenomenology in multiple personality disorder: Implications for diagnosis and treatment. In B. G. Braun (Ed.), *Dissociative Disorders 1988: Proceedings of the fifth international conference on multiple personality/dissociative states* (p. 8). Chicago: Rush.

Ludwig, A. M. (1983). The psychological functions of dissociation. *American Journal of Clinical Hypnosis*, *26*, 93–99.

Miller, J. G. (1978). *Living systems*. New York: McGraw-Hill.

Putnam, F. W. (1985). Dissociation as a response to extreme trauma. In R. P. Kluft (Ed.), *Childhood antecedents of multiple personality disorder* (pp.66–97). Washington, DC: American Psychiatric Press.

Putnam, F. W. (1989). *Diagnosis and treatment of multiple personality disorder*. New York: Guilford.

Sinnott, J. D. (1984). Postformal reasoning: The relativistic stage. In M. L. Commons, F. Richards, & C. Armon (Eds.), *Beyond formal operations* (pp. 298–325). New York: Praeger.

Spiegel, D. (1986). Dissociation, double binds and posttraumatic stress in multiple personality disorder. In B. G. Braun (Ed.), *Treatment of multiple personality disorder* (pp. 63–77). Washington, DC: American Psychiatric Press.

Spiegel, D. (1988). Commentary: The treatment accorded those who treat multiple personality disorder. *Journal of Nervous and Mental Disease*, *176*, 535–536.

3

Age-Related Changes in Visual Processing May Result in Continuing Cognitive Development

JULIE R. BRANNAN AND CAMERON J. CAMP

Continued cognitive development beyond adolescence must have its basis, to some degree, in corresponding changes within the biological systems of individuals. Recent research in visual perception lends support to this claim. In this chapter, we will review relevant research and the adaptive utility of continued growth beyond adolescence.

Specifically, we will discuss visual-sensory-processing changes with age that are related to the idea of continuing cognitive development across the life span. It may be particularly useful to rethink the common assumption that all physiological or sensory changes with age are necessarily detrimental. In fact, these changes may help create a population of older adults who are optimally suited to certain tasks that are important to society and the continuation of the species.

There is evidence that the human visual system processes many aspects of visual information in parallel along two separate pathways (e.g., Breitmeyer & Ganz, 1976; Weisstein, Ozog, & Szog, 1975). Although this dichotomy is to some extent artificial (see Lennie, 1980), it is useful in that it serves to organize available knowledge. One of these pathways is referred to as the *transient* system, and the other is called the *sustained* system. The transient aspect of visual processing responds optimally to stimuli with abrupt on- and off-sets and high temporal frequencies; is optimally sensitive to low spatial frequencies (that is, broad patterns carrying form and shape information but very little detail); and produces a rapid, quickly decaying response. Because of these unique processing characteristics, the transient system might be best suited for holistic, global processing; the perception of motion; and the localization of objects in space.

In contrast, the sustained aspect of visual processing responds in a more prolonged fashion to stationary or slowly moving stimuli, higher spatial frequencies (that is, finer patterns carrying more detailed information), and low temporal frequencies. Its response characteristics would make it optimally suited for analytic, featural processing, involving the perception of pattern information and fine detail. In general, stimuli presented in the fovea (central vision) tend to activate the more sustained system, whereas the transient system becomes more active as stimuli move into peripheral vision.

There is neurophysiological evidence for such a functional dichotomy. Ganglion cells in the retina and lateral geniculate nucleus of the cat can be segregated into X and Y cells, which seem to process visual information differently (Enroth-Cugell & Robson, 1966). A second dichotomy is the magno-parvo segregation observed in monkeys, which may relate visual perception to cellular layers (see Livingstone & Hubel, 1987, 1988). These classifications are based on different data and are not completely interchangeable, but they do share several characteristics important for our purposes. In general, X cells and the parvocellular system respond in ways similar to the functional division of the sustained system (i.e., high spatial and low temporal resolution). On the other hand, Y cells and the magnocellular system seem related to transient functioning (i.e., low spatial and high temporal resolution). The transient/sustained dichotomy is perhaps the most appropriate model for psychophysically obtained data on visual changes with age, since it is a functional and not an anatomical division.

In spite of the fact that the sustained and transient systems are separate, they are capable of interaction. In particular, there is evidence from masking experiments that the transient system seems to inhibit the persisting response of the sustained system (Breitmeyer & Ganz, 1976). In order for a viewer to visually inspect an object, its image must fall on the center of the visual field. The sustained system then processes the visual information contained in the object. If attention is diverted to the periphery during this procedure, some process is required to prevent the blurring of the sustained information. This may be one function of the transient system, which is triggered by eye movements. Its stimulation inhibits the remaining sustained response from fixation. This inhibition of sustained response seems to be important in processes such as reading, where words might blur from one fixation to the next without some inhibitory process taking place (see Breitmeyer, 1983). For our purposes, this sustained/transient dichotomy (in particular, its interaction) provides a framework within which the pattern of changes seen with aging can be categorized and conceptualized.

There exists a fairly consistent pattern of changes in vision with increasing age. In general, spatial acuity declines and contrast sensitivity decreases, particularly at high spatial frequencies and when stimuli are moved or drifted (Owsley, Sekuler, & Siemsen, 1983). Various aspects of temporal processing seem to change, also suggesting a decline in temporal resolution with age (see Kline & Scheiber, 1982). One of the most pervasive changes in temporal-visual processing with age is that older adults find it more difficult to distinguish between two stimuli presented closely in time; the stimuli seem to fuse, or persist. Brannan and colleagues (Brannan, Sekuler, & Phillips, 1988b; Brannan, Sekuler, Phillips, & Chan, 1988a) have recently investigated age-related differences in temporal processing. The stimuli were spatially localized patterns with various peak spatial frequencies (from low to high). On each trial, two stimuli were briefly presented and subjects were asked to tell whether they had seen two separate stimuli or one continuous stimulus. Time intervals between stimuli were varied. Adults in their 70s needed more time between stimuli to detect two separate pulses than adults in their 20s. This difference increased at high spatial frequencies. The need for additional interstimulus time suggests that the information from the first pulse was persisting into the second pulse for older adults. A longer time between pulses was required for older adults to detect both stimuli as separate presentations.

Kline and Schieber (1981) first proposed that differential aging of the transient and sustained systems could explain the above-mentioned temporal- and spatial-visual-processing changes seen with age. Since then, additional evidence has supported this suggestion (for example, Sturr, Church, Nuding, Van Orden, & Taub, 1986; Sturr, Church, & Taub, 1985; Sturr, Kelly, Kobus, & Taub, 1982; Sturr, Van Orden, & Taub, 1987), although it does not always hold true (Sturr, Church, & Taub, 1988). There is some physiological foundation to the idea that there may be differential developmental courses for these channels within the visual system. X cells tend to develop before Y cells. Also, in studies on early visual deprivation in the developing visual system, Y cells are selectively impaired over X cells (Kratz, Sherman, & Kalil, 1979). It may be that the mechanisms underlying our concept of a transient system are particularly vulnerable to damage. A selective transient deficit could not only lead to deficits in tasks believed to be mediated by a transient system (for example, the detection of the temporal order of two briefly presented stimuli), but might also lead to a paradoxical strengthening of the sustained system due to its disinhibition. This disinhibitory component of the transient decrement theory of visual changes with age could account for persistence changes. Brannan and colleagues (1988b) found that changes in two-pulse sensitivity with age (that is, increased temporal persistence) were consistent with a model incorporating decreased inhibition in older adults.

There is evidence of temporal persistence changes with age in other sensory modalities as well. Older adults have a higher auditory-click fusion threshold, suggesting that clicks persist at high temporal frequencies. Older adults often complain of finding sentences more difficult to understand than single words; their higher auditory-click fusion threshold suggests that each word in a sentence may be persisting, or blurring, into the next. Axelrod, Thompson, and Cohen (1968) reported that older adults were impaired in the ability to perceive sequentially presented shocks to the fingers. Although spatial analogues are more problematic in nonvisual sensory systems, these data suggest that separate transient-like and sustained-like temporal pathways may be present in various sensory modalities.

The consequence of these physiological and perceptual changes in the aging visual system is a limitation of information-processing capacity. The end result of these changes is to alter perception to the world with age. The selective decrement of the transient pathway decreases sensitivity to high temporal frequencies, leading to a loss of temporal resolution and an increased persistence of visual images. This loss of temporal resolution is compounded by the disinhibition of the sustained pathway, which is predisposed to the detection of slow motion and low temporal frequencies. A shift to low temporal frequency information could lead to an emphasis on the detection of temporal invariants in the environment. In addition to age-related psychophysical changes, there are changes in the optics of the eye that result in a loss of sensitivity to high spatial frequencies. This produces a visual system that is less effective in detecting fine detail in the environment and instead perceives its global component. Taken together, various age-related changes in vision produce an organism optimized to extract the global invariants of visual information in the world.

Changes in the perception of the world would undoubtedly necessitate changes in cognitive skills. With age, the ability to attend to detail and abrupt changes could decline. This would be replaced with a concentration on developing an overall perspective to the environment. Information would be analyzed within a global framework rather than by reflex reactions to limited (localized) and transient information.[1] These changes in cognition would not necessarily have to be limited to visual information processing. This mode of analysis could be generalized to deal with various situations and within other sensory modalities.

It is not unexpected that physiological changes in an organism that alter its perceptual capacity should have such far-reaching effects as the alteration of cognitive behavior or capabilities. What is perhaps surprising is that innate age-related physiological changes might precede and direct the form of the cognitive changes. As such, cognitive changes observed in adult development could to a great extent be a reflection of physiological changes in perceptual systems. Even more significant, such changes may represent not necessarily an inevitable decay but rather an adaptive shift toward an organism with different processing capacities that are equally valuable in coping with the environment.

The hypothesis that physiological changes with age could direct cognitive development has been the subject of recent theories of cognition. Pascual-Leone (1984) has described how physiological changes in adulthood and old age can lead to qualitative changes in adult cognition. Functional potential bases of physiological processes (*silent operators*) begin to decline with increasing age. For example, some physiological base must underlie the changes in visual persistence reported by Brannan and colleagues (1988a, b). As a result, this functional breakdown causes mental structures supported by these physiological processes (*macrostructures* and *superstructures*) to become less available. In his words, "This functional breakdown disturbs adaptation and forces new selective cognitive growth" (p. 212). Thus, growth and structural integration become confined to more limited domains. However, within domains, an individual is still supported by silent operators, enabling continued development and qualitative change. Therefore, if a selective transient loss mediates increased visual persistence in older adults, then cognitive functions subserved primarily by the sustained system could strengthen, allowing continuing development.

In this vein, Rybash, Hoyer, and Roodin (1986) described a similar model in which adult cognitive development is described as a process of knowledge *encapsulation*, involving the development of specific areas of expertise in domains that are salient to the individual. Over time, declining resources such as attentional capacity become more devoted to a smaller number of domains of information. As a cohort, older adults might be said to have more expertise in living or life experiences (real-world knowledge) than younger adults, leading to a greater likelihood of the development of constructs such as "wisdom" with advancing age. A visual system that has become uniquely suited to processing within a global framework might enhance such cognitive changes in older adults.

The ability to generate macrostructures depends in part on the ability to lose lower-level information. Commons and Hallinan (in press) have suggested that sensitivity to detail must be suppressed in order to see the overall patterns required in higher levels of cognitive development. Pascual-Leone (1984) described the general process of scheme creation as a way to reduce relevant information to its purest form; individuals creatively condense the functional essence of a scheme while disregarding unnecessary content or structural details. Camp (1988) has discussed the idea that older adults may be more suited to discover invariants within the environment as a function of both their increased level of knowledge and their decreased memorial abilities. The changes that occur in visual channels over the normal adult life span may contribute to changes in other cognitive systems, leading to overall qualitative changes in the way individuals have come to know the world over time.

To conclude, visual changes in aging may be thought of as helping to create a population of different, but equally valuable, processors. Younger people may be more suited to attending to rapid changes and making a quick response, whereas older adults are ideally suited to attending to (or perhaps discovering) steady states, and making more cautious, reasoned responses. Thus, both groups would provide obvious adaptive advantages for the species.

NOTES

1. Elias, Elias, and Elias (this volume) argue that inability to attend to detail could potentially result in an overdominance of detailed information for some individuals. Kaplan (1988) has proposed that the aging process results in a greater reliance on feature analysis as opposed to contour analysis. From such a viewpoint, this reliance may not indicate an organism better suited to featural analysis but rather a failing system that requires more attention. Whereas known spatial-processing changes in the aging visual system could be consistent with declining featural analysis, temporal-processing losses could not be accounted for under this hypothesis.

REFERENCES

Axelrod, S., Thompson, L. W., & Cohen, L. D. (1968). Effects of senescence on the temporal resolution of somesthetic stimuli presented to one hand or both. *Journal of Gerontology, 23,* 191–195.

Brannan, J. R., Sekuler, R., Phillips, G., & Chan, C. (1988a). Stimulus persistence in young and older adults: The effects of reduced retinal illumination. *Investigative Ophthalmology and Visual Science, 29,* 432.

Brannan, J. R., Sekuler, R., & Phillips, G. (1988b, November). *Temporal processing in young and older observers.* Paper presented at the annual meeting of the Psychonomic Society, Chicago.

Breitmeyer, B. G. (1983). Sensory masking, persistence, and enhancement in visual exploration and reading. In K. Rayner (Ed.), *Eye movements in reading: Perceptual and language processes* (pp. 3–30). New York: Academic.

Breitmeyer, B. G., & Ganz, L. (1976). Implications of sustained and transient channels for theories of visual pattern masking, saccadic suppression, and information processing. *Psychological Review, 83,* 1–36.

Camp, C. J. (1988). In pursuit of trivia: Remembering, forgetting, and aging. *Gerontology Review, 1,* 37–42.

Commons, M. L., & Hallinan, P. W. (in press). Intelligent pattern recognition: Hierarchical organization of concepts. In M. L. Commons, R. J. Herrnstein, & S. M. Kosslyn (Eds.), *Quantitative analyses of behavior: Vol. 8. Pattern recognition and concepts in animals, people, and machines.* Hillsdale, NJ: Erlbaum.

Enroth-Cugell, C., & Robson, J. G. (1966). The contrast sensitivity of retinal ganglion cells of the cat. *Journal of Physiology, 187,* 517–552.

Kaplan, E. (1988). A process approach to neuropsychological assessment. In M. Dennis, E. Kaplan, M. Posner, D. Stein, & R. Thompson (Eds.), *Clinical neuropsychology and brain function: Research measurement and practice (master lecture)* (pp. 374–383). Washington, DC: American Psychological Association.

Kline, D. W., & Schieber, F. (1981). Visual aging: A transient/sustained shift? *Perception and Psychophysics, 29,* 181–182.

Kline, D. W., & Schieber, F. (1982). Visual persistence and temporal resolution. In R. Sekuler, D. Kline, & K. Dismukes (Eds.), *Aging and human visual function* (pp. 231–244). New York: Liss.

Kratz, K. E., Sherman, S. M., & Kalil, R. (1979). Lateral geniculate of dark-reared cats: Loss of *Y*-cells without changes in cell size. *Science, 203,* 1353–1355.

Lennie, P. (1980). Parallel visual pathways: A review. *Vision Research, 20,* 561–594.

Livingstone, M. S., & Hubel, D. H. (1987). Psychophysical evidence for separate channels for the perception of form, color, movement, and depth. *The Journal of Neuroscience, 7,* 3416–3468.

Livingstone, M. S., & Hubel, D. H. (1988). Segregation of form, color, movement, and depth: Anatomy, physiology, and perception. *Science, 240,* 740–749.

Owsley, C., Sekuler, R., & Siemsen, D. (1983). Contrast sensitivity throughout adulthood. *Vision Research, 23,* 689–699.

Pascual-Leone, J. (1984). Attention, dialectic, and mental effort: Toward an organismic theory of life stages. In M. L. Commons, F. A. Richards, & C. Armon (Eds.), *Beyond formal operations: Vol. 1. Late adolescent and adult cognitive development* (pp. 246–258). New York: Praeger.

Rybash, J. M., Hoyer, W. J., & Roodin, P. A. (1986). *Adult cognition and aging*. New York: Pergamon.

Sturr, J. F., Church, K. L., Nuding, S. C., Van Orden, K., & Taub, H. A. (1986). Older observers have attenuated increment thresholds upon transient backgrounds. *Journal of Gerontology*, *41*, 743–747.

Sturr, J. F., Church, K. L., & Taub, H. A. (1985). Early light adaptation in young, middle-aged, and older observers. *Perception and Psychophysics*, *37*, 455–458.

Sturr, J. F., Church, K. L., & Taub, H. A. (1988). Temporal summation functions for detection of sine-wave gratings in young and older adults. *Vision Research*, *28*, 1247–1253.

Sturr, J. F., Kelly, S. A., Kobus, D. A., & Taub, H. A. (1982). Age-dependent magnitude and time course of early light adaptation. *Perception and Psychophysics*, *31*, 402–404.

Sturr, J. F., Van Orden, K., & Taub, H. A. (1987). Selective attenuation in brightness in brief stimuli and at low intensities supports age-related transient channel losses. *Experimental Aging Research*, *13*, 145–149.

Weisstein, N., Ozog, G., & Szog, R. (1975). A comparison and evaluation of two models of metacontrast. *Psychological Review*, *82*, 325–343.

4

Normal Aging and Disease as Contributors to the Study of Cognitive Processing in Aging

JEFFREY W. ELIAS, MERRILL F. ELIAS, AND P. K. ELIAS

The concept of disease as distinguishable from normal aging (i.e., physical changes unrelated to disease) has many implications for the study of cognitive processes. In this chapter we consider some of these implications, discuss disease-age relationships, and offer a potential means for dealing with disease as it affects cognitive functioning in old age.

While calling the reader's attention to the potential role of disease processes as they affect cognitive functioning, the authors recognize the utility of choosing individuals for study who theoretically represent optimal aging or disease-free aging. Even in the study of cognitive function related to disease processes, the age-equivalent control group is a necessity. We hope the reader will benefit from our discussion and come to accept the idea that "normal" and "pathological" aging processes may in some cases be a matter of degree that may be measurable.

IMPLICATIONS

The assumption that a distinction can and should be made between disease processes and nondisease processes in the study of cognitive function places great responsibility on the cognitive researcher. Specifically, it requires that the distinction must be observable experimentally or clinically in such a way that the variance attributed to each process can be clearly identified. Ignoring for the moment the potential difficulty of distinguishing between disease processes and nondisease processes, it is clear that a consideration of the concept is necessary and has positive implications for aging. One positive implication is that if certain pathological conditions can be avoided, then the loss of cognitive capacity in old age is less likely or will be minimal. The notion of the possibility of a ''more pure aging process'' leads eventually to an emphasis on preventative measures that are always more cost-effective than treating disease once it has occurred. For example, programs designed to prevent age- and work-environment–related pathological conditions are receiving increasing attention in legislative proceedings.

The loss of cognitive capabilities with age may be feared as much as the loss of physical capabilities. In many cases, one may compensate more easily for the latter. Therefore, finding little difference between young and old adults, or little change over time in cognitive processes, is interpreted as a positive finding. To the extent that the researcher can distinguish disease from nondisease states, he or she is prevented from attributing more cognitive change to the aging process than is necessary. Historically, life span developmental psychologists have focused on the careful separation of aging effects from age/cohort effects because some proportion of age-related cognitive decline can be attributed to cohort (Schaie & Parr, 1983). A similar concern has been directed toward age/disease effects. Some of the systematic variance attributed to age/cohort effects is related to health status (Elias, Elias, & Elias, 1990). A focus on health as it affects cognitive functions is a refining of the study of cohort effects. Cohort membership is thus based on susceptibility to disease, its detectability, disease awareness, treatability, treatment efficacy, and financial capability (e.g., health insurance programs).

An emphasis on the discrimination between healthy and nonhealthy individuals focuses attention on the need for accurate and timely clinical diagnosis and accurate and sensitive behavioral measurement. Behavioral researchers should not assume that clinical medical diagnosis and behavioral measures are unrelated entities. With respect to dementia or depression, cognitive dysfunction, defined behaviorally, is a primary symptom of a clinical syndrome.

CHANGING CONCEPTS OF DISEASE

From a clinical medicine perspective, the method of distinguishing between a disease state and a nondisease state is not without error. Evans (1988) noted that the modern concept of disease in medicine has gone through an evolution of thought. Initial notions of disease states resulted from the capacity to perform autopsies and relate pathological findings to symptoms. In the nineteenth century, the discovery of infectious agents resulted in the emergence of etiology as an important concept in diagnosis. These influences on medical philosophy resulted in a model that emphasized disease as an entity that was definable and diagnosable because these were identifiable, single, necessary, and sufficient causes intruding on the ''victim.'' Evans (1988) also noted that eventually it became recognized that individual differences in the form of susceptibility constituted an important variable to be considered in the study of disease. It was also recognized that susceptibility could be manipulated via preventive measures designed to remove causes or lower susceptibility. The effectiveness of these practices and the development of pharmacology and immunology have resulted in an increase in life expectancy and in the current emphasis on the study of chronic disease. Chronic disease states provide more difficulty than acute disease states for the behavioral researcher and the clinician because the point at which the disease is diagnosed and the point at which it can be, or is, treated are often the same. In chronic disease states, however, the actual length of time the disease has been present (often without significant symptomatology) is unknown.

Point of onset of disease is an important variable in both medical and behavioral research. Depending on the particular disease, it may be described as: (a) the point of seeking treatment, (b) the point of noticeable disease onset, (c) the point of dysfunction, or (d) some combination of these factors with an emphasis on the ones most accurately known. In some cases the point at which a disease is treated may be considered the point of disease onset by the physician. The consequences of point of onset as associated with the age of the individual will vary with the nature of the disease and its relationship to the aging process. For example, with Alzheimer's disease or Huntington's disease (Finch, 1988), an early onset (i.e., at a younger age) may indicate a more progressive disease state. By contrast, a later disease onset of Parkinson's disease appears to have more impact on some cognitive functions than an earlier onset (Netherton et al., 1989).

AGE-DISEASE RELATIONSHIPS

The capability for accurately distinguishing between particular disease states and between disease states and nondisease states is, without question, of major importance to the clinical and the behavioral researcher. It is important to realize, however, that not all disease processes have the same relationship to the aging process. Figure 4.1 shows the relationship of age to disease onset for four diseases that severely affect cognitive function: schizophrenia, Huntington's disease, Parkinson's disease, and Alzheimer's disease. It can be seen that the onset of each disease and its relative occurrence have a distinct relationship to age. The age of maximum vulnerability to each disease is quite different. Thus, age as a risk factor for each disease has to be considered quite differently. Understanding the relationship of the disease process to age is of vital importance to both clinical medicine and cognitive psychology. Although firm theoretical perspectives have not yet emerged, several models or perspectives are now being developed.

Kohn (1985) has approached the categorization of disease processes by considering them in terms of their frequency and association with the aging process. He has provided the following taxonomy.

Category 1. There are diseases that are universal, progressive, and irreversible with age. Atherosclerosis as a chronic vascular system disease falls within this category. Atherosclerosis is considered universal because it occurs in all populations and because some sign of atherosclerotic deposit can be found at a very

Figure 4.1
Age of Onset of Dopaminergic-Related Diseases Shown by Percentage of Huntington's Disease, Schizophrenia, Parkinson's Disease and Alzheimer's Disease

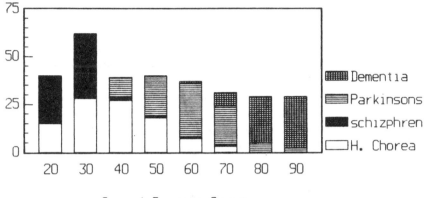

Age of Disease Onset

young age. This is a disease that is truly developmental in nature, but the point at which it becomes a major factor in the functional capabilities of an individual varies greatly.

Category 2. There are diseases that are common but not universal and not inevitable. Cancer qualifies as such a disease. Cancer is often age-related, but different types of cancer have different relationships with age (e.g., lung cancer incidence decreases after age 70, and colon cancer incidence increases sharply in older age groups), and tends to affect subgroups within a population.

Category 3. There are diseases for which age represents a vulnerability factor once the disease is present rather than a risk factor for susceptibility to initially contracting the disease. Illnesses related to lung function, for example, pneumonia, colds, and flu, fall into this category.

Normal aging within this conceptualization is found to share criteria similar to those found for category 1 disease processes. Aging defined as clear physiological change is universal and inevitable, and occurs even under optimal circumstances. For the cognitive psychologist, such a similarity in criteria between normal aging and a disease process seems to equate normal aging with disease. From the perspective of a pathologist such as Kohn, normal aging and disease are seen as points on a continuum that has quite a bit of variability from one individual to the next (Elias, Elias, & Elias, 1990).

If one accepts this definition of normal aging and category 1 disease processes, then it should be understood that the study of cognitive processes in normal aging is also the study of category 1 disease processes, whether diagnosed or nondiagnosed, treated or nontreated. This raises the issue of whether one may be studying the process of optimal aging rather than normal aging if the entire distribution of disease processes is not present in the aging sample. That is, what is normal in old age may not necessarily correspond with what is considered healthy. Furthermore, actual functional capability may vary greatly among individuals with similar health statuses.

GENETICS AND AGING

Category 2 diseases occur under even the most favorable conditions for the control of category 1 diseases. This is given support by longevity studies conducted in pathogen-free environments. For mice (*Mus musculus domesticus*), such environments have lengthened life expectancy considerably in the normal lab environment to points beyond 3 to 4 years (Martin & Bryant, 1988); that is, "normal aging" and category 1 disease processes have been minimized.

Martin and Bryant (1988) reported that in AB6F1 hybrid male mice, who were genetically identical and had nearly identical environments, a number of animals developed a variety of neoplasms as they aged. Some contracted lymphoma early on and died at about 18 months, while others developed lymphoma at 36 months. Postmaturational events involving a series of independent somatic mutations were proposed to account for the cancer. The probability of such postmaturational events was thought to be determined by gene loci controlling DNA repair, free-radical activity, and other events such as chromosomal segregation. These genes are thought to act in the maintenance of what is referred to as macromolar integrity (Martin & Bryant, 1988). What is demonstrated here is a model of pathogen-free aging that is in part dependent on the integrity of housekeeping functions. If these housekeeping functions go awry, they contribute to the vulnerability of the system that they help to maintain. Within this particular model, disease may affect certain subgroups only, and a percentage of the population would be expected to develop neoplasms with age regardless of attempts to control the environment. One can make the inference that similar conditions exist in humans.

If one were interested in the characteristics of this population in general, those with obvious disease states would have to be included for study. In choosing a representative sample for study, the appropriate stratification techniques should be used to insure appropriate sample representation of the expected numbers of mice with neoplasms. If such a sampling technique is not employed, then one is either studying optimal aging (i.e., a sample at only one end of the distribution for category 1 processes) or treating the disease process as if it does not represent a normative aging process. This is a position that may be hard to justify.

THRESHOLD AND VULNERABILITY MODELS OF DISEASE

Three of the diseases shown in Figure 4.1, Huntington's disease, Parkinson's disease, and Alzheimer's disease, can be considered diseases that manifest themselves subsequent to a threshold loss of neurons and neuronal connections, and a subsequent imbalance of neurotransmitters. Each of these diseases involves a loss of dopaminergic neurons to a point where a threshold of normal function has been crossed. The study of disease involving dopaminergic systems has led Finch (1988) to propose that there are age-related phenomena that are *eugeric*. *Pathogeric* phenomena are age-related phenomena that are secondary to disease processes. Eugeric phenomena are more generally distributed with age and are not considered pathological in nature, although the normal progression of these processes may lead to a disease state. The point at which a phenomenon changes from eugeric to pathogeric may depend on a relative imbalance of systems or the crossing of a threshold of homeostatic balance.

Parkinson's disease (PD) is an example of a disease state that is reached when a threshold of cell loss has been reached and a balance in neurotransmitters has been disrupted. Parkinson's disease is thought to manifest itself when there has been an 80% loss of the dopaminergic cells in the nigrostriatal area that project to the neostriatum. Such cell loss is hypothesized to begin normally in midlife and progress in proportion to the life span (Finch, 1988; Langston, 1988). A 20% to 40% loss of striatal dopamine receptors over the life span is considered normal. Since the incidence of PD is about 1 in 100, then about 99% (assuming appropriate diagnosis across all age groups) of the population will not progress, with or without toxic insult, to a point where the disease will manifest itself. Parkinson's disease results in a variety of cognitive changes beyond that expected from normal aging, and in some cases can lead to dementia (Elias et al., 1990; Netherton et al., 1989; Passafiume, Boller, & Keefe, 1986; Taylor, Saint-Cyr, & Lang, 1987).

Given the incidence of Parkinson's disease, it cannot be considered in the universal category, but it can be considered age-related, with age as a major risk factor for developing the disease state due to its clear association with loss of dopaminergic cells. There are no markers for the disease process, nor does it show any strong genetic relationships. Therefore, it is difficult to determine any degree of risk beyond age. Two means by which the normal aging process could result in the disease threshold being reached include individual differences in the rate at which dopaminergic cells are lost in the nigrostriatal area and individual differences in the original number of cells that are present there (or some combination of both; Finch, 1988).

Huntington's disease is another dopaminergic-related disease process that occurs when a threshold of cell loss is reached (Finch, 1988). In Huntington's disease there is a severe loss of striatal neurons and a subsequent imbalance of neurotransmitters. The same models proposed for Parkinson's disease can be proposed for the accelerated loss of striatal neurons in Huntington's disease; however, the expression of Huntington's disease occurs much earlier. Moreover, the disease has a definite genetic relationship, and there are genetic markers that indicate disease susceptibility. The cognitive deficits associated with early Huntington's disease are severe and usually result in dementia.

Figure 4.2 shows data gathered by Chui and colleagues (Chui et al., 1986)

Figure 4.2
**Neuronal Counts in Three Subcortical Nuclei for Parkinson's Disease (PD),
Alzheimer's Disease (AD), and Nondemented Elderly Controls**

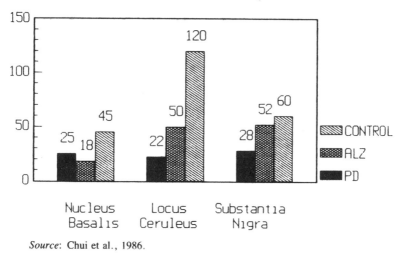

Source: Chui et al., 1986.

from small samples of individuals with Alzheimer's disease, Parkinson's disease, or no disease symptoms. In these data the differential cell loss in the nucleus basalis meyert (cholinergic), nigrostriatal area (dopaminergic), and locus ceruleus (noradrenergic) is clearly illustrated. Thus, disease processes where a threshold of cell loss must be reached before symptoms become apparent are ultimately diseases resulting in a change in the homeostatic balance of the neurotransmitters. These are not single-neurotransmitter disease processes even though treatment or attempts to develop treatment may focus primarily on one type (e.g., Alzheimer's and acetylcholine replacement, Parkinson's disease and levodopa or L-dopa treatment).

Although Alzheimer's disease is considered a disease driven primarily by cholinergic dysfunction associated with basal forebrain neurons, considerable thought is being given to the role of the locus coeruleus in this disease as it determines microvascular circulation. The model, as explained by Scheibel, Duong, and Tomiyasu (1986), has several components. With Alzheimer's disease there are changes in the vascular wall structure and the loss of a perivascular neural plexus. The structural changes in the walls of the small cerebral vessels affect functioning of the blood-brain barrier. The innervation of the parenchymal brain vessels forming the blood-brain barrier comes from several sources. According to Scheibel and colleagues (1986), the most well-documented source is the locus ceruleus, with some evidence of cholinergic innervation from the basal forebrain area. A change in the permeability of the blood-brain barrier has long been implicated in the development of Alzheimer's disease.

In developing a cerebrovascular model for the origin of senile dementia,

Roberts (1986) also implicated the locus coeruleus and pointed to the particular age-related vulnerability of the catecholaminergic systems. This model also ties in the immune system, free-radical production, and the role of trophic factors in maintaining cellular integrity. These three factors are the primary factors discussed in the consideration of overall models of physiological aging. Roberts (1986) went a step further and described a hypothetical neurobehavioral relationship that depends on the interrelationship of the cholinergic and noradrenergic systems and the balance between the two systems as they affect excitation and inhibition of neural circuits and thus affect a balance in cognitive functioning.

A discussion of disease processes that seem to involve a point of critical neuronal loss or function eventually leads to a discussion of age-related vulnerability to diseases in which the primary manifestation is cognitive. While schizophrenia currently could not be considered a disease that involves a critical neuronal loss, it is a cognitive disorder that shows a definite age-related vulnerability.

There is a developing body of evidence with respect to schizophrenia (Murray, Lewis, Owen, & Foerster, 1988; Weinberger, 1987) and neurotoxin-related Parkinson's disease (Langston, 1988) that age-related processes lead to an increased vulnerability to lesions of the brain. In the case of schizophrenia, it is suggested that developmental neuronal and cognitive abnormalities predate the onset of schizophrenia (Murray et al., 1988; Weinberger, 1987). Furthermore, there is a long latency period between structural insult and behavioral dysfunction. The onset of schizophrenia typically occurs in late adolescence to early adulthood. It is suggested that brain development and change in the form of myelinization, cell death, retraction of axonal processes, and synaptic elimination continues through adolescence and early adulthood, and it is proposed that at the point of myelinization, previously undetected damage to neurons can become apparent (Murray et al., 1988). Feinberg (1982/83) has suggested that the synaptic elimination process that takes place with the maturing brain may reveal a "faultily wired" system of neuronal interconnections. Weinberger (1987) has suggested more specifically that such developmental processes reveal early lesions that primarily affect the function of both the dorsolateral prefrontal cortex and the mesocortical dopamine system which projects from the midbrain to the prefrontal cortex. Research by Chapman and Chapman (1985) indicated that frontal lobe cognitive dysfunction is related to symptoms of schizophrenia in young adults prior to any diagnosis. That is, signs of frontal lobe dysfunction and cognitive vulnerability predate the onset of the behavioral disorder. The development of schizophrenia may depend on an environment that either enhances or minimizes the frontal lobe–mesocortical dopaminergic dysfunction.

A second vulnerability model is based on the effects of toxins on the dopaminergic system. The nigrostriatal system is highly vulnerable to certain toxic compounds that damage cells to a point where a Parkinsonian syndrome develops (Elias et al., 1990; Langston, 1988). One such compound is MPTP (1-methyl–4-phenyl–1,2,3,6-tetrahydropyridine), a compound that is not considered to be toxic until it crosses the blood-brain barrier (Langston, 1988). Once across the blood-brain barrier, however, MPTP is rapidly transformed into the highly toxic MPP+. MPP+ shows a very high affinity for the dopamine re-uptake system.

The effects of MPTP toxicity increase with age (Langston, 1988), and this fact has been related to the age-related increase in the enzyme MAO-B and the age-related increased efficiency in converting MPTP to MPP+. Age-correlated vulnerability in this case is a function of the increase in activity with age in the enzyme MAO-B and the affinity of the particular toxin for the dopamine re-uptake system. Recent attention has been focused on the catecholamine system in terms of free-radical production and the cytoxic nature of catecholamines (Carlsson, 1986). The autoxidation (quinoid) products of catecholamines are considered highly reactive compounds, and may contribute to the special age-related vulnerability of catecholamine neurons and the loss of cells in the striatum and the locus ceruleus. Attention is called also to any condition that might result in ischemia, since the protective mechanisms against free radicals are less functional following ischemia and the subsequent return of oxygen.

The recent success of the drug deprenyl, a type B–selective monoamine oxidase inhibitor, for the treatment of Parkinson's disease (Shoulson et al., 1989) fits well with the findings of Langston (1988) and Carlsson (1986). To the extent that monoamine oxidase activity and the formation of free radicals was involved in nigrostriatal degeneration, deprenyl was expected to slow the progression of disease. The degree of delay in starting levodopa therapy was chosen as the measure of success of treatment. After 12 months of the study, it was observed that the risk of reaching the point of levodopa therapy was reduced by 57%. The importance of the use of the antioxidant Vitamin E by itself or in conjunction with deprenyl is still being evaluated.

It cannot be overlooked that the peculiarities of the production and metabolism of catecholamines are involved in a number of the more severe cognitive disorders that show age-related vulnerability. Likewise, it should not escape attention that a number of personality and life event factors could serve to enhance or reduce the potential for depression. Depression is a condition that results in high levels of monoamine oxidase activity and altered catecholamine metabolism. High levels of steroids which are related to anxiety and depression are known to be toxic to cells in the hippocampus and hypothalamus (Finch, 1988; Meaney, Aitken, Berkel, Bhatnagan, & Sapolsky, 1988). Depression as a chronic condition may serve to enhance the vulnerability of the catecholaminergic systems. Environmental and behavioral variables could either aggravate or buffer against this kind of vulnerability.

VULNERABILITY INDICES

Given these descriptions of disease processes and their varying relationships with age, it would seem that the aging process can be described as one of increasing vulnerability. In addition to an increased vulnerability to the specific diseases discussed above, there is an increased vulnerability to other serious illnesses or to increased mortality and morbidity once the primary disease has developed.

Focusing on the distinction that might be made between disease-related and nondisease-related aging, it seems unlikely that any random selection procedure regarding older individuals is likely to select individuals who are disease-free. However, all individuals within *any* age group are disease-vulnerable. It may very well be, particularly with respect to cognitive processes and aging, that attempts to distinguish between normal and pathological aging are, as Evans (1988) stated in regard to physical disease processes, "an attempt to separate the undefined from the indefinable" (p. 40).

Recent data collected by Stern, Tetrud, Martin, Kutner, and Langston (1990) illustrates this point very well. These investigators studied six patients who had been exposed to MPTP but were asymptomatic for Parkinson's disease. Positron emission tomography found these individuals to have a reduced uptake of labeled 6-fluorodopa into the striatum despite their lack of significant motor symptomatology. Cognitive performance on category naming and a visual construction task was impaired in these individuals relative to age-equivalent controls. However, performance on these tasks was not impaired relative to that of other individuals who had been exposed to MPTP and were showing motor symptoms for Parkinson's disease. The authors pointed out that in this circumstance a cognitive change preceded the motor symptoms of the disease. They suggested that a threshold of dopaminergic loss had been reached and that cognitive function had declined regardless of the degree of dopaminergic dysfunction needed to develop motor signs of Parkinson's disease. By contrast, performance on the Stroop Color Word Test found the asymptomatic MPTP subjects performing more poorly than controls but significantly better than subjects who had been exposed to MPTP and were showing motor signs of Parkinson's disease. These results supported the notion that cognitive function declined in a graded fashion as dopamine stores were reduced, starting from normal aging, to MPTP asymptomatic individuals, and then to MPTP symptomatic individuals.

Samples of "healthy" individuals must be described as samples with an inherent distribution of vulnerabilities to disease. We feel that one should not attempt to distinguish between variance attributable to normal aging (so-called "healthy" samples) and variance attributable to pathological aging. Rather, one should attempt to identify the processes and factors that contribute to cognitive performance across the life span and to detail their relative expected frequency, time of influence, and expected contribution to cognitive processes.

Essentially, this would involve the development of a vulnerability index tied to age. To meet this requirement, it would be necessary to recognize age as a variable that has historical and social as well as physiological components. This notion is similar to a functional aging concept. However, the focus in this case is on cognitive function and factors that might lead to its vulnerability. For example, it appears that what has come to be called "primary memory," as exemplified by digit span memory performance, is relatively invulnerable to a number of insults to the nervous system (Squire, 1987). Therefore, for these insults, vulnerability of primary memory functioning at age 60 might be similar to vulnerability at age 25. Secondary memory, by contrast, has been found to be more vulnerable at age 60 (Poon, 1986); however, the factors involved in this vulnerability beyond chronological age per se remain to be determined. The diagnosis of a specific disease state may or may not add to this vulnerability. For example, in some disease processes such as Parkinson's disease (Elias & Hutton, 1989), not all persons with the disease would be equally vulnerable to secondary memory dysfunction. Factors other than the disease itself would also contribute to vulnerability in this group.

In some cases, a careful examination of the factors that contribute to cognitive function might reveal that the disease state per se is not a major contributor, but rather produces a major bias toward certain factors being present in a population. Research in the area of hypertension and cognitive function by Merrill Elias and colleagues is a primary example of such a finding (Elias, Robbins, & Schultz, 1987). Using such cognitive measures as reaction time, IQ performance, the Halstead Reitan Impairment Index, and the TPT tests as dependent measures of cognitive function, Elias et al. found that age, education, anxiety, and depression were better predictors of cognitive performance than hypertension alone.

Any attempt to develop an index of cognitive function will result in the appearance of measurement issues. Simply deciding what variables should remain in or out of the equation is a major feat. An understanding of how a vulnerability index might be developed can be gained by studying the concept of functional aging (Birren, Munnichs, Thomae, & Marois, 1983) and subsequent attempts to measure cognitive function based on this concept.

Fozard and Costa (1983) provided a valuable start to the development of a vulnerability index in their study of memory function as it relates to personality, general perspectives of ability, and endocrine function. Using data gathered from men involved in a longitudinal study of "normal" aging (the Normative Aging Study), measures of speed of retrieval from primary, secondary, and tertiary memory (defined by paradigm) were found to have varying relationships to such personality characteristics as extraversion, urgency, anxiety, imaginativeness, and depression. The relationships of personality to speed of memory retrieval varied depending on the task and the age of the individual. For example, depression was found to slow simple decision making in older men, but was unrelated to cognitive function in the more complex tasks. When information was retrieved from secondary memory stores, extraversion was related to slower retrieval in younger individuals and faster retrieval in older individuals. The variable of openness to experience was related to faster recognition of letters in familiar and unfamiliar sets in older men but not younger men. Fozard and Costa (1983) pointed out that in considering personality variables, one has to distinguish those factors with more stability across the life span (i.e., extraversion) from those reflecting more transient mood states such as anxiety or depression.

In their discussion of this data, Fozard and Costa (1983) endorsed a distinction between normal and pathological aging. The concept of a vulnerability index would include definable disease or probable disease as a factor in the index, but would not attempt to distinguish "definable" or "probable" as they contribute to cognitive functioning. On an individual basis, a disease process might have a differential weight depending on a number of factors such as premorbid ability, premorbid functional capacity, breadth and depth of support, age of disease onset, illness coping, and physiological functional capacity.

Studies focusing on physiological indices of aging also can contribute toward the development of a vulnerability index. Sampling from the same population as Fozard and Costa (1983), Borkan and Norris (1980) tested 1,086 males on a variety of capacities and correlated performance with chronological age. Variables most highly correlated with chronological age included forced expiratory volume ($r = -.698$), vital capacity ($r = -.606$), creatine clearance ($r = -.602$), systolic blood pressure ($r = .538$), handgrip strength ($r = -.501$), and tapping time ($r = .468$). More cognitively oriented variables like simple and choice reaction time had correlations with age below $r = .30$.

In the Jyväskylä Studies on Functional Aging (Heikkinen et al., 1984), the approach was to measure functioning in several areas of physical, mental, and social capacity. A review of cognitive studies related to chronological age found several variables correlating r at a level of .40 and higher, including memory tasks. One of the more reliable variables that was highly correlated with age was vibratory sensitivity measured at 100 hertz (Hz).

It should be pointed out that the variables noted in these studies relating performance to age have not been extensively tested in respect to cognitive vulnerability; in other words, there have been no systematic attempts to develop a vulnerability index in which age is one among many correlated variables. Further, correlations with age do not automatically make a physiological parameter a strong component of a vulnerability index that is focused on cognitive ability.

The statistical issues involved in developing such an index cannot be underestimated. Issues of reliability of measures, scaling of measures, shared variance, and suitability of linear models to describe threshold phenomena require considerable attention. Discussion of these issues is beyond the scope of this chapter, but the reader is directed toward such sources as Davies (1983); Elias, Elias, and Elias (1990); Elias, Robbins, and Schultz (1987); and Schaie and Parr (1983). Davies (1983) draws attention to issues of correlational interpretation, measurement criteria, measurement of change, and compensatory relationships between combinations of variables. Elias and colleagues (1990) discuss design biases, measurement of disease, and control of demographic and personal variables. Schaie and Parr (1983) discuss the historical nature of the relationship between variables and estimates of cohort.

SUMMARY

The suggestion has been made that the attempt to discriminate between normal and pathological aging as it affects cognitive functioning might be reconsidered such that poor health or disease states, as well as age-related physiological changes occurring universally, become component factors in an overall index of cognitive vulnerability. It is expected that such an approach to the relationship of disease and cognitive function would result in disease states per se having different effects depending on the variable combinations and weights of other factors in the index. This should lead to a greater understanding of disease as it affects cognitive function and would serve as an excellent introduction to the shifting sands of predictive relationships when age, disease, and cognitive function are in the same equation. Special attention has been drawn to factors that affect catecholamine metabolism as a potential organizational focus for considering age, disease, and cognitive function.

REFERENCES

Birren, J. E., Munnichs, J., Thomae, H., & Marois, M. (Eds.). (1983). *Aging: A challenge to science and society*. New York: Oxford University Press.

Borkan, G. A., & Norris, A. H. (1980). Assessment of biological age using a profile and physical parameters. *Journal of Gerontology, 35* (2), 177–184.

Carlsson, A. (1986). Brain neurotransmitters in normal and pathological aging. In A. Scheibel, A. Wechsler, & M. Brazier (Eds.), *The biological substrates of Alzheimer's disease* (pp. 193–204). New York: Academic.

Chapman, L. J., & Chapman, J. P. (1985). Psychosis proneness. In M. Alpert (Ed.), *Controversies in schizophrenia: Changes and constancies* (pp. 157–174). New York: Guilford.

Chui, J., Mortimer, J. A., Slager, V., Zarow, C., Bondareff, W., & Webster, D. D. (1986). Pathological correlates of dementia in Parkinson's disease. *Archives of Neurology, 43*, 991–995.

Davies, A. D. (1983). Is there a need to estimate functional age? In J. E. Birren, J. Munnichs, H. Thomae, & M. Marois (Eds.), *Aging: A challenge to science and society* (pp. 346–360). New York: Oxford University Press.

Elias, J. W., & Hutton, J. T. (1989). Cognitive change in Parkinson's disease. In J. T. Hutton & R. L. Dippel (Eds.), *A practical guide to the care of patients with Parkinson's disease* (pp. 132–146). New York: Prometheus.

Elias, M. F., Elias, J. W., & Elias, P. K. (1990). Biological and health influences on aging. In J. E. Birren & W. K. Schaie (Eds.), *Handbook of the psychology of aging* (pp. 80–102). New York: Academic.

Elias, M. F., Robbins, M., & Schultz, N. (1987). Influence of essential hypertension on intellectual performance: Causation or speculation? In J. W. Elias & P. H. Marshall (Eds.), *Cardiovascular disease and behavior* (pp. 107–149). Washington, DC: Hemisphere.

Evans, J. G. (1988). Aging and disease. In D. Evered & J. Whelan (Eds.), *Research in the aging population* (pp. 38–57). Chichester, U.K.: Wiley.

Feinberg, I. (1982/83). Schizophrenia: Caused by a fault in programmed synaptic elimination during adolescence? *Journal of Psychiatric Research*, *17*, 319–344.

Finch, C. E. (1988). Neuronal and endocrine approaches to the resolution of time as a dependent variable in the aging process of mammals. *The Gerontologist*, *28*, 29–42.

Fozard, J., & Costa, P. (1983). Age differences in memory and decision making in relation to personality, abilities and endocrine function: Implication for clinical practice and planning policy. In J. E. Birren, J. Munnich, H. Thomae, & M. Marois (Eds.), *Aging: A challenge to science and society* (pp. 276–294). New York: Oxford University Press.

Heikkinen, E., Arajarui, R., Era P., Jylita, M., Kinnunen, V., Leskinen, A., Leskinen, E., Masseli, E., Pohjolainen, P., & Rahkila, P. (1984). Functional capacity of men born in 1906–1910, 1926–1930, and 1946–1950: A basic report. *Scandinavian Journal of Social Medicine*, *533*, 1–93.

Kohn, R. R. (1985). Aging and age-related diseases: Normal processes. In H. A. Johnson (Ed.), *Relations between normal aging and disease* (pp. 1–44). New York: Raven.

Langston, J. W. (1988). Aging, neurotoxins, and neurodegenerative disease. In R. D. Terry (Ed.), *Aging and the brain* (pp. 149–164). New York: Raven.

Martin, G. M., & Bryant, E. M. (1988). Genetics of aging and disease models. In R. D. Terry (Ed.), *Aging and the brain* (pp. 1–16). New York: Raven.

Meaney, M. J., Aitken, D. H., Berkel, C., Bhatnagan, S., & Sapolsky, R. M. (1988). Effect of neonatal handling on age-related impairments associated with the hippocampus. *Science*, *239*, 766–768.

Murray, R. M., Lewis, S. W., Owen, M. J., & Foerster, A. (1988). The neurodevelopmental origins of dementia praecox. In P. Bebbington & P. McGuffin (Eds.), *Schizophrenia and the major issues* (pp. 90–106). Oxford: Heinemann Professional.

Netherton, S. D., Elias, J. W., Albrecht, N. N., Acosta, C., Hutton, J. T., & Albrecht, J. W. (1989). Changes in the performance of Parkinsonian patients and normal aged on the Benton Visual Retention Test. *Experimental Aging Research*, *15*, 13–18.

Passafiume, D., Boller, F., & Keefe, N. C. (1986). Neuropsychological impairment in patients with Parkinson's disease. In I. Grant & K. M. Adams (Eds.), *Neuropsychological assessment of neuro-psychiatric disorders* (pp. 374–383). New York: Oxford University Press.

Poon, L. (Ed.). (1986). *Clinical memory assessment of older adults*. Washington, DC: American Psychological Association.

Roberts, E. (1986). Senile dementia of the Alzheimer's type: A possible cerebrovascular origin and some therapeutic suggestions. In A. Scheibel, A. Wechsler, & M. A. Brazier (Eds.), *The biological substrates of Alzheimer's disease* (pp. 241–266). New York: Academic.

Schaie, K. W., & Parr, J. (1983). Concepts and criteria for functional age. In J. E. Birren, J. Munnichs, H. Thomae, & M. Marois (Eds.), *Aging: A challenge to science and society* (pp. 249–263). New York: Oxford University Press.

Scheibel, A. B., Duong, T., & Tomiyasu, U. (1986). Microvascular changes in Alzheimer's disease. In A. Scheibel, A. Wechsler, & M. Brazier (Eds.), *The biological substrates of Alzheimer's disease* (pp. 177–192). New York: Academic.

Shoulson, et al. (The Parkinson's Study Group). (1989). Effect of deprenyl on the progression of disability in early Parkinson's disease. *The New England Journal of Medicine, 321*, 1364–1371.

Squire, L. R. (1987). *Memory and brain*. New York: Oxford University Press.

Stern, Y., Tetrud, J. W., Martin, W.R.W., Kutner, S. J., & Langston, J. W. (1990). Cognitive change following MPTP exposure. *Neurology, 40*, 261–264.

Taylor, A. E., Saint-Cyr, J. A., & Lang, A. E. (1987). Parkinson's disease. *Brain, 110*, 35–51.

Weinberger, D. R. (1987). Implications of normal brain development for the pathogenesis of schizophrenia. *Archives of General Psychiatry, 44*, 660–669.

5

Reconceptualizing the Nature of Dialectical Postformal Operational Thinking: The Effects of Affectively Mediated Social Experiences

In this chapter I will discuss the respective roles of affect and social experience, particularly that of education, in stimulating dialectical thought and dialectical experiencing in young adults. Taking Michael Basseches's (1984) description of dialectical thinking as ideally suited both as a descriptive and as a prescriptive model of young adult development, I will criticize its exclusively intellectual focus. I will argue that the psychological and causal theory Basseches employs— namely, the genetic epistemology of Piaget (1947/1960, 1967/1971, 1972)— accounts for this bias. Furthermore, in taking intellectual structural development as its principal concern, I will argue that affective and educational factors are neglected. These factors could be better integrated if researchers adopted an information-processing theory (Greenberg & Safran, 1987; Pascual-Leone, 1983, 1984) with insights deriving from a Vygotskian perspective (Wertsch, 1985) and the sociology of knowledge (Berger & Luckman, 1966; Bowers, 1984).

Basseches describes dialectic as "developmental transformation occurring by means of constitutive and interactive relationships" (Basseches, 1984, p. 22). *Developmental transformation* is defined as developmental movement through forms. In a dialectical ontology, forms are secondary to the movement of which they are a part. This movement has a direction toward greater inclusiveness. *Constitutive* refers to a relationship in which things become what they are as a result of the relationship that makes them while they in turn make it (internal relations). *Interactive* refers to the continuous movement that goes on as elements change as a result of their relationships with each other and the whole of which they are a part.

Dialectical thinking is thinking that is inspired by the idea of the dialectic.

Formal operational thinking, on the other hand, does not contain the idea of dialectic; it views forms themselves as the real entities and the relationships between them as external and secondary. Formal operational thought tends to conceive of things in static, fixed terms, and fails to conceptualize how things relate to larger totalities.

For example, a formal operational thinker might see a relationship between two people as secondary to the persons making it up. People are conceived of as static fixed *things* that *have* relationships but are in their *essence* unaffected by them. A dialectical thinker would see the relationship as primary and the people in it as constituted and continually changed by their reciprocal interactions with each other.

In viewing dialectical thought from a Piagetian perspective, one tends to consider these "moves of thought" as constituted by logical operations. This is particularly so when dialectical thought is considered as a fifth stage in the sequence proposed by Piaget. Basseches presented his proposal in the context of other work such as that of Arlin (1975), Riegel (1973), Koplowitz (1984), and many others who have argued in various ways for a structure of thinking unique to adults. Given that the earlier stages are defined and constituted by the underlying logical operations that develop by means of self-regulatory mechanisms (reflective abstraction and equilibration), as a fifth stage in this kind of development, dialectical thought would itself have to be organized by a similar structure (or organized whole) emerging from the re-equilibration of formal operational structures.

Since Piagetian stage theory takes as its object the ontogenesis of the idealized epistemic subject and not the development of a concrete acting subject situated in a particular moment in time and history, the theory tries to extract what is most general for all persons at all times. Piaget argued that this could be done by investigating logical structural development. I will not examine here the problems in applying this approach to childhood or adolescence, as has been done by Broughton (1981), but will concentrate instead only on the problems as I see them with respect to the modeling of adult development.

AFFECT AND SOCIAL EXPERIENCE IN PIAGETIAN THEORY

In tracking only the trajectory of emerging logical structures, one is left with a picture of an active subject that has no particular reason to be active nor anything particular on which to act. In discussing the role of affect, Piaget says that it provides the energetics or fuel for intellectual structuring (Piaget, 1981), and hence that it provides the motivation or tendency to action.

Affect can generally be described as feeling or emotion, and throughout the history of psychology it has been connected in various ways with visceral responses and cognition. The James-Lange theory viewed emotion as a by-product of physiology, W. B. Cannon critiqued the visceral reductionism inherent in this model, and Stanley Schacter reinterpreted emotion or affect as the cognitive evaluation of undifferentiated visceral arousal (Gregory, 1987). Cognitive theorists today identify the evolutionary adaptive significance of emotion and argue that the reciprocal interactions between emotional and cognitive systems need to be studied. In fact, affect develops from a hard-wired foundation and is capable of learning, as cognition is. Affect can be described as consisting of schemes in the same way as cognition, and hence as embodying useful information about the organism and the environment. The difference between cognition and emotion lies in the kinds of schemes formed and in their neurological localization.

Piaget argued that affect does not itself provide any structuring to the forms of cognition that develop. In fact, there is an implicit bias in Piaget's theorizing that holds that affect is something that has to be controlled by intellectual or structural regulations, perhaps reflecting his own cultural upbringing. Piaget's concern was with the more deliberate and conscious aspects of life and not its more spontaneous and unconscious functioning. The principle of what I shall call serendipity was absent from his theorizing. Affective development was described as occurring in sequence with cognitive ontogenesis, and as eventuating in the establishment of normative scales of values and the emergence of will at the time of concrete operations.

As for the role of social experience, Piaget (1947/1960) argued that social stimulation may enhance development by means of the social pressures existing for such things as cooperation, perspective taking, and the need to justify one's position to others, as when children in play must justify their actions or their point of view to others. However, the *kinds* of social experiences do not contribute to the specific *kinds* of logical structures said to develop. The symbolic universe as mediated to the child through its language and socialization has no specific role in fostering the particular kinds of logical structures that develop. The structures that do develop are not related to the kinds of language that a child may experience; rather, they have their specific forms prefigured in the basic conditions of the biological organization of life (Piaget, 1967/1971). Development was said to consist of the reflective abstraction of these forms, whose coherence and necessity cannot be traced to the internalization of environmental structure.

INTELLECTUAL OPERATIONS AND THE LEARNING PARADOX

If the source of new forms in cognitive development is not due to affect or social-educational experience, as Piagetian theory holds, then the source of intellectual form must be due to the structuring activity of the intellect itself. This raises the issue referred to by Fodor as the inductivist fallacy (Chomsky & Fodor, 1980; Fodor, 1980) or by Pascual-Leone (1980) as the learning paradox. Essentially, this argument states that one cannot learn what one does not know, because in order to learn what one does not know, one would require some means of assimilating it. In order to assimilate it, one would have to, in a sense, already possess it. Applied to Piagetian theory, Fodor (1980) argued that one cannot learn a richer logic by means of a weaker logic, and Bereiter (1985) questioned how a structure could generate another structure more complex than itself. The argument assumes that learning occurs by the production of hypotheses that are then either confirmed or rejected. The system must, however, possess the hypothesis first in order to test it. It cannot test a hypothesis that it does not have. In other words, one cannot know to look underneath a rock unless one's conceptual system indicates that the rock exists in the first place.

The Piagetian answer to the learning paradox is that development occurs through "reflective abstraction" from action schemata (Piaget, 1967/1971), but as applied to adult dialectical development, this would entail that dialectical structure must have some kind of precursor form in the biological processes that Piaget described. Given that dialectics has been most often used in the analysis of human social and historical processes, this would seem to imply some anticipation by these biological mechanisms of later social developments at a time in our early molecular evolution prior to any human history.

The learning paradox is a result of the view that learning is a matter of hypothesis formation and confirmation (Fodor, 1980), and that one system of logic cannot produce another more powerful system of logic without having to frame hypotheses regarding the latter more powerful system from elements of the less powerful, earlier one. These hypotheses can then be confirmed or disconfirmed by specific feedback mechanisms; all this is thought to be explained by learning theory and the current philosophy of science (Campbell, 1974; Lakatos & Musgrave, 1970; Piattelli-Palmarini, 1980). What cannot be explained—except by resort to nativist theory according to Fodor—is the mechanism of hypothesis formation. Where do new ideas or new structures come from?

If a certain conceptual system—for example, some kind of robot—encounters a new and unknown world, it can seek to understand that world by projecting hypotheses onto it and editing out the hypotheses that are found inadequate while retaining those that work. However, if there is something in the world that has no equivalent in the system's repertoire of hypotheses, nothing adequate can be projected in the first place. If the robot's repertoire of hypotheses consists entirely of "greeps," and the robot has been dropped by its uncaring makers into a world of "snarves," it will be unable to cope.

Campbell and Bickhard (1987) pointed out that this argument is based on what they term "encodingism," or a picture theory of the mind in which cognition is said to reflect in a one-to-one correspondence the reality it knows. Hypotheses are like pictures. They advocate an interactive-systems perspective on knowing that manages to avoid the dismal conclusion reached by Fodor that development cannot occur. However, the source of novelty in such a system still has to be explained, as Campbell and Bickhard agreed that the source of new system organization comes from within the system (Campbell & Bickhard, 1987, p. 54).

This debate may strike some as analogous to the activities of medieval theologians who are said to have debated how many angels could dance on the head of a pin. However, this issue can be given a practical twist when we apply it to trying to understand why an individual might want to move from what is described as a dualistic, multiplistic, or even relativistic, framework to a more dialectical framework. One has to ask the question: Why change the structures one already has? Why try to develop new structures to replace old ones when the old structures are still strongly active in their control of current mental functioning? Furthermore, how is it that old organizations can develop into new organizations on their own when it is argued that one can only assimilate content to the existing structures one already has? How could one set about to construct a dialectical approach to experience when one may have no idea what a dialectical approach is? If cognitive reorganization involves moving into areas one presently does not understand, why would anyone want to make the leap from present intellectual securities into unknown and unchartered realms?

What exactly would be required to induce somebody to reconceptualize or re-negotiate the terms of, for example, a marriage, when he or she can see the relationship only in a fixed way and has no means of perceiving how it could be viewed dialectically? Why would a person want to try to see things differently when he or she has no idea of what this "seeing differently" involves?

SUGGESTIONS FOR WAYS OUT OF THE LEARNING PARADOX

To answer this, we must extend the nature of our inquiry into the broader context of the emotions and feelings that individuals have in concrete social situations. People must desire change—even though they may have no clearly formulated conception of what it will consist—and they must feel that to make the change that they will have some direction and support. Endogenous intellectual structures in and of themselves may be too conservative to bring about such change, particularly as described in Piagetian theory, which tends to emphasize the priority of assimilation over accommodation in structural development.

Cognitive structures are systems with conservative tendencies. Individuals assimilate the situations which they face using their existing cognitive structures, and insofar as the situation can be readily understood using the existing structure, the structure is reinforced. It is only when novel aspects of a situation stretch the existing cognitive structures beyond their limits that new structures are likely to develop. (Basseches, 1986, p. 108)

Accommodation will only occur if it has to; that is, if assimilation has previously failed. Pertaining to the potentially nondialectical nature of intellectual functioning is Perkins's (1986) observation that in informal reasoning tasks, high I.Q. subjects, as compared to others, were not necessarily as successful in generating ideas on the other side of the argument. They concentrated their energies instead on building arguments for their own side, producing more ideas in support of their own point of view than did normals.

I would like to propose that for dialectical development to occur, what would seem to be required is some affective goal orientation on the part of the individual, and some appropriate environmental structuring and stimulation in the form of human mediation on the part of the environment. The functioning of the ego (Kegan, 1982; Loevinger, 1976) must be nondefensive and secure enough to enable a willing suspension of taken-for-granted beliefs so that change can be sought in a positive manner. The view that the detection of cognitive inconsistency or ambiguity alone is a sufficient cause for the appropriate affect is too simple; the person needs to want to do something about that conflict as well as to be able to perceive its existence. They need to apprehend the problem, desire to change it, and have help from others. They can then enter into dialogue with others (friends, family, teachers, and therapists) who can provide the mediation into culturally transmitted symbolic universes (Berger & Luckman, 1966) which will, in time, become psychologically internalized as part of the person's own meaning-making activity (Carlsen, 1988).

We can see that the resources for change can come from the social sphere. As Meacham and Emont (1989) have argued, mental sets are broken in interaction with others. Problems do not have to be solved by isolated individuals. Repeated experiences with what can be called social problem solving can bring the individual to come to possess what Bowers (1984)—borrowing from Habermas—called "communicative competence." What has occurred in the form of dialogue in interaction with others becomes dialectic in the individual's consciousness.[1]

PERSONALITY AS AFFECT AND COGNITION

Pascual-Leone (1983, 1984) argued for an information-processing model of personality that is relevant to understanding how affect can relate to dialectical cognition. In his model, cognitive and affective schemes are interconnected such that the activation of one type of scheme can lead to the activation of the other. Personality may be defined as the recurring and consistently cofunctional activation of affective and cognitive structures. It is important to differentiate his conception from other developmental perspectives on the personality that include stages of development that are described as dialectical, such as those of Fowler (1982), Loevinger (1976), and Kegan (1982). Each of these conceptions argues that dialectical functioning is not based solely in intellectual structures but is grounded in personality structures as well.

While neo-Piagetian, Pascual-Leone's theory is strongly grounded in information-processing and neuropsychological research, and the "stuff" of which the mind is said to be made consists not of logical structures but of schemes, although defined somewhat differently than in Piagetian theory. Schemes are the basic unit of knowledge or mental representation in the brain of generalized routines for interacting with the objects of the world. Schemes can be built up through coordination with other schemes, and are defined neurophysiologically as patterns of coactivation in the brain. Personality is the molar-level description of the interconnections of myriads of cognitive and affective schemes. In Pascual-Leone's theory, personality is not seen as one structural entity; it is, rather, constituted by the result of the activity of many different schematic units managing to appear united, but without a "little man" running the show from behind the scenes in the manner of the homunculus criticized by cognitive science.

If we use these kinds of models to describe dialectical thought, we shall have to say something about personality, and thus describe affective processes as well as cognitive processes. From several points of view, we can see that the development of dialectical processes involves more than intellectual structural development.

THE IMPORTANCE OF DOUBT

Looking at adult intellectual development from a non-Piagetian perspective as we have been doing, we can argue that by describing sequential invariances in intellectual operations or logical abilities, we may be looking in the wrong direction for the real commonalities to that development. The question would seem to be not the argument over whether what is most common and unique in adult thinking—and what discriminates it from children's or adolescent's thinking—should be described as relativistic, dialectical, or metasystematic logical structure. The focus should instead be on studying how affect and education interact in moving the adolescent through the alternatives of either dogmatism or skepticism that can ensue after operational thought has developed. Chandler (1987) argued that a theory of adult development should be phrased in terms of the responses adolescents construct after the questioning and challenging of their epistemic certainties. This is precipitated by such factors as the awareness of the inherent subjectivity that is attributed to knowledge. The various responses constructed may be described as dialectical or relativistic, but there may also be other styles available that are not currently accounted for in our efforts to explain. Chandler argued that all these forms can be subsumed by the term "postskeptical."

It is argued that what underlies development is the adolescent's coming to take his or her conceptualizations of the world as problematic (Boyes, Chandler, Ball, & Hala, 1985). The prerequisite for this is the ability to operate on propositions (formal operations), enabling the ability to reflect and operate on one's knowledge structures as if they were constructions, and not to take them as if they were simple reflections of "what is." Such reflection involves the realization that subjectivity is intertwined with each objective statement that is made.

Aside from the experience of doubt, we might also examine certain phenomena associated with loss as described by the psychiatrists Colarusso and Nemiroff (1981):

The first crack in the armor appears to come in late adolescence when intrapsychic loss is felt keenly and normally experienced through a loosening of ties to the parents. A sense of history develops with a recognition of a personal past, present, and future. . . . [T]he dawning recognition is quickly defended against by the optimism and idealism of the young adult—an attempt . . . to deny the "two fundamental features of human life— the inevitableness of eventual death, and the existence of hate and destructive impulses inside each person" (Jacques, 1965, p. 505) . . . Gradually the belief in the inherent goodness of man, a central characteristic of the idealism of youth, is replaced by "a more contemplative pessimism" (Jacques, 1965, p. 504) . . . as awareness of the power of hate and destructive forces which contribute to man's misery, tragedy, and death increases. (p. 76)

These kinds of affective changes can be studied as they interact with the cognitive developments that may be unique to adulthood. The ways in which such interactions can be formulated are outlined below.

SOCIETY, DIALECTICS, AND ATTENTION

In going beyond a Piagetian perspective on adult development (Broughton, 1984), it is possible with an information-processing theory and a Vygotskian linguistic perspective to conceptualize what occurs in adulthood as changes in the processing of attentional strategies. Dialectical thinking can be seen as consisting of the flexible deployment and allocation of attention working with the currently functioning semantic structures such that new structures are brought into the "field of centration" (Pascual-Leone, 1983) or working memory as old structures are being modified (Irwin & Sheese, 1989).

One's socially circumscribed and linguistically bounded culture influences what can be conceptualized or attended to in one's equally circumscribed span of attention. Therefore, one's culture, as mediated by one's language, is important as a means of controlling attention and creating the conceptual structures for acting on mental schemes (Vygotsky, 1962, 1978). In order to develop dialectically, the cultural environment must contain the material with which to begin; developing in a dialectical manner in any given society (Bowers, 1984) is contingent on the symbolic and conceptual potentials existing in that society (Dobert, Habermas, & Nunner-Winkler, 1987). Societies can be said to differ with respect to the degree to which they foster not only the thinking of certain ideas but also the potential to rethink such ideas in the light of new perspectives.

Among the necessary conditions that have to be present in a sociocultural environment are pluralism (Perry, 1970), tolerance, support, challenge, change, and a nonauthoritarian atmosphere. Another important factor may be the presence of what Bowers (1984) termed a "liminal space" in the social and political environment. This could come about by having taken-for-granted attitudes made problematic—that is, no longer granted their previous sources of legitimation. Bowers defined liminal space as the conceptual openness created in periods of cultural transition when the individual relativizes his or her thinking about social and personal realities. However, in order for this to work, this experience must not be felt as threatening, or a regression into earlier patterns of thinking and behaving will occur. These kinds of factors—and the linguistic skills necessary to conceptualize them—could precipitate an individual into becoming able to dialectically monitor his or her own attentional processes and thus enter into the negotiation of the "social construction of reality," namely, to realize that reality is socially constructed by participants in a dialogue (Berger & Luckman, 1966). When this is encouraged in education, we speak of the empowering of the student. When one's focus is on the therapeutic process, attention should be given to creating the conditions of confirmation, continuity, and contradiction (Carlsen, 1988), which provide individual legitimation while at the same time building the basis for self-initiated change.

In Pascual-Leone's work (1983, 1984; Pascual-Leone & Goodman, 1979), attention is employed by executives, which are higher-level, goal-directed, processing units, that direct the processing of schemes over time by activation from their corresponding mental energy. These executive structures control the activation of schematic units, but they themselves also require activation components in the form of releasing conditions that can be triggered by content schemes or affect schemes. Executive-driven processes, unlike Piagetian operatory structures, have releasing conditions linked to stimulus input, and are contextually generated by perceptual pattern-matching processes. The internal context for activating executive processes includes one's internal and affective states or schemes (Bower, 1981; Lang, 1983) which are themselves triggered by innate perceptual-motor schemata or learned emotional schemata linked to stimulus patterns.

In order to think dialectically, different conflicting elements or schemes must be brought into the span of mental attention. This could be done by previously learned executives, or else it could be done through the boosting derived from affect schemes or content schemes that have been activated in the course of processing the environment (particularly in interaction with others in the human linguistic environment). If one is going to arrive at novel dialectical shifts in attention, one is going to have to produce performances or thoughts that are not a part of one's current functioning executive repertoire. For example, in order to solve an interpersonal problem, it may be necessary to think of the subject— for example, marriage—not as a fixed thing but rather as an evolving structure constituted by each partner in dialogue. This concept would presumably not be a part of the formalist vocabulary of someone who would be described as dualistic.

In order to break out of the learning paradox, new executives must be generated on the basis of the present functioning of old executives. This is where serendipity plays a role in what would otherwise be only conservative intellectual processing. I will mention that serendipity is defined by the concise *Oxford Dictionary* as "the faculty of making happy and unexpected discoveries by accident." Conditions must be ripe to allow for thoughts to occur that would not be predicted from a knowledge of a person's previous thinking patterns.

In discussing the learning paradox, I noted that the difficulty arises in determining the mechanisms of hypothesis formation. Although somewhat tentatively, I believe that I can provide at least some idea of where we should be looking for an answer:

1. We should conceptualize the movement into dialectical thinking as the acquisition of particular attention-mobilizing executives, not the re-equilibration of dialectical structure from formal operational structure.

2. The problem should be seen as one of determining how nondialectical executives can produce dialectical executives.

3. Creation of this sort can be precipitated by allowing for serendipitous processing in the activation and formation of cognitive structures. Order must emerge, but it can only come about if a certain chaos is tolerated or even encouraged. Given enough affective investment—and therefore the required mental energy—there will follow an executive-driven search for relevant elements. This will allow the activation of numerous experiential schemes.

4. The direction of attentional processes can be channeled via the intervention of symbolically structured social-learning experiences, namely, teachers, friends, salient emotional events, and so forth.

5. This will lead to the formation within attention of what are termed ephemeral or virtual schemes; a process that can be aided by the skillful interventions of educators, therapists, or family members. These ephemeral and virtual structures do not exist as part of the individual's permanent cognitive repertoire. Their coming into the span of attention is temporary and somewhat fortuitous at this time. A person with these virtual schemes only possesses them as a function of what the environment has facilitated at the time.

6. In order that the person be able to use and spontaneously exert effective control over these virtual schemes in the future, they must apply and be consolidated with repeated use, thus being converted into habitual schemes or executives that could then be activated in the future by the person's own control processes. Anderson (1983) called this proceduralization and automatization. The scheme's activation would then be the result of internal personality schemes, and would not be dependent on socially facilitating experiences.

AFFECTIVE SCHEMATA AND CHANGE

Although these are not the only possibilities that could be suggested for solving the learning paradox (other suggestions are offered in Bereiter, 1985), I have focused here on affective processing and the mediation of socially structured educational experiences. I shall now point out other ways that dialectical thinking might come about, and in the process I will get around the problems posed by the learning paradox, at least as it applies to the development of dialectical thinking.

Affective arousal or energizing and the activation of affect schemes that conflict with intellectual structures can often bring about changes in personality. Often this is the intent in therapeutic procedures that use emotional arousal to access unprocessed emotional schemata (Greenberg & Safran, 1987). Greenberg and Safran argued for a perspective that sees emotion as biologically relevant information cuing an organism to the state of its interactions with the environment. Often this information is not attended to as a result of repression or suppression, which are themselves the result of early socialization experiences. Processing emotional schemata can induce changes in conceptual schemata. Frequently people fail to attend to the functioning of emotional schemata because of cognitive prohibitions. Inducing experiences of intrapsychic contradiction is a means of bringing to awareness antitheses and contradictions to cognitive structures or beliefs—in this case, thoughts or feelings that have, until now, been denied or suppressed.

Another way this can be achieved was described by Pascual-Leone (1983) as occurring as the result of aging. With deterioration of the physiological hardware (or silent resources—specifically M for mental capacity or working memory and I for the interruption mechanism), mental energy is no longer available to keep apart or compartmentalize one's structures for dealing with the processing of interpersonal or social situations. Now one must confront discrepancies between one's differing schemes or representations of self and others that were previously activated only in situation-specific circumstances. In youth, these contradictions were easily suppressed by the interruption mechanism, but they are now brought into the open with the failure of these inhibiting mechanisms. In confronting these conflicts, one has to engage in what are specifically intrapsychic dialectical operations.

Labouvie-Vief (1982) has written of the de-automatization or "freeing-up" of dystonic equilibria that occurs in adulthood. Dystonic equilibria are the cultural patterns the child has introjected in a passive manner because of his or her own limited processing abilities in childhood. In adulthood, these can be reactivated and disinhibited as the maturing individual actively reprocesses their cognitive and affective structures in a more self-referential and reflexive manner. This kind of processing in adulthood has been noted in a clinical context by the psychiatrist Roger Gould (Gould, 1978), who describes how the adult's childhood fears, taboos, and monsters have to be faced and reworked in adulthood. More recently, Labouvie-Vief and colleagues (Labouvie-Vief, Hakim-Larson, & Hobart, 1987) have noted the changes in defense mechanisms and coping strategies that occur as a function of development, where the more overtly repressive styles of defense come to show decreased frequency.

EDUCATION AND SOCIALIZATION

Bowers (1984) discussed ways in which dialectical thinking might be stimulated by social interaction, and particularly education. One of the changes in curriculum that he proposed is the use of a more phenomenological method that relates symbolic or abstract material to the subjective life-world as experienced by the student; the concepts taught would be perceived as more concrete and thus less susceptible to reification by the student. Another approach is to historically contextualize subject matter and employ a cross-cultural method that will facilitate an outlook that relativizes and historically situates concepts that would otherwise be taken as given, and thereby objectified. These kinds of methods are considered to make problematic the student's natural attitude toward what is socially defined as "reality."

Bowers has argued that the objective is the fostering of a student's communicative competence. This concept—taken over from Habermas's work (1979)—describes the characteristics required of individuals to be able to enter into an active role in the negotiation and construction of their own and others' social reality. This can occur only if they possess the facility with the cultural traditions in which they have been raised to come to be able to symbolize their own conceptual map-making experiences, thus taking a critical stance toward their own socialization, of which their education is also a part.

One medium of communication in education is writing. Some people working in the area of composition (Elbow, 1986) have argued for the way in which writing favors dialectical thinking, and others have noted (Hays, Brandt, & Chantry, 1988) how much developmental level effects composition processes. The use of pre-writing heuristics (Young, Becker, & Pike, 1970) contains much that implicitly could be informed by developmental theories and research (Irwin, 1989). Writing, through overcoming the communicative barriers traditionally set down by geography and history, builds on the communicative competence of students.

What these other disciplines lack—at least traditionally—is a precise conception of the ontogenesis of this communicative competence; what I am arguing here is that this could be the task of research in adult development; specifically, what is currently termed postformal research.

In conclusion, what is crucial to note is that this communicative competence is not entirely either history- or culture-free, but rather is relative to the traditions and language games with which the individual interacts. Consequently, it should be seen that modeling this development by simple formal or abstract organizations of logic would be to miss what is most important about the phenomenon—its essentially social nature (Broughton, 1987).

NOTE

1. It is important to note that an individual's dialectical processes may be represented at a conscious level of serial processing requiring effort and attention, or that they may exist at a preconscious or tacit level (Greenberg & Safran, 1987) of parallel processing that has not been automatized and does not require conscious effort (Schneider & Shiffrin, 1977). It is thus important, when carrying out one's protocol analyses, to make a methodological distinction between dialectical thinking that can be explicitly articulated and

dialectical thinking that occurs but is not necessarily explicated verbally. In either case, dialectical strategies, executives, or schemata would generally be context-bound and frequently associated with emotional-processing schemata and their activation (Bower, 1981).

REFERENCES

Anderson, J. R. (1983). *The architecture of cognition*. Cambridge, MA: Harvard University Press.

Arlin, P. K. (1975). Cognitive development in adulthood: A fifth stage? *Developmental Psychology, 11*, 602–606.

Basseches, M. (1984). *Dialectical thinking and adult development*. Norwood, NJ: Ablex.

Basseches, M. (1986). Cognitive-structural development and the conditions of employment. *Human Development, 29*, 101–112.

Bereiter, C. (1985). Toward a solution of the learning paradox. *Review of Educational Research, 55*(2), 201–226.

Berger, P., & Luckman, T. (1966). *The social construction of reality: A treatise in the sociology of knowledge*. New York: Penguin.

Bower, G. (1981). Mood and memory. *American Psychologist, 36*(2), 129–148.

Bowers, C. A. (1984). *The promise of theory: Education and the politics of cultural change*. New York: Longman.

Boyes, M., Chandler, M., Ball, L., & Hala, S. (1985, June). *A paradigmatic view of adolescent identity formation*. Paper presented at the meeting of the Canadian Psychological Association, Halifax, Nova Scotia.

Broughton, J. M. (1981). Piaget's structural developmental psychology. *Human Development, 24*, 78.

Broughton, J. M. (1984). Not beyond formal operations but beyond Piaget. In M. L. Commons, F. A. Richards, & C. Armon (Eds.), *Beyond formal operations: Late adolescent and adult cognitive development* (pp. 395–411). New York: Praeger.

Broughton, J. M. (1987). An introduction to critical developmental psychology. In J. M. Broughton (Ed.), *Critical theories of psychological development* (pp. 1–30). New York: Plenum.

Campbell, D. (1974). Evolutionary epistemology. In P. A. Schlipp (Ed.), *The library of living philosophers: Vol. 14, I & II. The philosophy of Karl Popper* (pp. 413–463). Lasalle, IL: Open Court Publishers.

Campbell, R. L., & Bickhard, M. H. (1987). A deconstruction of Fodor's anticonstructivism. *Human Development, 30*, 48–59.

Carlsen, M. B. (1988). *Meaning-making: Therapeutic processes in adult development*. New York: Norton.

Chandler, M. (1987). The Othello effect: An essay on the emergence and eclipse of skeptical doubt. *Human development, 30*, 137–159.

Chomsky, N., & Fodor, J. (1980). The inductivist fallacy. In M. Piattelli-Palmarini (Ed.), *Language and learning: The debate between Jean Piaget and Noam Chomsky* (pp. 255–275). Cambridge, MA: Harvard University Press.

Colarusso, C. A., & Nemiroff, R. A. (1981). *Adult development: A new dimension in psychodynamic theory and practice*. New York: Plenum.

Dobert, R., Habermas, J., & Nunner-Winkler, G. (1987). The development of the self.

In J. M. Broughton (Ed.), *Critical theories of psychological development* (pp. 275–301). New York: Plenum.

Elbow, P. (1986). *Embracing contraries: Explorations in learning and teaching*. New York: Oxford University Press.

Fodor, J. (1980). On the impossibility of acquiring "more powerful" structures. In M. Piattelli-Palmarini (Ed.), *Language and learning: The debate between Jean Piaget and Noam Chomsky* (pp. 142–162). Cambridge, MA: Harvard University Press.

Fowler, J. (1982). *Stages of faith: The psychology of human development and the quest for meaning*. Cambridge: Harper & Row.

Gould, R. L. (1978). *Transformations: Growth and change in adult life*. New York: Simon & Schuster.

Greenberg, L. S., & Safran, J. D. (1987). *Emotion in psychotherapy: Affect, cognition, and the process of change*. New York: Guilford.

Gregory, R. (1987). *The Oxford companion to the mind*. Oxford: Oxford University Press.

Habermas, J. (1979). *Communication and the evolution of society* (T. McCarthy, Trans.). Boston: Beacon.

Hays, J. N., Brandt, K. M., & Chantry, K. H. (1988). The impact of friendly and hostile audiences on the argumentative writing of high school and college students. *Research in the Teaching of English, 22*, 391–416.

Irwin, R. R. (1989, July). *The dialectics of writing: Relations between cognitive-developmental factors and perception of the writing process in young adults*. Paper presented at the Fourth Adult Development Symposium, Boston.

Irwin, R. R., & Sheese, R. L. (1989). Problems in the proposal for a "stage" of dialectical thinking. In M. L. Commons, J. D. Sinnott, R. A. Richards, & C. Armon (Eds.), *Adult development: Vol. I. Comparisons and applications of developmental models* (pp. 113–132). New York: Praeger.

Jacques, E. (1965). Death and the mid-life crisis. *International Journal of Psychoanalysis, 46*, 602.

Kegan, R. (1982). *The evolving self: Problem and process in human development*. Cambridge, MA: Harvard University Press.

Koplowitz, H. (1984). A projection beyond Piaget's formal-operations stage: A general system stage and a unitary stage. In M. L. Commons, F. A. Richards, & C. Armon (Eds.), *Beyond formal operations: Late adolescent and adult cognitive development* (pp. 272–295). New York: Praeger.

Labouvie-Vief, G. (1982). Dynamic development and mature autonomy: A theoretical prologue. *Human Development, 25*, 161–192.

Labouvie-Vief, G., Hakim-Larson, J., & Hobart, C. J. (1987). Age, ego level, and the life-span development of coping and the defense processes. *Psychology and Aging, 2*(3), 286–293.

Lakatos, I., & Musgrave, P. (1970). *Criticism and the growth of knowledge*. Cambridge: Cambridge University Press.

Lang, P. J. (1983). Cognition in emotion: Concept and action. In C. Izard, J. Kagan, & R. Zajonc (Eds.), *Emotion, cognition, and behaviour* (pp. 192–226). New York: Cambridge University Press.

Loevinger, J. (1976). *Ego development*. San Francisco: Jossey-Bass.

Meacham, J. A., & Emont, N. C. (1989). The interpersonal basis of everyday problem solving. In J. D. Sinnott (Ed.), *Everyday problem solving: Theory and applications* (pp. 7–23). New York: Praeger.

Pascual-Leone, J. (1980). Constructive problems for constructive theories: The current relevance of Piaget's work and a critique of information-processing simulation psychology. In R. Kluwe & H. Sapada (Eds.), *Developmental models of thinking* (pp. 263–296). New York: Academic.

Pascual-Leone, J. (1983). Growing into human maturity: Toward a metasubjective theory of adulthood stages. In P. B. Baltes & O. G. Brim (Eds.), *Life-span development and behaviour* (Volume 5, pp. 118–156). New York: Academic.

Pascual-Leone, J. (1984). Attentional, dialectic, and mental effort: Toward an organismic theory of life stages. In M. L. Commons, F. A. Richards, & C. Armon (Eds.), *Beyond formal operations: Late adolescent and adult cognitive development* (pp. 182–215). New York: Praeger.

Pascual-Leone, J., & Goodman, D. (1979). *Intelligence and experience: A neo-Piagetian approach.* (Department of Psychology Reports, No. 81). Toronto: York University.

Perkins, D. (1986, April). *Reasoning as it is and as it could be: An empirical perspective.* Paper presented at the meeting of the American Educational Research Association, San Francisco.

Perry, W. (1970). *Forms of intellectual and ethical development during the college years.* New York: Holt, Rinehart & Winston.

Piaget, J. (1960). *The psychology of intelligence* (M. Piercy & D. Berlyne, Trans.). Totowa, NJ: Littlefield, Adams & Co. (Original work published 1947)

Piaget, J. (1971). *Biology and knowledge: An essay on the relations between organic regulations and cognitive processes* (B. Walsh, Trans.). Chicago: University of Chicago Press. (Original work published 1967)

Piaget, J. (1972). *The principles of genetic epistemology* (W. Mays, Trans.). London: Routledge & Kegan Paul.

Piaget, J. (1981). *Intelligence and affectivity: Their relationship during child development* (T. A. Brown & C. E. Kaegi, Trans.). Palo Alto, CA: Annual Reviews.

Piatelli-Palmarini, M. (1980). *Language and learning: The debate between Jean Piaget and Noam Chomsky.* Cambridge, MA: Harvard University Press.

Riegel, K. F. (1973). Dialectic operations: The final period of cognitive development. *Human Development, 16,* 346–370.

Schneider, W., & Shiffrin, R. M. (1977). Controlled and automatic human information processing: I. Detection, search, and attention. *Psychological Review, 84,* 1–66.

Vygotsky, L. S. (1962). *Thought and language.* Cambridge, MA: MIT Press.

Vygotsky, L. S. (1978). *Mind in society* (M. Cole, V. John-Steiner, S. Scribner, & E. Souberman, Trans.). Cambridge, MA: Harvard University Press.

Wertsch, J. V. (1985). *Culture, communication, and cognition: Vygotskian perspectives.* New York: Press Syndicate of the University of Cambridge.

Young, R., Becker, A., & Pike, K. (1970). *Rhetoric: Discovery and change.* New York: Harcourt, Brace, & World.

6

Bridging Paradigms: The Role of a Change Agent in an International Technical Transfer Project

LYNN JOHNSON

There are many professions in which long-term positive behavioral change on the part of one or more individuals or groups of individuals is the desired outcome. However, the factors that cause change and the learning/change process that occurs are only partially understood. Using a descriptive case study, this chapter will offer support for the hypothesis that postformal reasoning as one step beyond Piaget's formal operational reasoning (Commons, Richards, & Armon, 1984; Kramer, 1983; Kramer & Bopp, 1989; Sinnott, 1989b) plays a part in the learning process. A postformal thinker is characterized by conscious self-referential thinking in which formal truth and logic systems are selectively ordered and used dependent on a given context (Sinnott, 1989c). The theoretical argument will be made that if the "teacher/facilitator" is interacting cognitively with the learner at a postformal level at least part of the time, then the learner is more likely to learn how to define and solve problems more effectively and more creatively. In addition, the learner may learn how to reason postformally and to generalize what has been learned across different contexts which could enable the learner to make long-term behavioral changes. It is hypothesized that it may be possible to help individuals move to higher cognitive levels, including the level of postformal operations, through two-way communication involving an empathetic facilitator who operates postformally and can bridge various ways of looking at the world or at paradigms. *Paradigm* as used in this chapter refers to an individual's overarching cognitive and emotional framework for interpreting experience: one's construction of reality. If an impetus for restructuring one's cognitive structure or shifting paradigms is communication with others (Meacham, ch. 9, this volume), then communication in a group context with a post-formal facilitator should accelerate this process.

These hypotheses will be explored within the specific context of a technical transfer program, under the auspices of the Agency for International Development (AID), in which rural subsistence women in Honduras were organized into cooperative groups and taught how to raise, maintain, and market imported breeds of pigs in small pig farms (Johnson-Dean, 1986).[1] This particular situation was selected because it appears that only one facilitator in the technical transfer program operated with postformal reasoning, while the other facilitator and group participants primarily used formal operational reasoning, and that this affected outcomes. This example provides a real-life, nonformal adult-learning context for examining the role of postformal reasoning.

This discussion centers on a specific time, place, and process, and the empirical data are limited. The suggestions and hypotheses discussed are not based on experimental research but rather are theoretical in nature. Nevertheless, it is hoped that this chapter may suggest new ways of enabling people to move to levels of more complex thought, which might increase their adaptability, enlarge their problem-finding and -solving space (Arlin, 1984, 1989), and promote the learning process along with long-term, complex behavioral change (Perry, 1975). This discussion may also provide insights into the learning/change process itself.

BACKGROUND

In 1984, AID funded a small-scale livestock project in Honduras. The objective of this project was to empower rural subsistence women through training, technical assistance, and financial support so that they could develop an ongoing business of raising, marketing, and selling new breeds of pigs, and thus increase their standard of living. These breeds were originally imported from the United States and, although they were much larger and leaner than, and thus superior to, the traditional domestic pig, they required far more care and had to be raised in pig farms. Four villages were selected to participate in this 3-year project. During the first year, approximately 10 to 15 women per village were organized into a group. Each group was assigned a facilitator, a project staff woman who acted as moderator, mentor, and change agent to each of two groups. The project sought to develop camaraderie among the women through a series of group activities that emphasized recognition, value, and respect for each of the members and their experiences, perspectives, and ideas. Along with providing emotional support for these women, at a cognitive level the formation of these groups and the subsequent group activities also laid the foundation for introducing new paradigms and encouraged the women to move to levels of more complex thought, thereby increasing their problem-solving abilities.

The project planners believed that the success of the development project was dependent on the formation of cooperative groups and the empowerment of women through group activities so that they could make their own informed decisions about the pig project enterprise and its future. The planners did not focus on the extent to which the women learned the technical information conveyed, but rather on whether the women could define and solve problems and generalize this ability to different contexts. It was believed that whether long-term behavioral change would occur was dependent on the success of the four groups in their ability to problem solve and deal with changes. Nine months after the start of this project, two of the four groups were successfully keeping pigs. Although these groups did encounter difficulties, the abilities of the women in these two groups to define and solve problems seemed greater than that of the members of the other two groups. The facilitator of the more successful groups appeared to operate at a postformal level, and it is suggested that this ability was a major factor in the groups' success.

THE LEARNING PROCESS

Sternberg (1988) described the acquisition of knowledge as occurring through the following mechanisms: (a) selective encoding, sifting out relevant from irrelevant information; (b) selective combination, synthesizing discrete information into a unified whole; and (c) selective comparison, integrating new information with that already acquired. For selective comparison and subsequent generalization, as defined in learning theory, to occur, individuals seem to take what has been learned and incorporate that new information into their existing body of knowledge such that they structure their reality in a new way (Ginsburg & Opper, 1969). Perhaps all types of learning and knowledge acquisition are maximized when the teacher and learner operate at a postformal level during the encoding, combination, and comparison processes. Since it appears that postformal reasoning may not be that common, it may not be possible for both the teacher and the learner to operate with complex cognitive thinking. However, if the information is communicated by someone operating postformally who can help to bridge the new information into an individual's existing paradigm and who can dialogue with that individual during the selective encoding, combination, and comparison processes, then new paradigms will still be created and learning will be made generalizable.

INTRODUCTION OF INFORMATION

The introduction of new information is an essential component of the learning/change process, and it must be presented in such a way as to be understandable and acceptable to the learner. It must relate to the previous knowledge or skill level of an individual so that it can be incorporated into the learner's cognitive framework. It should be recognized that information of any type is not value-free. All information is conveyed and interpreted at different cognitive stages and viewed through individual filters that are formulated by beliefs, values, emotions, experiences, cultural systems, and context.

Filters may be judged more disparate in a cross-cultural context, yet these filters exist intraculturally as well as interculturally. Each individual has a different set of filters, and for information to be communicable, it must be at least somewhat acceptable to the belief, value, and cultural systems of the receiver. A person's belief and value systems, however, are not static entities; they change over time and circumstance, and may vary even within the same time frame dependent on the context of interaction with others. Perhaps one of the most effective ways of shifting paradigms is through group interaction and discussion, and through analysis of the new information (Meacham, ch. 9, this volume). At the same time, it is important to remember that the individual relates not only to the group but also to his or her family, other groups, society, and culture. As Sinnott has pointed out (ch. 16, this volume), each of these sources affects perceptual filters and thus affects the individual's decision-making process. If change is being promoted, it is essential to examine the context in which new (or previously unattended to) information is introduced, and to recognize that any individual is part of a nested set of systems.

WHAT ALLOWS SYSTEMIC CHANGE TO HAPPEN?

The ability of individuals to shift paradigms or to operate postformally seems to be dependent on a critical level of "chaos" in which their present paradigm or paradigms can no longer adequately make sense of the world (Kelly, 1955; Perry, 1975). There must be a sufficient level of dissatisfaction with the status quo to make change acceptable and to permit the encoding of new information even though the amount of disorder or discomfort increases. The individual, group, culture, and society must also maintain enough flexibility to allow such a change. Viewing such change from a General Systems Theory (GST) approach, it is important to recognize that individuals, groups, cultures, and societies may be thought of both as systems and as parts of a larger system, and that they are all interrelated and affected by each other. When looking at the process of change, it may be helpful to review system characteristics from GST that influence it (Sinnott, 1989a, p. 57):

1. The system must permit more information to enter . . . flexibility, but under bounded control.
2. Systems resist disorder.
3. Change means temporary increase in disorder.
4. Systems monitor and control the amount of disorder.
5. Surviving systems contain the seeds of their own change, and are programmed to get to the next highest level of order.
6. Surviving systems balance potentials and activated processes.
7. Surviving systems fit many contexts.
8. Surviving systems are programmed to interfere with each other.

9. Nonsurviving systems have the same parts as surviving systems, but different processes. (p. 57)

System, as it is used in the context above, could describe the intra-individual processes of the participating women, the cooperative groups as entities, the village culture, or the Honduran society as a living system. It is important to remember these system characteristics when analyzing and assessing the change process within a given situation. There are many factors that affect whether change occurs. In the four project villages, entropy existed; it was not too great, and provided the motivation for change. Almost any change that might enhance the villagers' economic situation would be considered. For the villagers to accept a new way of raising pigs and the fact that women should market the pigs on a long-term basis, there needed to be a cognitive shift in values and cultural beliefs, primarily in the women, but also throughout the system and the women's interrelationships. It was also essential that the project be economically successful so that the financial gain would balance the amount of disorder created by the change. An important part of the long-term acceptance of this change process and the resultant cognitive shifting was the communication that occurred internally within the groups, between the groups and other development project personnel, and between the groups and other groups within the same village. In many of these interactions, individuals were operating from different paradigms; through the juxtaposition of these paradigms and the facilitator's ability to bridge between them the likelihood of the incidence of postformal reasoning and the adoption of a paradigm that would accommodate these changes increased.

Project personnel realized from previous experience that certain information, particularly information that challenged established cultural concepts and realities, needed to be introduced to, and discussed with, other members of the community as well as the women in the project. The concept of maintaining pigs in pig farms and the idea that women should market the pigs was totally new. Women traditionally cared for small domestic animals, and over half the women in the pig project had previously kept pigs tethered near their houses. These pigs scavenged for food, and their maintenance was relatively low. When it came time to sell the pig, however, the man of the house would take the pig to market, sell it, and keep the profits. The pig project was thus not only introducing new breeds of pigs and a different way of caring for them, it was also introducing change in familial relationships and the economic structure of the family and the village. The project personnel recognized that they needed acceptance, and ideally support, from the women's husbands and other male village leaders. These changes could not be introduced without a recognition of the impact on other relationships and without giving the women emotional support and increasing their power. As a result, project personnel (who were all women) met with the village leaders and the participating women's husbands several times, and explained how the project would operate and what the women would be expected to do if they were to receive the money for constructing the pig farms and the technical support of the project. The project staff thus made the acceptance by the entire village of a new reality (women marketing the pigs) a condition of bringing the project to the village.

TWO-WAY COMMUNICATION: A MEANS TO MORE COMPLEX THOUGHT

Communication between Teacher and Learner

Communication between development project personnel and project participants was only one part of a complicated communication process. Thus, it was essential that the two-way communication between "learners" and development project personnel be ongoing and attempt to take into account all communication, including what occurred within the participants' nested relationships.

Many development programs assume that information need flow in only one direction from the "teacher" or "expert" to the "learner," and that the only change that occurs is on the part of the learner. However, two-way communication, Freire's "dialogue" (1971), in the introduction of information and its application to daily living seems critical for the learner to maximize selective encoding, combination, and comparison, and to increase generalization and the complexity of cognitive reasoning. It also may be essential for any long-term behavioral change to occur (O'Sullivan-Ryan & Kaplun, 1981; Wickramasinghe, 1982). As Meacham has stressed (ch. 9, this volume), complex cognitive reasoning is a function of shared communication and a social-mind perspective. Although individuals and groups can sometimes be coerced into short-term behavioral change, for sustained behavioral change to occur, individuals should be able not only to wed the factual information with previously known facts and concepts, but also to incorporate and internalize the underlying belief and value systems that accompany such information into the already existent belief, value, and cultural systems embedded in experience and emotion which comprise individuals' cognitive structures. In many development projects this does not happen, and as soon as the funding stops and the outside motivation for change stops, the project ceases and life returns to what existed before the introduction of the development project.

It is precisely because belief and value systems are not static entities that two-way communication between the learner and the teacher seems to be necessary if complex change is to become internalized. It must be a give-and-take process in which the ultimate goal is a compromise position and the roles of teacher and learner are exchanged by the participants. The teacher also learns from the learner, and both systems change.

Two-way communication presents concurrent but usually dissimilar paradigms or reality constructs. In other words, it highlights two disparate views of truth. The more continuous the two-way communication, the greater the possibility that paradigms will shift closer to each other. If one accepts that "truth" is simply a different way of looking at reality and not an absolute value, then the learning process and an ability to problem solve should be viewed in a different way (Sinnott, in press). Effective two-way communication involves more than expressing one's viewpoints; it also connotes an ability to listen, analyze, exchange, reevaluate, and incorporate other views into one's own conceptual framework. This seems to require, at least on the part of one of the parties, relativistic thinking and an ability to move among mutually contradictory frames of reference, which in turn leads to the development of the most expansive problem-solving space possible and a cognitive structure capable of accommodating such solutions. Without a constant flow of two-way communication and a recognition of the varying paradigms, no true consensus on goals or outcomes can be reached among the parties. The internalization of such a consensus and the acceptance and incorporation of compromise paradigms are an indication of postformal thought (Arlin, 1984; Kramer, 1983; Riegel, 1976) and the basis for long-term behavioral change. People who are able to define their own needs, who have an equal say in the decision-making process that attempts to resolve those needs, and who share reality constructs with common goals or outcomes will be the ones who accept development projects and internalize those goals.

Movement to More Complex Cognitive Levels

Sinnott (1984) has elaborated on Piaget's cognitive stages in defining the interpretive complexity of interpersonal communication; sensorimotor; preoperational; concrete operational thought; formal operational thought; and postformal or relativistic thought. On the sensorimotor level, a person reacts with an emotional, knee-jerk response. In the preoperational stage, the self is not viewed as a separate entity but rather as a reflection of the identity of another. Concrete operational thought recognizes the self as separate from others but can only conceive of others and their actions as an extension of self. Formal operational thought orders relationships into a logically consistent closed system in which rules and principles are viewed as absolute, universal, and nonrelative. Postformal reasoning is self-referential and relativistic, and attempts to synthesize new components into a continually expanding cognitive framework that formulates reality (i.e., a paradigm), while acknowledging that there are other paradigms and that one can shift between them dependent on the context and task at hand.

Not all people can operate on the higher levels of interpretive complexity, but all people appear to move among their own levels dependent on the situation and interaction with others (Basseches, 1984; Ford, 1987). It appears that through the communication process itself, and the resulting conflict and recognition of incongruity on the part of the receiver between what was received and the complexity of the communication sent, a gradual shift to more complex modes of thinking may occur. This is the same shift toward cognitive complexity that Inhelder and Piaget (1958) noted in the attempted resolution of conflicts between aspects of experience and the knower's cognitive structure. If this is true, then by increasing two-way communication, the opportunities for expanding problem-solving space and reordering cognitive frameworks toward relativistic thought increase. Whether or not it is possible to help people operate at a higher cognitive level remains to be seen, for little research has been conducted in this area. Certainly it may be possible to help people recognize that there are different levels of reasoning and that their level of empathy and self-confidence may be increased to allow the restructuring of thinking in more complex ways leading to the development of new paradigms. However, this does not necessarily mean that they will be operating at a postformal level. The shift may be due to a sensorimotor response or to a complete change from one paradigm to another such as might occur within formal operational thought. If, however, the affected people selectively choose a paradigm that enhances their problem-solving ability at any given time and are able to do this with new changes, then they probably are operating with postformal reasoning. For example, if the participating women could consciously choose a male-dominant family economic style the majority of the time and a female-dominant economic style when dealing with the pigs and the pig project, acknowledging that both styles could make sense but that one may be more accommodating and appropriate than another at a given time, these women would appear to be operating at a postformal level.

COOPERATIVE GROUPS FOR ENHANCING COMPLEX, COGNITIVE THOUGHT

Cooperative groups with a mentoring facilitator, as described in Kindervatter's *Women Working Together for Personal, Economic, and Community Development* (1983) were established for the participating women. One of the first activities of the facilitators of the cooperative groups was to recognize, legitimize, and respect the members' varying points of view and opinions, and to encourage the verbalization and acceptance of each of the members' experiences, values, beliefs, and realities. This reinforcement and empowerment in a culture and situation in which the women's views were rarely asked for and even more rarely regarded as worthwhile was critical to developing their self-confidence and an attitude that they could change their lives for the better. Other activities focused on defining resources within the group, as well as cooperative problem solving and decision making. In these exercises, the facilitators were to attempt to bridge the participant's realities through discussion and to find some mutually understandable common ground by means of what seemed to be postformal reasoning. The planned interaction with the mentoring facilitator seemed to occur in two of the groups, namely those of the postformal facilitator. In the other two groups, the formal operational facilitator's views dominated the group discussions, and empowerment did not appear to occur. The facilitator was unable to leave her own discriminatory framework, much less shift among paradigms or act as a bridge among the disparate constructs of the participating women.

THE POSTFORMAL FACILITATOR

Although no measurements such as those described by Commons and colleagues (1984), Sinnott (1989b), or Rankin and Allen (this volume) were taken to document the existence, or frequency, of postformal thought on the part of the facilitators or group participants, it appeared from my long-term directed observation that the complexity of the level of reasoning among the women varied, and that only one facilitator exhibited indications of postformal thought. This facilitator appeared to be able to adopt multisystem perspectives on problems and help the women in her two groups consider options that would normally be outside their paradigms. She appeared to demonstrate most of Sinnott's (1984) criteria for the presence of relativistic operations in her conversations. The second facilitator, on the other hand, seemed to view actions and thoughts as strictly right or wrong, as rigidly defined by her cognitive framework.

One example of relativistic postformal reasoning occurred in one of the group meetings I attended. There was an argument over how the group's money was being spent. Some of the women thought that the treasurer was taking some of the money for her personal use. A discussion led by the postformal facilitator ensued, in which the facilitator defined the problem from alternative points of view and explored the causes of the situation. She then suggested both abstract and practical solutions to those problems; refocused on the most pragmatic solution for that specific time and place, which encompassed a change in process; and communicated this to the group members in a way they could understand. The facilitator ultimately suggested that the treasurer provide the group with a listing of all past income and expenditures with receipts, and in the future should prepare a monthly report on the account. (Although this may seem an obvious solution to the reader, none of these women had maintained financial accounts before, and record keeping was not generally done.) Based on my discussions and personal interactions with the less successful facilitator, it seems that her solution would have been to judge the treasurer and, if she found her guilty, to replace her. This second facilitator viewed the world in terms of absolutes, and did not seem to value the ideas or opinions of the participant women. There was no evidence of relativistic thinking on her part, nor a recognition that there could have been more than one solution to the problem.

ROLE OF THE FACILITATOR

The concept of a change agent is essential to most development projects, and is defined as the teacher or person who initiates the intervention or introduces new information (Rogers, 1983). Perhaps the role of the change agent should be reexamined and redefined as a facilitator who, by operating in a postformal reasoning mode, is able to see and empathize with other realities and act as a bridge between differing realities. A teacher is often thought of as the expert who transfers information in a one-way communication. The teacher holds the ''right'' reality, and there is a moralistic judgment that the learner's paradigm is the only one that must change. This attitude conveys to the learner that she or he is incompetent and unable to learn. This perception may well be responsible for the failure of at least some development projects. In the case discussed here, the formal operational facilitator was comparable to the traditional change agent, and her two groups took much longer to make group decisions and to assume responsibility for the pig project.

When the emphasis is not on the presentation of the information but rather on helping people achieve new levels of cognitive reasoning, the abilities required of facilitators will be very different from those of traditional change agents. Facilitators must suspend absolute moral judgments about varying paradigms. They must be able to disassociate from their own paradigms complete with their incumbent value and emotional judgments, and be able to shift among other reality constructs (Benack, 1984). It is essential that facilitators recognize different people's realities as different but equal, although certain realities may be more adaptive and thus ''better'' in certain situations or at a given time. Facilitators should be able to make relativistic ethical and practical judgments as to the validity of certain paradigms. They must be able to operate at a postformal cognitive level or, as defined by King, Kitchner, Davison, Parker, and Wood (198 `   .t Stage 7, the highest cognitive level. At this level there is a premise that knowledge is subjective and relativistic, but that through constant critical inquiry and monitoring over a period of time, certain knowledge claims can be validated.

The extent to which facilitators can shift paradigms seems to be dependent on their ability to empathize with others intellectually and emotionally. They, like all people, do not operate solely in the postformal mode, but rather move among stages of interpretive complexity. At times they may revert to sensorimotor or gut emotional reactions, or to a lower cognitive level, but the extent to which this occurs will negatively affect their effectiveness in working with others. The facilitators' capacity to shift paradigms enables them to perceive interrelationships in new ways, to identify cognitive patterns that permit a larger problem-finding space, and to integrate, in building-block fashion, previous knowledge to new information. Facilitators explore new possibilities and express ways of looking at things in contexts that are understandable from varying points of view. They are continually seeking compromise solutions that are acceptable to all parties.

There were numerous reasons for the selection of the facilitators in the pig project, but their ability to operate at a postformal level was not officially one of them. One of the facilitators seemed to operate at a postformal level most of the time when working with her groups, but the other facilitator did not. The latter did not believe that the women were truly capable of making their own decisions, and generally assumed the role of teacher instead of facilitator. The women in her groups appeared much less empowered, much less capable of solving problems, and were from 3 to 6 months behind the other two groups in terms of the project's time table. There were many reasons officially given for the disparity between the groups. The success of the groups may not have been totally dependent on the facilitators' cognitive and communicative abilities, but these certainly seemed to be important factors.

CONCLUSION

This experience suggests the following: (a) postformal reasoning on the part of the teacher/facilitator is critical to the learning process, and may increase the learner's cognitive complexity and the possibility of postformal reasoning, thus promoting long-term behavioral change on the part of the learner; (b) two-way communication in which the teacher and learner shift and bridge realities is an essential component of the postformal reasoning process; and (c) effective communication cannot occur without empathy. In this descriptive case study, it appeared that some learners could attain postformal reasoning, but this was dependent on the facilitator's abilities to empower them through two-way communication to a greater sense of self-confidence and an increased ability to problem solve and make decisions. The analysis of this particular case study suggests that the role of the change agent in development projects should be reexamined, and that research should be done on the cognitive complexity and emotional characteristics of good facilitators.

It is recommended that further research with regard to development projects should be conducted to ascertain: (a) whether the cognitive levels of the participants change during the course of the project; (b) the relation between the participants' cognitive complexity level and the likelihood of long-term behavioral change; (c) if such a relationship does exist, the most effective ways for helping participants progress to higher cognitive levels; and (d) whether the facilitator's functional cognition level is a factor in change. If it is shown that there is a direct relationship between the participants' cognitive levels and long-term behavioral change, then much more time and attention should be paid to helping the participants operate at a postformal level, and facilitators should be selected for their postformal-reasoning capabilities and skill at helping others achieve postformal reasoning. Just as Lee and Armstrong (this volume) suggest that master teachers and good therapists might be identifiable by their level of cognitive ability, the ability to reason postformally may be a good indicator of the effectiveness of facilitators and other change agents. As part of the evaluation process of development projects, it would be worthwhile to attempt to measure the level of the participants' cognitive complexity before, during, and after the project, and to correlate this to long-term behavioral change and successful problem solving. These case studies would provide a nonformal educational context for studying positive adult development and/or postformal operational thought.

It is also recommended that applied research be conducted in other contexts to further examine the relationship between teacher/learner and the role that postformal reasoning plays in the learning process with different age groups.

Since a large part of our present educational system is dependent on traditional teacher/learner roles and since adult education is modeled after successful educational systems for young people, such research would be more than justified.

NOTES

This work was done as a research study for an Interdisciplinary Master's degree through New Mexico State University and was supported financially by an Inter-American Foundation Fellowship, a Women in Development (AID) Fellowship, and a Title VI Foreign Language and Area Studies Fellowship for Latin America through the Center for Latin American Studies at New Mexico State University. The views expressed in this chapter are the author's and do not necessarily reflect the views or opinions of the awarding organizations.

1. The author worked with the "Small-Scale Livestock for Rural Farming Women Project" from July through December 1985, preparing and presenting videotapes on technical aspects of pig keeping to the project participants and evaluating the effectiveness of these videotape programs as a communication tool.

REFERENCES

Arlin, P. K. (1984). *Adolescent and adult thought: A structural interpretation*. In M. L. Commons, F. A. Richards, & C. Armon (Eds.), *Beyond formal operations: Late adolescent and adult cognitive development* (pp. 258–271). New York: Praeger.

Arlin, P. K. (1989). *The problem of the problem*. In J. D. Sinnott (Ed.), *Everyday problem solving: Theory and applications* (pp. 229–237). New York: Praeger.

Basseches, M. (1984). *Dialectical thinking and adult development*. Norwood, NJ: Ablex.

Benack, S. (1984). Postformal epistemologies and the growth of empathy. In M. L. Commons, F. A. Richards, & C. Armon (Eds.), *Beyond formal operations: Late adolescent and adult cognitive development* (pp. 340–356). New York: Praeger.

Commons, M. L., Richards, F. A., & Armon, C. (Eds.). (1984). *Beyond formal operations: Late adolescent and adult cognitive development*. New York: Praeger.

Ford, D. H. (1987). *Humans as self-constructing living systems: A developmental perspective on behavior and personality*. New York: Erlbaum.

Freire, P. (1971). *Pedagogy of the oppressed*. New York: Herder & Herder.

Ginsburg, H., & Opper, S. (1969). *Piaget's theory of intellectual development: An introduction*. Englewood Cliffs, NJ: Prentice-Hall.

Inhelder, B., & Piaget, J. (1958). *The growth of logical thinking in the child*. New York: Basic Books.

Johnson-Dean, L. (1986). *The effectiveness of videotape programs as a communication tool in the small-scale livestock for rural farming women project, Honduras*. Unpublished manuscript, New Mexico State University, Las Cruces.

Kelly, G. A. (1955). *The psychology of personal constructs*. New York: Norton.

Kindervatter, S. (1983). *Women working together for personal, economic, and community development*. Washington, DC: OEF International.

King, P. M., Kitchener, K. S., Davison, M. L., Parker, C. A., & Wood, P. K. (1983). The justification of belief in young adults: A longitudinal study. *Human Development, 26*, 106–116.

Kramer, D. A. (1983). Post-formal operations? A need for further conceptualization. *Human Development*, *26*, 91–105.

Kramer, D. A. (1989). A developmental framework for understanding conflict resolution processes. In J. D. Sinnott (Ed.), *Everyday problem solving: Theory and applications* (pp. 133–153). New York: Praeger.

Kramer, D. A., & Bopp, M. (Eds.). (1989). *Transformation in clinical and developmental psychology*. New York: Springer.

O'Sullivan-Ryan, J., & Kaplun, M. (1981). Communication methods to promote grass-roots participation. A summary of research findings from Latin America, and an annotated bibliography. *Communication and Society*, *6*, 62–137.

Perry, W. B. (1975). *Forms of intellectual and ethical development in the college years: A scheme*. New York: Holt, Rinehart & Winston.

Riegel, K. (1976). The dialectic of human development. *American Psychologist*, *31*, 61–89.

Rogers, E. (1983). *Diffusion of innovation*. New York: Free Press.

Sinnott, J. D. (1984). Postformal reasoning: The relativistic stage. In M. L. Commons, J. D. Sinnott, & C. Armon (Eds.), *Beyond formal operations* (pp. 298–325). New York: Praeger.

Sinnott, J. D. (1989a). Changing the known; knowing the changing: The general systems theory metatheory as a conceptual framework to study complex change and complex thoughts. In D. A. Kramer & M. Bopp, (Eds.), *Transformation in clinical and developmental psychology* (pp. 51–69). New York: Springer.

Sinnott, J. D. (1989b). *Everyday problem solving: Theory and applications*. New York: Praeger.

Sinnott, J. D. (1989c). Life-span relativistic postformal thought: Methodology and data from everyday problem-solving studies. In M. L. Commons, J. D. Sinnott, F. A. Richards, & C. Armon (Eds.), *Adult development: Vol. 1. Comparisons and applications of developmental models* (pp. 239–278). New York: Praeger.

Sinnott, J. D. (in press). Teaching in a chaotic new physics world: Teaching as a dialogue with reality. In P. Kahaney (Ed.), *Teachers and change: Theoretical and practical perspectives*. New York: Columbia University Teachers College Press.

Sternberg, R. J. (1988). *The nature of creativity* (pp. 125–147). New York: Cambridge University Press.

Wickramasinghe, L. (1982). Toward a new extension strategy from promotion of innovations to participatory communication. In *1981 training for agriculture and rural development* (pp. 59–71). Rome: Food and Agricultural Organization of the United Nations.

7

Relativistic Operations: A Framework for Conceptualizing Teachers' Everyday Problem Solving

DIANE M. LEE

At the end of Carlos Castaneda's *A Separate Reality* (1971), Don Juan retorts to Castaneda, "Your mind is set to seek only one side of this" (p. 310). "You're chained," Don Juan explains. "You're chained to your reason" (p. 313). Don Juan knew that to be fully human, Castaneda had to free himself from literal, closed perceptions of meaning and to become involved in "making with open eyes the decisions that give shape to one's life" (Kaufmann, 1973, p. 4).

Like Castaneda, to be fully human, teachers must make decisions that fund a diversity of meanings. They must engage the subjective, and often rely on intuition as they confront problems that are in flux, contextual, and open to multiple solutions. These are the ill-structured problems Churchman referred to as "the richer problems of everyday life," life's "wicked problems" (1971, p. 144).

Sinnott's (1984, 1986, 1989) stage of postformal reasoning, called relativistic operations, provides a structure for describing problem posing and problem solving with problems of the "wicked" sort. Relativistic operations account for problems with unclear parameters that are sensitive to context, for the acceptance of contradiction as a basic feature of physical and social reality, and for the presence of subjectivity in adult reasoning.

The purpose of this chapter is to illustrate the usefulness of Sinnott's criteria for postformal thinking, or relativistic operations, as a framework for conceptualizing one teacher's problem posing and problem solving. In the first section of this chapter, characteristics of formal and postformal thought will be discussed, and the relevance of relativistic operations to teachers' everyday problem solving will be outlined. The second part of the chapter will present the application of

Sinnott's criteria for determining the presence of relativistic thought: one teacher's problem posing and problem solving.

BACKGROUND

In Piaget's scheme of cognitive development, mature adult thought is characterized by the presence of formal operations. Three abilities in particular enable formal operational thinkers to conceptualize phenomena from within the logico-mathematico domain and to engage in scientific thinking (Inhelder & Piaget, 1958). First, formal operational thinkers can create a reversal in the relationship between reality and possibility. Second, they can think about the nature of thinking. Third, they can generate abstract hypotheses and test them by the manipulation and isolation of a crucial set of variables; that is, they can engage in hypothetico-deductive forms of thought.

However, like Castaneda, formal operational thinkers are conditioned to seek only one side of a problem. In other words, formal operational thinkers view knowledge in fixed, absolute, and static terms. Formal thinkers consider problems from a closed-system perspective, and so regard the presence of contradictions as a temporary condition to be eliminated from the system. Acceptance of only one viewpoint gives rise to seeking and acknowledging only one correct solution. Thus, problem solving is likely to take precedence over problem posing. In sum, formal operational thought does allow for competent problem solving but only when the problems are well-structured; that is, when there is a single correct solution that can be found by applying explicit rules within a closed system.

Life's problems, however, are seldom well structured. Indeed, problems confronted in the increasingly complex social environment in which the adult finds him- or herself are more likely to be of the ill-structured sort. As the adults' world broadens and they are exposed to multiple perspectives, certainty breaks down and the limitations of formal thought are realized. Consequently, postformal thinkers view knowledge as relativistically true and contextual, and not as fixed, absolute, or static. They regard contradiction as a necessary feature of reality, and will attempt to integrate conflicting views into coherent wholes. Thus, problems are conceptualized within an open-systems context, and subjectivity is allowed to enter into their analyses. Furthermore, they will engage in problem posing as well as problem solving. Unlike formal operational thought, postformal thinking permits competent problem solving when problems are ill-structured.

As noted, relativistic operations, Sinnott's stage of postformal reasoning, provide a useful framework for describing problem posing and problem solving with ill-structured problems. Relativistic operations should be especially relevant for understanding the everyday problem posing and problem solving of teachers when the following characteristics are present: (a) the problem space is broad, (b) the problem-solving process includes an element of necessary subjectivity and conscious self-reference, and (c) there is an acceptance of contradiction as an inescapable feature of reality (Lee, 1989).

When teachers conceptualize classroom problems of the ill-structured type, the potential set of admissible information is quite large. Teachers must choose which information to include in representing a problem before solving it. With everyday problems of the ill-structured variety, teachers ask many questions. Germane are questions such as: What must I teach? For whom? For what purposes? Who should decide? How will I assess my teaching? How will evaluate students' learning? Teachers realize that there may be as many answers and interpretations as there are students, administrators, and parents touched by the results of their deliberations, not to mention the numerous perspectives of experts. Thus, there are often multiple goals rather than just one. Classroom problems are deemed important and are, by definition, social (Tom, 1984). Multiple solutions are recognized, although frequently only one may be enacted at any moment in time.

This broad problem space, coupled with the recognition that everyday classroom problems are inherently social, requires teachers to allow subjectivity into their problem solving. As noted by Cavanaugh and his colleagues (Cavanaugh, Kramer, Sinnott, Camp, & Markley, 1985), "objectivity breaks down as multiple perspectives are included in one's analysis, and choices must be made about the meaning of an event by the various individuals involved in the event as they live the event" (p. 152). As teachers attempt to analyze the multiple realities of classroom experiences, they must abandon the notion of knowledge being separate from the knower in favor of a dialectic wherein the knower and the known are "co-present, each modifying and shaping the other" (Gowin, cited in Greene, 1988, p. x). Thus, teachers are called on to be self-conscious, that is, to be aware of one's own and others' perspectives so that they may be more fully aware of the possible consequences of alternative courses of action on the persons involved and on the meanings they are creating in relationship. The call to action research, critical inquiry, and hermeneutics in education reflects such awareness.

Teachers' everyday problem solving so conceived necessitates an acceptance of contradiction. The acknowledgment of multiple perspectives and multiple vantage points often gives rise to contradictory yet equally valid information. Harding (1987, p. 288) noted that it is the ability to interpret contradiction that allows one to discriminate dilemmas from other events requiring choices. Dilemmas, she noted, are typically ill-structured problems wherein the choices are not just two different options but rather are incompatible alternatives requiring the recognition of the contradictory nature of their outcome. Dilemmas are inextricably woven into teachers' everyday experiences, so much so that practitioners and researchers alike often refer to dilemmatics as the language of schooling. As noted by Lather (1987), the question in education today is, "How am I to learn to think in a world of contradictory information?" to which the respondent on this study added, "How am I to think in a world in which personal meanings differ and yet the meanings of all individuals concerned are considered valid?''[1]

Thus, it was from this conception of problem solving and teaching that I have employed relativistic operations to illustrate one teacher's problem posing and problem solving.

PROCEDURES

A primary purpose of this study was to illustrate the feasibility of using relativistic operations as a framework for describing and explaining teachers' everyday problem solving. With this in mind, the decision was made to present an in-depth analysis of one teacher's problem posing and problem solving. The methodological character of this work took the form of participant observations during actual classroom activity and interviews after the observations. Audiotapes of classroom dialogues and interviews with the researcher were transcribed and analyzed, and narratives from six classroom sessions and three interviews with the teacher were used. Fragments from both sources were selected, and are presented as illustrations of the presence of relativistic operations. After a draft of this chapter was finalized, the participant responded to it and added a question (see note 1) and an additional statement (see section titled "Parameter Setting").

The methodology used in this study adds to the expanding body of literature investigating the nature of mature, adult thought. The case reported was built on a specific problem identified by the participant. Underlying this approach is a commitment to the notion that inquiry into everyday problem solving should indeed consider problems grounded in the phenomenological structure of experiences deemed significant by the participants. To date, most of the research on relativistic operations has been conducted in laboratories using problems contrived by the researchers. Although useful, such studies shed little light on participants' problem posing, and raise serious questions about the ecological validity of laboratory tasks (Labouvie-Vief, 1979). Another important feature of this study was that practice formed the starting point for the inquiry. Thus, this study led to further development of Sinnott's theoretical model of postformal reasoning as well as to understanding further the practice of a master teacher.

The participant in this inquiry, Dr. Andrews (a fictitious name), is a full professor in educational policy, planning, and administration at a large university. She is an adult woman who has taught for many years at both the elementary and university levels, although the crux of her experience is at the university level. She is considered to be a master teacher as determined by her numerous years of experience; her student evaluations, which are uniformly high; and her colleagues' appraisals (Berliner, 1986). Observations were made throughout one semester during a graduate course that she taught on curriculum theory. Those of her deliberations that meet the criteria for relativistic operations, both during class in dialogue with her students and in her thinking outside class during the interviews, are presented. Utterances are not necessarily presented in the order of occurrence, but rather as they illustrate elements of relativistic operations.

Two questions guided this study: First, "Are the everyday problems identified by a master teacher useful illustrations of relativistic operations?" Second, and relatedly, "Are criteria for determining the presence of relativistic operations useful for helping us think about teachers' everyday problem solving?" It was expected that the real-life problems of an expert teacher would provide good examples of the criteria determining relativistic operations. It was also expected that these operations would bring to the fore this teacher's tacit knowing, while providing a way of framing our understanding of how a teacher poses and solves problems during the ebb and flow of classroom activity and in the process of reflecting on those activities.

FINDINGS

Findings are organized around the eight operations determining the presence of relativistic operations. Excerpts from observations and interviews are presented as illustrations of the criteria of postformal reasoning as defined by Sinnott (1984, pp. 314–315). Deliberations not illustrating the operations are not presented. Similarly, not all the utterances satisfying the criteria have been included. Thus, some of the intensity and complexity of Dr. Andrews's deliberations have been lost in this presentation.

Problem Definition

The first operation to be considered is problem definition. Problem definition regards defining problems in a specific chosen way. It involves a statement of the meaning and demands of the problem for the problem solver. As noted by Arlin (1984), it "represents the ability of the adults to ask generative questions of themselves, their life's work, and of the phenomena that surround them" (p. 264).

Dr. Andrews defined the problem as follows:

What are some of the future directions curriculum theory can, should, take? Many important issues are timely in curriculum development. . . . We always have multiple strands of thought and sometimes one strand is more prominent than another. We can't deal with any one of these alone. . . . As a teacher of curriculum I continually put myself and my professional experiences in question.

In focusing her problem on the future directions curriculum theory and research could and should take, Dr. Andrews considered many issues to be timely, including her own personal interactions with the field, namely, her life's work in this area; issues raised currently in the literature, namely, by other experts in the field; and issues identified as pertinent by the students, namely, issues they confronted during the course of their experiences in schools as students, teachers, principals, and parents (summary of transcripts). By asking what directions curriculum theory could and should take, Dr. Andrews posed her problem within a frame of possibility and responsibility. Stated this way, her deliberations lead to complex, relativistic understandings. For example, her language indicates that she deems the curriculum field as changing and as necessarily open to multiple perspectives. As multiple perspectives are taken into account, subjectivity enters her conception and analysis of the problem. The limitations of a formal, objective logic are realized in her display of relativistic thought.

Parameter Setting

The operation of parameter setting involves naming key variables to be combined or made proportional in the problem other than those given in the problem demands. Often the person will explicitly state key variables. Dr. Andrews identified several key factors to be included in the problem set.

A major area for the future relates to how we get small groups to collaborate. . . . There are multiple strands of thought among professionals from different disciplines that need to be interwoven. . . . We have to realize that curriculum is a complex issue and that it is difficult to look at just one aspect. We have to look at the research, at what's been written, at teachers' roles, etc. We can't deal with any one of these alone. . . . This is going to call for a reconceptualization of what we mean by curriculum work. . . . We need to look at the direction society is moving, at a particular locale so that we engage thought that is in keeping with a community. . . . [W]e haven't pushed to the limits what our public is ready for [and] . . . we must deal with the tension. . . . We need to reevaluate teacher education programs [and] . . . consider five year programs with longer internships and at least a three year induction. . . . The nine month school year is another issue to be looked at. . . . [P]erhaps we need to develop summer programs that operate under the aegis of the schools . . . with teachers being paid professional salaries. . . . We always need some people on the cutting edge. . . . I am continually asking myself, "Am I providing what's worthwhile?"

Unlike highly structured problems where the choice of elements to be included in the problem space is largely predetermined and closed, with ill-structured problems the potential set of usable elements is broader. Selection, then, becomes an important factor in the creation of multiple solutions and in the range of operations that can be used as a system to relate and order information, information that is oftentimes contradictory. In selecting a wide range of potentially usable elements to be included in the problem space, Dr. Andrews called for the kind of logic that characterizes relativistic thought. She called for reconceptualization, and in doing so entertained the possibility that new rules for interpreting the problem would emerge and that contradictory information would likely be encountered. Recognizing that logico-mathematico knowledge is insufficient, she also included personal knowledge (as defined by Gardner, 1983) in her representation of the problem. Thus, ever-present in her thoughts was the need to include interpersonal as well as self-understanding in her analysis. As Dr. Andrews noted after reading this chapter, "Knowledge can't be separated out. All knowledge is personal."

Metatheory Shift

Metatheory shift refers to the production of abstract and practical (real-life) solutions as well as a shift between conflicting abstract and real a prioris. This shift is stated by the person. The solution always includes problem definitions.

Dr. Andrews began tackling future directions at a theoretical level by invoking some of the prominent voices in curriculum theory. She moved from the theoretical to her own lived experiences and those of her students. She also suggested some solutions based on logic gleaned from theory as well as knowledge gleaned from experience.

[Schwab] suggested we move from the Tylerian rationale to the practical [and] . . . essentially then we're looking at students, at teachers, at the setting, at what's being learned. But we're looking at it in the here and now and looking at the various kinds of decisions that teachers make when they're dealing with all these aspects at once. . . . Tyler's is a very linear kind of process while Schwab is trying to take into account the complexity of the process. . . . [T]here are several kinds of things that we can take out of the work that Schwab did that helps when we look toward the future. One is, I think he leads us to looking at a clearly delineated focus. A focus that can be stated in a variety of ways. For example, let's go back to Stratemeyer. . . . Foshay was talking about six aspects of humanness. . . . You can turn to the work of Kohlberg[,] . . . of Gilligan. . . . The question is, of course, of moving commitment to action. What works in theory is not always what works in practice. My plan for this evening was just to talk about what future directions curriculum should take. But as I hear you talking I think we need to back up and talk more about effecting change. . . . We also need to look at our language. It's very useful to take some of our common jargon and develop an analysis of it. For example, Scheffler does a linguistic analysis of what we mean by human potential.

In this narrative Dr. Andrews affirmed the need to focus on rethinking old information. She attended to the problem of making the theoretical relate to truths of everyday practice. For her, curriculum "oughts" are practical concerns to be translated into action. The practical refers not to technical or managerial know-how but rather to a sense of the practical as communicative understanding and social wisdom. She acknowledged that educational decisions are made amid the ever-changing context of real classrooms, in the here-and-now of educational experiences, with the orientation of those persons involved in the experiences in mind. In doing so, she rejected the one-dimensional givens of empirical-analytic science as the only source of knowledge from which to draw as one tackles curricular problems. Instead, she favored curriculum knowledge that is tied to classroom experiences, critical analysis, interpretation, and interpersonal communication.

Process/Product Shift

A process/product shift occurs when a problem solver describes a process as one answer and an outcome as another answer; that is, when a problem solver decides to solve for a dynamic or for a particular content solution. Often there is a statement that finding the solution is actually a never-ending process. With a process/product shift there may be a discussion of process differences in arriving at two different outcomes.

Whenever you talk about future directions you're caught in a spiral of constant questioning. ... Whether I'm writing or teaching I always ask myself this question [What are the future directions curriculum theory and research should go?]. As times change and new students enroll, the answers vary. ... I guess I change, too. My deliberations always seem to include consideration of students' needs, the department's needs, my needs, and so on. ... The issue is academic freedom. But with that goes responsibility. ... [W]hen you're locked in you pick up what's been called for by someone else. You have to use that book even if the kids didn't like it. That's not for me. I prefer to be actively responsible.

At this point a student interjected:

That's personal power. Being in control means you're open to making mistakes.

To this Dr. Andrews replied:

That's right and I've made many of them. And you say to yourself, "I should have done this and I should have done that. Why didn't I do that differently? I should have picked up on that." ... This is the role of reflection.

Dr. Andrews stated clearly that deciding what future directions curricularists should take was indeed a problem for which there was "no clear-cut point of terminating the questioning process." When asked how she responded to the questions she raised, she described both the process of her deliberations and the outcome in relative terms. Indeed, it is from within the dialectic of self- and mutual regulation that she reexamines the logical constraints of the problem as she has identified it. She accepted responsibility for her decisions, and called on reflection as a way to reconceptualize her deliberations and actions. This reconstructive process engages conscious choice emanating from intra- and interpersonal understanding, and thus acquires pragmatic, social, moral, and personal dimensions.

Multiple Solutions

This operation involves making statements that there are many correct solutions intrinsic to a problem with several causes, or that no problem has only one solution. In addition, the problem solver may create several solutions, recognizing that many solutions may be termed correct as the constraints of the problem are changed. Dr. Andrews articulated many possible solutions as the constraints of the problem shifted.

There are so many possibilities. . . . Some may be at odds with others and the demands made by various groups may be at odds. . . . Priorities may be arranged and rearranged as the semester runs its course, as students grow and change [but] . . . the curriculum issue is constant. . . . There are several ways to go about this. . . . We could continue what we're doing and look for methods . . . or we can continually look at what counts as school knowledge, how that knowledge is organized and transmitted, how persons make meaning together, what knowledge has leading-on power.

Perhaps the key term here is "possibilities," since that speaks directly to multiple solutions and reduces the likelihood of seeking just one right answer. As multiple perspectives are considered, uncertainty and contradiction are included in Dr. Andrews's cognitive structure. Accepting plurality and contradiction, Dr. Andrews affirmed both as essential features of reality. By envisioning possibilities, Dr. Andrews engaged a symbolically structured reality that encompasses herself and others as well as the meanings they create in relation and the products of their actions. She recognized the juxtaposition of responsibilities that are the teacher's lot when he or she is willing to include in the problem space the voices of others who "may be at odds." Her concern with leading-on power reflects her commitment to moving students to interpret their lived worlds and to opening their perspectives even wider.

Multiple Causality

Multiple causality is present when there is a statement that multiple causes exist for any event or that some solutions are more probable than others. Sinnott noted (1986, p. 315) that some persons state that the solution depends on all past relations of the persons in the problem. Dr. Andrews did consider the problem of determining future directions in curriculum by reflecting on her relations with the problem and with the persons involved both presently and in the past.

I think all curriculum development has a value connotation to it. One of the issues in curriculum development is to surface the values of teachers, of the students, and the community and then try to take all of these into account[,] . . . both those you're currently working with and those you've worked with previously. . . . Some call for predetermined objectives, others say values and objectives should emerge. . . . Ought there to be pre-determined objectives? Whose?

Dr. Andrews called for the integration of multiple frames of reference, and in doing so, reaffirmed her tolerance of others' beliefs and ways of life. This is characteristic of postformal thinkers as they carry out relativistic operations on reality (Sinnott, 1984, p. 320). Dr. Andrews did not limit her choices to one formal system but rather strove for consensual understandings and a maximal use of contradictory information. She sought to incorporate voices from the past and the present as well as those in conflict as she began to explore different ways of looking at curricular problems. Her words suggest the variability of individual and group opinions. As noted by Swoyer (cited in Leadbeater, 1986), this form of variability "is consistent with the Piagetian view that what is known is constituted by an active knower, but a relativistic position also insists that there is no universal or single way of doing this" (p. 292).

Pragmatism

In exhibiting this operation, persons may choose a best solution among several, or can choose the best variant of a solution that has two processes. They must, however, actually give more than one solution.

Dr. Andrews did state several solutions to her dilemma. She prefaced her discussion regarding what future directions curriculum should take by describing the process she undertook as she prepared for this course. She defined solutions based on the most recent thoughts expressed by other experts in the field, by the direction of her department, and by her own observations and experiences. By sharing her deliberations, she modeled a process that her students could emulate when confronted with the problem of determining future directions for curriculum theory and research.

During the AERA [American Educational Research Association] meetings I followed primarily sessions that had to do with alternative research methodologies and was gaining some new insights . . . that coupled with a long article that just came out on varieties of qualitative research . . . led me choose to discuss this today. . . . [O]ne of the other reasons I'm focusing on this a little bit is that I hear you talk and it appears that the direction you're moving is some form of qualitative research . . . and most of you get enough of the other [quantitative methodologies] in your research courses. . . . [P]ossibilities, curriculum should create possibilities. . . . [T]he question goes back to "What matters?" . . . Teacher as watcher. He's [Aoki] saying a teacher watches individuals and then determines his/her moves from what the teacher has perceived. This contrasts with the preplanned curriculum. . . . If we pick up on what Aoki is saying, then this too, this teaching for Being together, will be part of our curriculum. . . . It's one way of looking at curriculum. . . . It's the most contemporary. . . . [Y]ou use your own judgment. . . . It's hard to teach what I don't know well—I'm afraid to deviate . . . yet I do try to teach what's on the edge of my knowing. . . . There are two ways we could go about this. We could continue doing what has been prescribed, which is basically an implementation of what someone else has predetermined, or we could use multiple lenses. I prefer to use multiple lenses. I know I keep changing my mind. And that's not bad. . . . You have to know the setting, the context. . . . What does it mean to be a life-long learner and what kinds of opportunities need to be available? If I were to look at the major questions that need to be dealt with in the curriculum area, I think this would be first or close to it.

Dr. Andrews stated that there is no single way of determining what direction curriculum should take in the future. She prefers to enter her deliberations using multiple lenses, and she exhibited this process while defining multiple solutions. Her words reveal the primary place of self-reflection as she related external frames of reference to inner, self-conscious referents. Within this process she was able to transcend the status quo through social consciousness and active, thoughtful subjectivity, and in doing so, she assumed a relativistic position. Dr. Andrews rejected the idea of an absolute solution in favor of meaning making as an endless series of interpretations. Her words and actions suggest a belief in the "recovery of lost meanings and the creating of new ones" permitting "the opening up of 'possible worlds' " (Ricoeur, 1984, p. 16). Thus, it is within a self-reflective spiral that she challenges what is taken for granted and creates space for possibility.

Paradox

This operation is present when the person gives a direct statement or question about perceived, inherently conflicting, demands that are integral to the problem, not simply two solutions with different parameters. The person notices that two different things are being said at once, both of which could change the way the problem should be solved.

Paradox was not clearly present in Dr. Andrews's deliberations, and therefore this operation was scored absent. This is consistent with Sinnott's previous findings, wherein no individual research participant articulated a perfect profile of relativistic operations (1984). Furthermore, paradox was typically the operation that was absent.

DISCUSSION

Sinnott's model of relativistic operations did provide a useful frame for examining a master teacher's problem posing and problem solving. Dr. Andrews's deliberations demonstrated relativistic understanding that met the criteria for seven of the eight operations delineated by Sinnott (1984, 1986, 1989). In her conception of the problem, Dr. Andrews defined the problem space broadly, accepted contradiction as an inherent feature of reality, and included subjectivity and self-reference within the problem-solving process.

In her conceptualization and reconceptualizations related to what directions curriculum could, and should, take in the future, Dr. Andrews described the problem as ill-structured. Unlike well-structured problems wherein the problem space is conceived of as a necessarily closed, finite system (Newell & Simon, 1972), Dr. Andrews represented the problem broadly, describing a system that is open to multiple knowledge states that in turn could undergo a gradual alteration as the problem is revisited.

Recognition that knowledge is not fixed, absolute, or static demanded that Dr. Andrews synthesize conflicting experiences, thoughts, and values into a more encompassing and manageable whole. She displayed an acceptance of ambiguity and an awareness that all human judgment is somewhat flawed. She noted that persons make the best decisions they can with the knowledge they have while realizing that we never have all the knowledge or all the possible value configurations. Furthermore, her willingness to give legitimacy to multiple viewpoints was coupled with a willingness to assume responsibility for critically evaluating and choosing between alternatives. Competent decision making by postformal thinkers is marked by such personal responsibility and commitment.

Teaching, as many view the activity of teachers, is intersubjective. It is a dialogue between teacher and students that is directed toward the world; that is, a dialogue about something (Scudder & Mickunas, 1985). Dr. Andrews engaged in an educational dialogue with her students that was characteristically directed at understanding curricular issues. Recognizing that the subject influences the object that comes to be known, Dr. Andrews allowed subjectivity to enter her analysis. Thus, her thinking exhibited pedagogic tact and thoughtfulness.

Tact, as described by Herbart (cited in van Manen, 1988, p. 4), is a way of interacting that is dependent on feeling or sensitivity, and that manifests itself in everyday life in the process of making instant judgments and quick decisions. Regarded this way, tact is a way of seeing, listening, responding, and dwelling in the tensionality created by subjective decision making. Teachers interacting tactfully and thoughtfully are aware of the uniqueness of their situation in each moment of decision and of the consequences of their thoughts and actions for the students affected. Such interactions cannot be understood fully using formal operations, but rather require cognitive operations that can structure adults' interpersonal and everyday world and account for the unity of subject and object (Sinnott, 1984, p. 302). Relativistic operations did account for this unity, and permitted subjectivity to be ordered within the complex thought of this teacher, thereby exposing conceptualization that went beyond the "purely cognitive" (Schoenfeld, 1983).

CONCLUSION

In the real, lived world of classrooms, problems are messy and fraught with interpretations that are frequently incompatible, and demand action even when only tentative solutions are the best that anyone can construct. Relativistic operations have provided a compelling framework for analyzing this master teacher's problem posing and problem solving. Unlike formal operations, relativistic operations have unearthed the values, passions, and imagination that this teacher called on to meet the problems endemic to her profession.

This study of everyday problem solving is the study of an expert in her field. Denney (1985) has noted that the study of expertise is the study of everyday problem solving within areas of individual specialization. This awareness generates many questions. Do novice teachers demonstrate postformal thought, or are they more likely to exhibit formal operational or even concrete operational thought? If there are consistent differences in the cognitive abilities of master and novice teachers, might not this distinction be a more useful basis for identifying master teachers than the number of years in the profession? Do learners perform differently when they are working with a teacher who uses a complex, postformal mode of teaching than when they are working with a teacher who does not? Might not the modeling of postformal thinking free students to move beyond the literal, rigid interpretations permitted by formal operational thinking? Are the dynamics of interpersonal relations different when teachers use self-referential knowledge and interpersonal knowledge in their problem posing and problem solving than when they do not? How does a teacher with a low level of skill develop into a highly skilled performer capable of dealing with dilemmas in a postformal way? These questions, as well as many others, need to be investigated. A truly realistic understanding of these questions demands that all levels of cognitive abilities and adaptive possibilities be examined in the lived worlds in which problems arise. Thus, it is suggested that Sinnott's model of relativistic operations be used to analyze the everyday problem posing and problem solving of teachers and learners.

NOTE

1. Question added by the respondent after reviewing a draft of this chapter.

REFERENCES

Arlin, P. K. (1984). Adolescent and adult thought: A structural interpretation. In M. L. Commons, F. A. Richards, & C. Armon (Eds.), *Beyond formal operations: Late adolescent and adult cognitive development.* New York: Praeger.

Berliner, D. C. (1986, August/September). In pursuit of the expert pedagogue. *Educational Researcher, 15*(7), 5–13.

Castaneda, C. (1971). *A separate reality.* New York: Simon & Schuster.

Cavanaugh, J. C., Kramer, D. A., Sinnott, J. D., Camp, C. J., & Markley, R. P. (1985). On missing links and such: Interfaces between cognitive research and everyday problem solving. *Human Development, 28,* 146–168.

Churchman, C. W. (1971). *The design of inquiring systems: Basic concepts of systems and organizations.* New York: Basic Books.

Denney, N. W. (1985, March). *Everyday problem solving: How much potential?* Paper presented at the Third Annual George A. Talland Conference on Memory and Aging, New Seabury, MA.

Gardner, H. (1983). *Frames of mind*. New York: Basic Books.

Greene, M. (1988). *The dialectic of freedom*. New York: Teachers College Press.

Harding, C. G. (1987). A developmental model for the invention of dilemmas. *Human Development, 30*, 282–290.

Inhelder, B., & Piaget, J. (1958). *The growth of logical thinking from childhood to adolescence*. New York: Basic Books.

Kaufmann, W. (1973). *Without guilt and justice*. New York: Wyden.

Labouvie-Vief, G. (1977). Adult cognitive development: In search of alternative interpretations. *Merrill-Palmer Quarterly, 33*, 227–263.

Lather, P. (1987,). *Response to Allen Bloom*. Paper presented at Challenges and Visions for Undergraduate Teaching Conference, Springhill Conference Center, Minneapolis, MN.

Leadbeater, B. (1986). The resolution of relativism in adult thinking: Subjective, objective or conceptual? *Human Development, 29*, 291–300.

Lee, D. M. (1989). Everyday problem solving: Implications for education. In J. D. Sinnott (Ed.), *Everyday problem solving: Theories and applications* (pp. 251–265). New York: Praeger.

Newell, A., & Simon, H. (1972). *Human problem solving*. Englewood Cliffs, NJ: Prentice-Hall.

Ricoeur, P. (1984). Dialogues with Paul Ricoeur. In R. Kearney (Ed.), *Dialogues with contemporary continental thinkers: The phenomenological heritage*. Dover, NH: Manchester University Press.

Schoenfeld, A. H. (1983). Beyond the purely cognitive: Belief systems, social cognitions, and metacognitions as driving forces in intellectual performance. *Cognitive Science, 7*, 329–363.

Scudder, J. R., & Mickunas, A. (1985). *Meaning, dialogue, and enculturation: Phenomenological philosophy of education*. Lanham, MD: University Press of America.

Sinnott, J. D. (1984). Postformal reasoning: The relativistic stage. In M. L. Commons, F. A. Richards, & C. Armon (Eds.), *Beyond formal operations: Late adolescent and adult cognitive development* (pp. 298–325). New York: Praeger.

Sinnott, J. D. (1986). Prospective/intentional and incidental everyday memory: Effects of age and passage of time. *Psychology and Aging, 1*, 110–116.

Sinnott, J. D. (1989). *Everyday problem solving: Theories and applications*. New York: Praeger.

Tom, A. (1984). *Teaching as a moral craft*. New York: Longman.

van Manen, M. (1988, April). *Pedagogic thoughtfulness and tact*. Paper presented at the American Educational Research Association meeting. New Orleans.

8

Conflict and Cooperation in Adulthood: A Role for Both?

JOHN A. MEACHAM

That adult development and aging take place not in isolated, autonomous persons but instead in persons existing in close psychological relationship with each other is a commonplace. I take it as axiomatic, therefore, that positive development must include a striving for harmonious, rather than acrimonious, interpersonal relations. Thus, as we consider the nature of positive development in adulthood and aging and how such development might be promoted, a fundamental issue that must be confronted is the following: Why don't we observe less conflict and more cooperation among adults and within society as a whole? Perhaps we have neglected some benefit of conflict that might explain why it endures? On the other hand, perhaps we have neglected some disadvantage of cooperation that might help in understanding why it isn't more prevalent? I assume that most people, like myself, desire friendship and cooperation with others, yet sometimes when I earnestly seek cooperation, I end up in conflict with others. Why is this? In providing some tentative answers to these questions, this chapter touches upon dead rats, a kitten with only one eye, sex, washing dishes, and child rearing. The chapter also sets forth several pairs of terms: power and interests, true cooperation and false cooperation, conflict and discourse, and success and understanding.[1]

TRUE COOPERATION OR FALSE COOPERATION?

Questions such as ones just raised can be pursued by considering a bit of Americana, a story that is both familiar and paradigmatic of the American way of life, the story of Tom Sawyer, the glorious whitewasher. As Mark Twain

(1936) told the story, a deep melancholy settled down on Tom's spirit as he faced the thirty yards of board fence with his bucket of whitewash and his brush. As he thought of the "delicious expeditions" that the other boys would be taking that day, and of the fun that they would make of him for having to work, his sorrows multiplied. "At this dark and hopeless moment an inspiration burst upon him. Nothing less than a great, magnificent inspiration! He took up his brush and went tranquilly to work. Ben Rogers hove in sight presently—the very boy, of all boys, whose ridicule he had been dreading" (p. 42).

Most readers will recall that Tom was able to convince Ben Rogers and the other boys that in fact he *liked* whitewashing the fence. "I don't see why I oughtn't to like it. Does a boy get a chance to whitewash a fence every day?" (p. 44). Ben was quick to offer Tom his apple in exchange for the privilege of whitewashing the fence. By the middle of the afternoon, Tom's wealth included a kite, a dead rat and a string to swing it with, a key, a kitten with only one eye, and a brass doorknob. As Mark Twain related, "If he hadn't run out of whitewash, he would have bankrupted every boy in the village" (p. 46).

This hardly appears, at least upon first reading, to be a story of conflict and competition. Tom Sawyer controls access to the whitewash, the brush, and the fence; Ben Rogers controls access to his labor and his apple. The boys negotiate, and agree to a cooperative exchange. There has been no struggle, clash, controversy, disagreement, or opposition.

I turn now to a second bit of Americana, a bit not as celebrated as Mark Twain's story but equally representative of the American way of life. Yla Eason (1988) has recounted the story of Florine Mitchell's (not her real name) first day at a new job. As she and her new boss were riding in the elevator on their way to get desk supplies, he asked casually, "Would you slap my face if I made a pass at you?" Later, as they entered a storage room, he commented on how attractive she was and tried to kiss her. "Blocking his move, Florine announced, 'I don't go for that, and I wish you wouldn't try it again. As long as I've worked, I've never gotten involved with anybody on the job, especially my boss.' " Three days later, her boss declared that he liked her. When Florine made clear that she had a boyfriend, the boss told her to "Think about it" (p. 139). A few days later, he explained the details of an out-of-town trip and his expectation that Florine would accompany him. Florine thought about the mortgage payment she had to make and about her two sons, and realized that she could not quit this new job. "Think about it," her boss said. "If you want to hold onto your job, you had better *cooperate*." "No way in hell," Florine asserted. Less than two months later, she was fired.

Is this a story of conflict or a story of cooperation? The story of Florine Mitchell is potentially an example of cooperation. Her boss, like Tom Sawyer, controlled access to the workplace; Florine Mitchell, like Ben Rogers, controlled access to her labor and her body. Like Tom Sawyer and Ben Rogers, they could have negotiated and agreed to a cooperative exchange. There would be no struggle, clash, controversy, disagreement, or opposition. Some workers, both female and male, do exchange sexual encounters for raises and promotions.

What should we make of these two stories? They do not provide good examples of what we typically mean by conflict, so it appears we are forced to consider them as illustrations of cooperation. However, I don't feel entirely comfortable with what Tom Sawyer did to his friends, and it is not possible to accept or rationalize what Florine Mitchell's boss was attempting to do to her. (Unfortunately, as numerous surveys have shown, 50 to 80% of women in the workplace have been subject to verbal or physical sexual harassment.)

In my view, both these stories illustrate what I will term *false cooperation*. Although the negotiations between Tom Sawyer and his friends have the outward appearance, at least in the short term, of cooperation, what Tom perpetrated on his friends was a con job. That is, he swindled or defrauded them by first winning their confidence. Tom cleverly aroused in the other boys a desire that they originally did not have, to whitewash the fence, and then provided an opportunity for the boys to attain this desire if they would cooperate in providing not only their labor but also the kite, the dead rat, the key, the kitten, and the brass doorknob.

The apparent cooperation between the boys was a false cooperation because it involved deception: First, Tom did not reveal his own interest, his "magnificent inspiration," to get the other boys to whitewash the fence for him. Second, Tom manipulated the other boys in order to introduce an interest that was, at least on that glorious summer day, not their true interest. What came of this false cooperation? Mark Twain's story ends at this point, but we can guess that it would eventually occur to at least some of the other boys that placing their confidence in Tom was not warranted, as they came to understand that he had manipulated their interests for his own benefit. They would figure out that they had been conned by someone who had little regard for their own true interests.

The long-term consequence of such false cooperation is not true cooperation, but conflict. Tom Sawyer would eventually find that his friends were far less trusting, that they were more cautious in protecting their own interests, that they were more shrewd in their negotiations with him, and that they might even attempt in the future to defraud him.

What should we make of the story of sexual harassment? Of course, in hearing a story such as this it is difficult not to be outraged. I reject out of hand that there is anything in common between Florine Mitchell's situation and true cooperation. However, as I've suggested, the story is potentially an example of cooperation. Like Ben Rogers and Tom Sawyer, Florine Mitchell and her boss could have negotiated and agreed to a cooperative exchange. In this story we don't find the masking of interest and the manipulation of desire that we find in the confidence game that Tom Sawyer was running. The interest of the boss in having sex with the employee is clear; the interest of the employee in working to pay the mortgage and support her children is clear as well.

What is not right about the situation in which Florine Mitchell found herself is the asymmetrical power relationship between herself and her boss. The boss, who is in a position to fire any of his employees, holds far more power in any negotiations than do any of his employees, so that any apparent cooperation must be seen as merely a false cooperation, a reflection of the abuse of power by the boss.

Therefore, false cooperation can be based, first, on deception and disregard for the interests of others and, second, on the abuse of power. There is a third kind of false cooperation. Consider the story of Barbara Murray (drawn loosely from Chassler, 1984). For many years, she has chosen to defer her true interest—which is to push ahead aggressively in her career—in order to give time and energy to supporting her husband's career and raising her children. Barbara's family life appears tranquil—there is no open conflict between her interests and those of her husband and children. On a typical evening, her husband sits down to read the paper while Barbara goes into the kitchen to do the dishes. To her husband, she looks happy, or at least not unhappy. He considers that she is probably appreciating the change of pace after a hard day at work. Yes, he thinks, she is using the time well.

The next evening her husband is in a cooperative mood, so he decides to do the dishes and let his wife read the paper. Why, however, does he have the choice of doing or not doing the dishes, and Barbara does not? Why does she have to wait until the children are in school to vigorously pursue her own career? The excessive yielding of one's true interests in favor of another's is a third type of false cooperation. Barbara has deferred her own true interest for the sake of an outward appearance of cooperation within her family.

These three stories of false cooperation—involving deception and manipulation of the interests of others, abuse of power, and yielding of one's own true interests—all represent something that is inimical to positive development, for false cooperation leads to conflict. If cooperation can be either true or false, then the mere fact of cooperation among adults is, in and of itself, no certain criterion that they are progressing along a positive course of development or along the right course of action for protecting the environment, for a just society, or for world peace.

AVOIDING FALSE COOPERATION THROUGH DISCOURSE

How might we recognize and avoid false cooperation and at the same time better secure the possibility for true cooperation? Notably lacking in these three examples of false cooperation is a clear and forceful expression of true interest. In the first story, Tom masked his own true interest and, moreover, deceived the boys so as to induce an interest that was not true for them. However, if he had expressed his true interest, he might have found that the other boys were willing to volunteer to help him whitewash the fence and finish the work early so that they could all embark on a "delicious expedition" together. In the second story, Florine Mitchell made her interest clear, but only to her boss. She did not report the incidents of sexual harassment at the time they occurred. If she had expressed her interest more publicly, she might have been able to elicit support to prevent such incidents in the future. In the third story, Barbara Murray has kept to herself her interest in vigorously pursuing her career. However, if Barbara had expressed her true interest, she might have found that her husband and children were willing to help her achieve her goals.

A clear and forceful expression of true interest—that's a short and simple phrase, but to carry this out in practice might be difficult. What are some of the obstacles to a clear and forceful expression of true interest? Why were true interests not expressed in any of the three stories? Tom Sawyer was concerned that if he expressed his true interest—to go on a "delicious expedition"—the other boys would ridicule him. Expressing his interest in having them help with his work would lead, he feared, to conflict. Florine Mitchell was concerned that making a public charge of sexual harassment would aggravate her conflict with her boss. Barbara Murray was concerned that expressing her true interest in pursuing her career might introduce conflict into the apparently tranquil family relationship.

There is a paradox here. In all three stories only a false cooperation was achieved, and not true cooperation, because the actors were not willing to risk the conflict that might follow if they were to express their true interests. However, false cooperation will lead, in the long run, to conflict. True cooperation depends on a clear and forceful expression of true interests, and yet this would appear, at first glance, to also lead to conflict. We now have a partial answer to the question I raised in the introduction: Why do we not observe less conflict and more cooperation? The partial answer is that much apparent cooperation is merely false cooperation, and so leads to further conflict; and we often avoid the potential conflict that is associated with the clear and forceful expression of true interests that is necessary in order for true cooperation to be achieved.

How can we distinguish between conflict that is truly contentious and the apparent conflict associated with the expression of true interests? Let me introduce a distinction between these two types of conflict. I'll continue to refer to the first type, the bad type, as conflict; I'll refer to the second type, the good type, as discourse. In *conflict*, one is concerned primarily with self interest. One employs a variety of tricks to deceive the enemy and maximize one's own power. Conflict of this type does not lead to true cooperation.

In *discourse*, one is involved in those actions that are essential in converting a situation of false cooperation into one of true cooperation: First, there must be truthfulness; that is, a full expression of one's true interests so that there can be no deception and manipulation of other persons: Tom Sawyer should have been truthful. Second, there must be equality of power, so that any decision to cooperate is freely chosen and not constrained by tradition or status: Florine Mitchell's boss should not have abused his power in order to enforce her co-operation. True cooperation, when there is an initial asymmetrical power relationship, depends on either the achieving or the relinquishing of power in order to produce a relationship of equality. Third, there must be a sincere interest in the other person, including an active engagement in eliciting and supporting his or her interests, in order to prevent the false cooperation that arises through yielding: Barbara Murray's husband should have elicited and supported her true interests.

Discourse is risky. It is risky to express one's true interests, to give up whatever advantage in power one might have, and to take a sincere interest in another person. One risks loss of face, for one may be perceived by the other person as weak and perhaps willing to make concessions (Pruitt & Rubin, 1986, p. 156). Moreover, one risks revealing information about one's negotiating position, for the other person, knowing one's true interests, might seek to exploit this knowledge and gain a competitive advantage. Committing oneself to discourse requires one to *trust* another person, to trust that the other person will be sincere in taking one's own interests into consideration and therefore not seek further competitive advantage.

Self-Interest versus Relations with Others

What do we mean by trust? When we trust someone, we are expecting the other person to be socially responsible. A distinction can be drawn between two interpretations of social responsibility. The first is consistent with a philosophy of conflict and competition; the second is consistent with a philosophy of true cooperation. According to the first interpretation of social responsibility, I act responsibly toward others because it is in my own interest to do so. I expect to benefit from reciprocity; that is, I expect that sometime later, others will be socially responsible and helpful in return. Consequently, my motivation for being socially responsible is primarily self-interest.

However, there is a second interpretation of social responsibility. This depends on my conceiving of myself not as a self-contained individual, but rather "through my relations with others; I am completed through these relations and do not exist apart from them" (Sampson, 1988, p. 20). If I define myself in this way, then there is no distinct boundary between myself and others. Most important, "there is no fully separate self whose interests do not of necessity include others" (Sampson, 1988, p. 20). This second interpretation of responsibility is more consistent with the concepts of true cooperation and discourse. However, we often find the first interpretation easier to understand and accept, for the notion of self-contained individualism has long been a dominant theme in Western culture and particularly in American culture, especially on the frontier in the eighteenth and nineteenth centuries.

The distinction between social responsibility based in self-interest and social responsibility based in relations with others might be made more clear through recognizing that the Golden Rule is more consistent with the first interpretation, self-interest (McCarthy, 1978, p. 326): Do unto others as *you* would have them do unto you. This form of the Golden Rule assumes, as did Immanuel Kant in formulating the categorical imperative, a world of isolated, self-contained individuals who abstract from their own actions possible rules for social responsibility and then ask themselves whether they would like to have these rules applied to themselves. How arrogant is such a procedure!

It is simply not clear how a Golden Rule based only in self-reflection and self-interest has the *moral force* to restrain Tom Sawyer from conning his friends, to get Florine Mitchell's boss to back off, or to give Barbara Murray the power to decide for herself whether she will do the dishes or read the paper. Instead, any Golden Rule should be formulated in discourse: Abstract from your own actions a possible rule for social responsibility, and then submit the rule to others for their consideration.

Of course, there might well ensue considerable discussion and perhaps even some debate and conflict over what rules might be agreed to by all concerned. However, if such discussions can take place openly and publicly, in an atmosphere of equality of power so that the flow of ideas is not constrained by tradition or status, then the better argument will win out. A Golden Rule thus formulated in discourse, or any agreement for cooperation on whatever issue formulated in discourse, will then have sufficient force to prevent the false cooperation illustrated in the three stories.

Orientations toward Success versus Understanding

A second distinction between conflict and discourse reflects the goals or orientations of the persons involved. There are two principal orientations: an orientation toward success, and an orientation toward understanding (Habermas, 1984, p. 286). An orientation toward success requires the exercise of deception and domination to sustain even the appearance of cooperation, as illustrated above in the three stories of false cooperation. An orientation toward reaching mutual understanding leads to true cooperation. The terms or conditions of cooperation will be accepted as valid by both the participants, the agreement will rest on common convictions, and the agreement will not have been imposed by either party (Habermas, 1984, p. 287).

PROMOTING MUTUAL UNDERSTANDING

How can we move toward a better society in which adults are oriented less toward individualistic success and more toward reaching mutual understanding with others? One answer to this question is that we must turn our attention toward the development of an orientation toward understanding in our children, for it is they who will carry society and culture into the future. I recognize that it might at first seem inappropriate, in a volume on adult development and aging, to turn even briefly to matters of child rearing. However, in doing so I agree strongly with Erikson (1963; Meacham, 1989) that one of the major develop-

mental tasks of adulthood is the resolution of the issues associated with generativity, the seventh of eight life-course stages in Erikson's theory. Generativity
is primarily a concern for the next generation, although it includes motivations
toward productivity and creativity as well. For many individuals, generativity
is expressed as a choice of caring for the long-term well being of children and
grandchildren over caring for oneself (Erikson, Erikson, & Kivnick, 1986,
p. 84).

Therefore, I will turn to an illustration of child-rearing practices drawn from
the research of Baumrind (1971). In the course of an extensive investigation of
patterns of child rearing, Baumrind identified a small group of families in which
it appeared that, while the parents "almost never exercised control, they seemed
to have control in the sense that the child generally took pains to intuit what the
parents wanted and to do it" (p. 433). Let me quote briefly from an interview
with a mother about her four-year-old daughter Nina:

Interviewer (I): Describe Nina.

Mother (M): She's strong-tempered, which comes up because she's always been taught
that her opinions are valid. So if you disagree with her, she'll stand there and argue
all day if she feels differently.

I: How do you feel when she disobeys?

M: If you use the term disobeys, that sort of conjures up a negative feeling. Oftentimes
she just doesn't think the way I do. But I figure to a certain amount I've been here
longer—walked around on the earth longer, so I know more. Which isn't particularly
valid either.

I: Does Nina ever downright refuse to obey?

M: If from my point of view it's important, I'll pursue it. There have been times when
we've sat for hours and hours and yelled at each other—just incredible—really
stubborn, both of us. But most of the time, if I really feel it's not important, I'll
drop it.

I: Is it to her best interest in the long run that Nina learn to obey?

M: No. I've taught my kids to do whatever you want to do.

I: What decisions does Nina make for herself?

M: She makes all her own decisions and then we argue about them. (Baumrind, 1971,
p. 70)

On the surface, Nina is a self-centered, strong-tempered, opinionated, stubborn
child, who argues a lot with her mother. The description of the interactions
between Nina and her mother certainly appears to involve conflict. However,
recall that this family was selected as a harmonious family, in which the parents
did not exercise control over the children. Nonetheless, the parents seemed to
have control, in the sense that the children took pains to understand what the
parents wanted and then do it.

This brief interview illustrates a family and a pattern of child rearing oriented not toward success on the part of the parent but toward reaching a mutual understanding between parent and child. The interview illustrates how harmonious and cooperative relations can be based in discourse that has the appearance of conflict: "There have been times when we've sat for hours and hours and yelled at each other." However, when Nina and her mother argue, their arguing is not directed toward control or success, but instead toward reaching a mutual understanding with each other.

What emerges in such discourse is that each person comes to understand not only his or her own true interest but also the true interest of the other. This mother has been careful to not let her size, knowledge, and power constrain the flow of communication with her daughter. It seems reasonable to expect that when Nina grows up, she will be neither a perpetrator nor a victim of false cooperation. Instead, she will not deceive her friends, she will not tolerate sexual harassment, and she will decide whether or not to wash the dishes. She will experience positive development in adulthood and aging.

SUMMARY AND CONCLUSION

Because the setting forth of my argument has been primarily narrative in form, I should conclude with an explicit listing of my main points.

1. Cooperation based in an orientation toward success is false cooperation, characterized by deception of others, abuse of one's power, and yielding of one's true interests. False cooperation leads to conflict.

2. True cooperation depends on a clear and forceful expression of the true interests of both parties.

3. True interests are most easily expressed in discourse, in which there is equality of power and an orientation toward mutual understanding. Unfortunately, in our well-intentioned efforts to avoid the apparent conflict that might follow in the short term from entering into open discourse with one another, we too often pursue or acquiesce in a false cooperation that in the long term leads more certainly to the conflict we had desired to avoid.

4. Discourse is not easy, because there is in fact an unequal distribution of power in our society. One reason to be deeply concerned with the nature of false cooperation is that too often those who have used conflict and force to attain their power have then appropriated the concept of cooperation in an effort to retain power. Male, white Europeans certainly used conflict to attain their power (Rothenberg, 1988). Now that women, minorities, and Third World citizens are asking for social justice, those in power decry the use of conflict. Let's cooperate, they say, in a gradual process of social change that will last for generations. Thus, cooperate means, to those without power, keep your place in the status quo. However, to ask for social justice is to seek to enter into discourse. We should not avoid discourse merely because it might lead to conflict.

5. Finally, we must move not only beyond conflict but also beyond mere

cooperation. We must move from an orientation of achieving success in our relations with each other to an orientation of achieving mutual understanding.

It is encouraging that a number of authors who are currently wrestling with the issues raised in this chapter are converging on very similar conceptual frameworks and conclusions, although we continue to use somewhat different pairs of terms to describe our orientations. Kohn (1986), for example, has pointed to the different outcomes that follow from "competitive conflict," in which the competition serves merely to promote anxiety, distraction, suspicion, redundancy, and waste, as well as to make our self-esteem dependent on causing others to fail; as opposed to "cooperative conflict," which involves a sharing of resources, skills, and talents. Kramer (1989), in a review of styles of conflict resolution in intimate relationships, distinguished between levels of social-cognitive development that lead to understanding conflict resolution in terms of submission, coercion, or avoidance, on the one hand; and in terms of cooperative efforts to achieve solutions that satisfy both persons, on the other. In parallel fashion, Sinnott (ch. 14, this volume) describes a person involved in family decision making as shifting her problem-solving framework from a battle for rights to a balancing of many needs among many persons. Johnson (this volume) contrasts the actions of one facilitator, whose views of what was true or correct dominated the group, with those of a better facilitator, who suspended judgment, empowered the group members, and helped to legitimize and respect the members' varying points of view.

The contrasting pairs of terms and descriptions in the preceding paragraph are roughly equivalent in meaning to the dichotomy that I have set forth between conflict, false cooperation, and an orientation toward success, on the one hand; and discourse, true cooperation, and an orientation toward mutual understanding, on the other. Together, these converging conceptual frameworks provide the beginning of some answers to the issue raised at the outset regarding the nature of positive development in adulthood and aging and how it might be facilitated. Because we live in close psychological relationship with each other, positive development must include a continual striving for harmonious interpersonal relations. Why then, despite our shared sense that conflict is bad and cooperation is far better, do we continue to experience and observe so much conflict and so little cooperation both among adults and within society as a whole?

One answer is that positive development in adulthood and aging must be understood as development not toward achieving success but instead toward achieving mutual understanding with others. A second answer is that we must strive, not only in our relations with each other as adults but also in our child-rearing practices, to promote an atmosphere that permits and even encourages conflict when it is grounded in the three criteria for discourse: truthfulness, equality of power, and a sincere interest in others. It is only in discourse that the paradigms of conflict and cooperation can be bridged, and a role can be found for both.

NOTES

I am grateful to Ronald Irwin for his close reading of the chapter and the many incisive questions he raised, only a few of which I was able to address in the allotted space.

1. This chapter is based to a great extent in my reading of the work of Jurgen Habermas (1984; cf. McCarthy, 1978), more so than might be indicated merely from the formal citations.

REFERENCES

Baumrind, D. (1971). Harmonious parents and their preschool children. *Developmental Psychology, 4*, 63–72.

Chassler, S. (1984, August). Listening. *MS. Magazine*, pp. 51–53, 98–100.

Eason, Y. (1988). When the boss wants sex. In P. S. Rothenberg (Ed.), *Racism and sexism: An integrated study* (pp. 139–147). New York: St. Martin's.

Erikson, E. H. (1963). *Childhood and society* (2nd ed.). New York: Norton.

Erikson, E. H., Erikson, J. M., & Kivnick, H. Q. (1986). *Vital involvement in old age*. New York: Norton.

Habermas, J. (1984). *The theory of communicative action: Vol. 1. Reason and the rationalization of society* (T. McCarthy, Trans.). Boston: Beacon Press.

Kohn, A. (1986). *No contest: The case against competition*. Boston: Houghton Mifflin.

Kramer, D. A. (1989). A developmental framework for understanding conflict resolution processes. In J. D. Sinnott (Ed.), *Everyday problem solving: Theory and applications* (pp. 133–152). New York: Praeger.

McCarthy, T. (1978). *The critical theory of Jurgen Habermas*. Cambridge, MA: MIT Press.

Meacham, J. A. (1989). Autonomy, despair, and generativity in Erikson's theory. In P. S. Fry (Ed.), *Psychological perspectives of helplessness and control in the elderly* (pp. 63–98). New York: North-Holland.

Pruitt, D. G., & Rubin, J. Z. (1986). *Social conflict*. New York: Random House.

Rothenberg, P. S. (1988). How it happened: The legal status of women and people of color in the United States. In P. S. Rothenberg (Ed.), *Racism and sexism: An integrated study* (pp. 177–184). New York: St. Martin's.

Sampson, E. E. (1988). The debate on individualism. *American Psychologist, 43*, 15–22.

Twain, Mark [S. L. Clemens]. (1936). *The Adventures of Tom Sawyer*. New York: Heritage.

9

The Importance of Interpersonal Relations for Formal Operational Development

JOHN A. MEACHAM

Nothing was further from Piaget's mind than the caricature of a formal thinker, caring for nothing but his or her own formal context-free logical structures and constructing some new insight on the strength of personal introspection.

Hans Furth (1987, p. 168)

I would like to begin with a story about the balance-beam problem (Ferretti, Butterfield, Cah, & Kerkman, 1985; Inhelder & Piaget, 1958; Siegler, 1976), a problem that should readily be solved with the acquisition of Piagetian formal operational thinking in early adulthood. When I was an undergraduate student still majoring in engineering, I spent one summer working for a railroad as a member of a survey team. Five of us, along with several hundred pounds of equipment, rode around California in a huge, 1960s station wagon, establishing track lines at various sites along the railroad right-of-way.

One afternoon in late summer, when the peaches, apricots, and plums were all ripening in the Central Valley, we went fruit picking in the company car. We drove past many orchards, looking for one where the trees were covered with ripe fruit and where the grower and his workers were absent for the day. Finally we stopped along an infrequently traveled road, got out of the car, and wandered through an orchard enjoying the warm and juicy fruit and bringing armsful back to the car. After several trips from the orchard to the car without having been seen, we all got back in and the driver started the engine.

With no warning, the car tilted slightly and then dropped two feet, right through the road. We quickly climbed out and discovered that a small irrigation canal passing under the road had collapsed from the weight of our car. As the water rushed along, the hole grew larger, and our car slipped deeper below the level of the road. We were in a difficult situation, unable to get the car out of the hole. Someone with plum stains on his shirt would have to walk for help, likely to the home of the grower whose peaches, apricots, and plums were scattered around the back of the station wagon.

As we were standing by the car, lost in thought, a dump truck appeared in the distance, rumbling along the road toward us. The truck driver stopped; fortunately, he was not the owner of the orchard. He tied a cable to the back of his truck and to the front of our car, and tried to pull us out, but by then our car had sunk too far below the rim of the hole and could not be pulled forward. Now the situation began to look grim. Our college-educated, formal-operational survey team was without a solution to this dilemma. Our supervisor would learn that we had lost the company car at least 20 miles from the railroad right-of-way.

We stood for quite some time on that hot afternoon, listening to the buzz of insects and the hum of distant machinery, considering our predicament and advancing tentative but clearly unworkable solutions for each other's consideration. Fortunately, after involving himself in our exchanges, the truck driver provided a solution. Here is where the balance-beam problem becomes relevant. The driver raised the bed on the dump truck and then fastened the cable, still attached to our car, to the slightly lowered back end of the bed. Next, he lowered the bed on the dump truck, thus raising the back end of the bed just enough to raise the front of our car higher than the rim of the hole. The driver was then able to pull our car forward and out of the hole.

At the critical point in our discussion, it was the truck driver who understood, better than we, that the effect of the large weight of the car could be reduced by the short distance from the back end of the bed to the pivot, and that this combined weight and distance could be more than offset by the contraction of the piston under the forward end of the bed, multiplied by the long length of the truck bed. This is, of course, the same understanding that is required to solve the balance-beam problem. We thanked the truck driver and drove off to find the railroad.

There are, of course, diverse explanations for how the problem of raising the car from the hole was solved, and so I do not want to maintain that this one story provides strong evidence for any particular thesis. Nevertheless, it illustrates much of what I hope to communicate in this chapter. My main purpose is to raise the question of whether the system of logic that Piaget has termed formal operations must be conceived, as many other than Piaget appear wont to do, as residing within the single minds of individuals, or whether it might better be conceived as residing within the shared mental space of a group of persons. In pursuing the answer to this question, I hope to make some progress toward allaying five concerns regarding what seems to be the traditional view toward adult thought.

I will conclude that a figure-ground reversal in how we think of the relationship between formal operations and other aspects of adult functioning would be helpful, so that the stage of formal operations can be understood not as an unambiguously positive achievement and as a necessary foundation for further development in adulthood and old age, but rather as an optional development presenting some positive opportunities but also some serious dangers that the individual must strive to negotiate successfully. Thus, an adult apparently not reasoning in a formal operational manner might be regarded not as having failed to achieve this particular developmental stage, but instead as someone who is negotiating his or her way successfully beyond the dangers of formal operations.

CONCERNS REGARDING THE STATUS OF FORMAL OPERATIONS

I have been led to pose this question, of whether formal operational thinking resides within single minds or within a shared mental space, by a number of concerns: First, when assessments of formal operational thinking are carried out, it appears that not all adults reason at this level, even within college-educated groups. In a sample ranging in age from 17 to 80 years, Hooper, Hooper, and Colbert (1984, p. 30) found that the percentage of formal operational tasks that were passed ranged from 47% (correlation tasks) to 84% (abstraction tasks). Lunzer (1978) remarked that "even intelligent adults often appear strikingly inept when asked to tackle formal problems, that is, problems that require the use of inferential procedures on the basis of arbitrary associations between elements that carry no meaning for the subject" (p. 27). It would seem, then, that formal operations might be a poor foundation for further, positive development during adolescence and adulthood, because apparently so few adults achieve complete formal operations or the robustness of formal operations for those who do may be questionable. Furthermore, perhaps formal operations is not a normative and universal development but merely a deviant development for an elite few. (I will later argue against these suggestions.) In short, how can the notion that all adults are formal operational be reconciled with their lack of formal operations during standard assessments?

Second, despite the apparent infrequency with which people achieve formal operations, many adults seem to be engaged routinely and relatively effortlessly in endeavors that are positive features of adult functioning and that have been described by some as postformal operational (see, e.g., Commons, Richards, & Armon, 1984; Kramer, 1983; Sinnott, 1984, 1989). To avoid a lengthy digression in order to define and justify the notion of postformal operations, I will merely repeat phrases that have been used by others: dialectical, reflective, sensitive to moral concerns, perceiving or giving multiple solutions to problems, relativistic, accepting of contradiction, and so forth. Although there may be some disagreement as to what is common among these phrases, I take the essence of these phrases to be their social nature. Contradictions, moral issues, relativistic concerns, and so forth, arise in interpersonal relations, not for Robinson Crusoes. If much of what has been described as postformal operational is a common experience for many adults, then our conception of developmental stages and sequences is rather awkward, in that apparently many adults have achieved the advanced stage of postformal operations without first achieving the stage of formal operations.

A third concern with the traditional, single-mind account of formal operations is that appropriate interpersonal functioning may be disrupted and further development impeded, at least in the short run, by the onset of formal operations in adolescence. Elkind (1967), in a classic article on egocentrism in adolescence, described some of these dangers of early formal operations for social development, including the belief in a self-constructed personal fable, a romanticized and idealized story in which one is always fortunate and protected from harm (for example, I can drink heavily and still drive safely), and the belief in an imaginery audience, that one is always on stage, with all of one's behaviors and thoughts open to scrutiny by others.

More recently, Chandler (1987) described the adolescent's realization, brought on by the onset of formal operations, that meaning is not a property of objects (as it is taken to be in concrete operations) but rather a construction of persons, and so necessarily subjective. This realization involves a feeling of epistemological loneliness, an apparent loss of the possibility for shared and certain truths. Chandler described two typical outcomes of this epistemological loneliness. The first is incapacitating relativism and skepticism, according to which there are no grounds for holding beliefs with any confidence or for rational decision making. The other outcome is dogmatism; that is, committing oneself to some presumably unimpeachable authority by which one's beliefs can be certified as valid; for example, a religious faith or scientism ("rituals of methodological rigors," p. 147). Certainly one might become formal operational and survive the dangers that Elkind (1967) and Chandler (1987) have described. Nevertheless, might there not be a more positive route through adolescence and young adulthood, a route leading with more certainty to mature adulthood?

A fourth concern is with the tendency to view formal and postformal operations as complete systems or ends in themselves, without inquiring in greater detail into the purposes to which these systems might be put and the human motivations that provide the context for their functioning. What is needed is to understand the place of formal operations within the more encompassing systems of the self, the family, the community, societal institutions, and culture (see, for example, Rankin and Allen, this volume). As Broughton (1981, pp. 334–335) has noted, even Piaget focused on the individual to the neglect of cultural activities and institutions. Labouvie-Vief (1980, pp. 154–155) has also pointed to the need to understand the development of logic within the contexts of the tasks of adult life and the maintenance of social systems; that is, to understand formal operational thought not as an end in itself but as a tool toward more encompassing ends.

My fifth concern is that formal operations, conceived as residing within the isolated minds of individuals, is not consistent with several theoretical perspectives according to which individual cognition and consciousness are rejected as a basis for individual and societal development in favor of interpersonal relations, communication, and cooperation (Meacham, 1984). Vygotsky (1978), for example, argued that all cognitive abilities appear first in social interaction and only subsequently at the individual level. Habermas (1984) rejected intrasubjectivity as a starting point for understanding the individual and society, arguing instead for basing these in intersubjectivity, in the community of persons in dialogue (cf. McCarthy, 1978, p. 326). A related perspective was advanced by Harre (1984, p. 64), who argued that the primary reality is persons in conversation, with human minds brought into being only as secondary realities. In contrast to these views is the feeling that if thinking is removed from the material locus of the individual brain and considered to inhabit some indeterminate space among minds, then the status of formal operations as real is threatened. Pepper (1942, pp. 198, 211), however, made it clear that this is a concern occurring primarily within a mechanistic worldview but not necessarily in other worldviews such as organicism or contextualism.

The basing of developmental processes in interpersonal relations, communication, and cooperation is reasonably well accepted among researchers in infancy and childhood, who in the last decade have focused on family and peer interactions to expand their understanding of development in an enthusiastic, productive, and integrative fashion (e.g., Kaye, 1982; Nelson, 1985). Similarly, at the other end of the life course, the significance of interpersonal relations is well accepted as a unifying framework as, for example, in the work of Erikson (1963; Kivnick, 1985) and others (White, Speisman, Costos, & Smith, 1987). However, for the middle portion of the life course, adolescence and young adulthood, researchers typically place a premium on individual achievement, self-discipline, and autonomous thought, while the positive capacities for mature interpersonal relations and involvement in issues of value and meaning in life are of secondary importance and dependent on prior cognitive-structural achievements within the individual. Perhaps this last sentence overstates the case somewhat. What is needed is neither a rejection of cognition as a domain nor a conception of interpersonal relations as dependent on prior cognitive achievements, but rather an understanding of development through and beyond formal operations in terms of interpersonal and social relations.

FIVE DEVELOPMENTAL SEQUENCES

If one accepts the well-established significance of interpersonal relations in infancy and childhood and in late adulthood and old age, then the traditional

Figure 9.1
Possible Developmental Sequences and Types

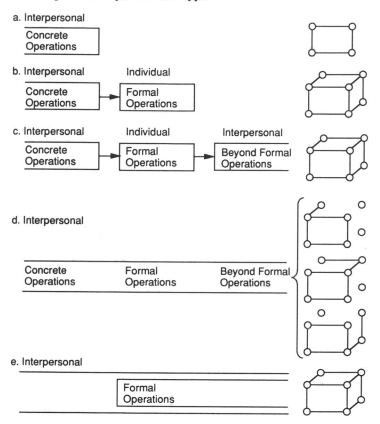

(a) Avoid formal operations; (b) single-mind formal operations; (c) two awkward transitions; (d) social mind; (e) single-mind formal operations within social mind. Sensorimotor and preoperational stages are not shown.

perspective emphasizing individualistic, self-contained cognitive processes as a major, normative achievement of adolescence and young adulthood presents two awkward developmental transitions requiring an explanation; first, in early adolescence, from interpersonal to individualistic, and second, during adulthood and aging, beyond formal operations to interpersonal. A more parsimonious developmental theory would emphasize the continuity of interpersonal relations as the basis for developmental progress. In this context, individualistic, self-contained cognition in adolescence can be argued to be deviant. Such an approach suggests at least the following possible developmental sequences (see Figure 9.1). These sequences in turn might provide a rough typology of individuals with respect to their passage through formal operations.

First, one developmental sequence for moving "beyond" formal operations is to avoid this development entirely (Figure 9.1,a). Granted, there might be some disadvantage in not having formal operations at one's command, but perhaps for some individuals positive development in adulthood and aging consists in avoiding the dangers of emotional upheaval inherent within the transition to and achievement of formal operations; for example, the problems of the imaginary audience and personal fable described by Elkind (1967), the incapacitating skepticism and dogmatism described by Chandler (1987), the false and dangerous belief that one can have complete knowledge, the positivistic separation of fact from value, and the illusion that life can be understood in black-and-white terms (Meacham, 1990). To progress in development not only presents opportunities but also entails risks of losing what is familiar and workable and venturing toward what is unknown and uncertain. Is it not reasonable that a few individuals might, in this trade-off of opportunities and risks, decide not to progress further? Such a decision might be reflected, for example, in the avoidance by some students of mathematics, logic, science, and similar studies.

A second developmental type is the individual who progresses through the first developmental transition, from interpersonal to individualized cognition, and then becomes stuck at this stage of formal operations (Figure 9.1,b). An individual of this type remains susceptible throughout adulthood to those dangerous symptoms of individualistic formal operations described earlier (Chandler, 1987; Elkind, 1967). While it might be argued that formal operations might be advantageous in certain occupational niches, and that with the complementary development of certain defensive structures one might have an outwardly adequate adult life, nevertheless, further positive development during adolescence and adulthood might require a second transition beyond these dangers of formal operations, a return to an interpersonal world of values and meaning (a third developmental type, Figure 9.1,c). Further developmental subtypes might be distinguished according to the age at which the second transition, from individualistic to interpersonal thought, is achieved. The content, values, and meanings associated with this transition will greatly color the conflict experienced by the individual according to whether the transition occurs, for example, in the 30s and early 40s or in the 60s (Meacham, 1989).

A fourth developmental type is the individual who successfully negotiates the dangers of formal operations by achieving mastery over this powerful tool while at the same time retaining the firm foundation for thought, values, and meaning provided by interpersonal relations (Figure 9.1,d). For such an individual, the two awkward transitions into and out of individualistic, self-contained thought do not occur. The achievement of formal operations becomes not an end point in development, but merely another tool in the service of interpersonal relations, communication, and cooperation. This fourth developmental type is illustrated in the work of Johnson (this volume), who describes the best facilitator as the one who empowers the individual women through group activities and helps the group to legitimize and respect the members' varying points of view. Similarly, in the case study described by Sinnott (ch. 14, this volume), not only is there an interweaving of social and cognitive processes, but advanced cognitive processes during problem solving are more likely when there are close interpersonal relations. This fourth developmental type (Figure 9.1,d) is, I would argue, the preferred developmental type, in that one does not have to strive to get "beyond" formal operations if one has not permitted formal operations to become the dominant mode of functioning in the first place. Nevertheless, the self-contained, individualistic bias of our society and our psychology (Sampson, 1977) might make such a developmental sequence difficult for many persons to pursue successfully (Meacham, 1990).

What does it mean to say that one might be formal and postformal operational within the context of interpersonal relations, within the context of a social mind, a shared mental space? At the right-hand side of Figure 9.1, I present a visual metaphor (loosely borrowed from Fischer, Hand, and Russell, 1984, p. 45) in which lines, squares, and cubes represent increasing levels of structural development. The contrast between the single-mind and the social-mind perspective on formal operations is whether a particular structure—for example, the cube— is conceived as residing entirely within the mind of a single person or whether this cube becomes a complete structure only when the incomplete portions within the minds of several people (in the figure, three people) are brought together in communication and cooperation. For a very few individuals, a sufficient number of these parts of the cube might be constructed and routinely accessible as habitual actions during performance, so that we might say that a single mind has developed within the context of social mind (the fifth developmental type, Figure 9.1,e). There are, after all, a few individuals who are quite able to solve formal operational tasks alone.

IMPLICATIONS: RESPONSES TO THE FIVE CONCERNS

There are a number of implications, paralleling each of the five concerns raised earlier in this chapter, of this social-mind perspective on formal operations. First, assessment of formal operations should be carried out not with individuals but with groups of individuals. Suppose we were interested in whether someone is a "party type," that is, whether he or she has fun at parties and contributes to the enjoyment of other people at parties. We would not assess this person by putting him or her alone in a room with a bowl of peanuts and some balloons. We might instead plan parties for several weekends, with different people invited to each but with the person in question invited only every other weekend. If the parties that the person in question attends are more fun than the parties on the alternate, control weekends, then we would credit this person with being a party type, that is, a catalyst for enjoyable parties.

The problem of assessing formal operations for the truck driver in my introductory story is similar. If assessed in the traditional manner, that is, if he were asked to engage in formal operational thinking in isolation from others with whom he could discuss the problems, he might not have done as well on the balance-beam problem as the college-educated, professional members of the survey team. However, in the context of everyday problem solving (Meacham & Emont, 1988), a context in which the driver became involved in discussions about the problem of how to get the car out of the hole (an interpersonal and so a more appropriate adult setting for the assessment of formal operations), he was able to act as a catalyst and lead the group to the solution of the problem. The truck driver should be credited, from the social-mind perspective, with being formal operational.

From the social-mind perspective, to be formal operational does not mean to be able to solve formal operational tasks alone. Instead, to be formal operational means to be able to participate in conversation—in more general terms, to engage in action—with other people at a formal operational level. Given this criterion, all healthy adults could be shown to be formal operational, and formal operations might be seen as a normal healthy development, not as deviance; thus, my first concern, expressed earlier, is resolved. As Furth (1987) noted, "When adults use what Piaget calls operations, it is no longer the single 'I' who acts but the social 'I' (Piaget's 'epistemic' subject), who as participant of the group has identified with the knowledge regulations binding on all humans" (p. 126).

The second implication is that, if adults are formal operational in this social-mind sense, then many adults should have the opportunity for further, positive development beyond formal operations, by virtue of their immersion within a social world, a world of interpersonal relations. It is within interpersonal contexts that the need for relativism becomes apparent, that contradictions are brought to one's attention, that questions and doubts arise, that reasoning about values and the meaning of life becomes unavoidable (Johnson, this volume; Meacham, 1990; Sinnott, ch. 14, this volume). The various notions brought together within the phrase "postformal operations" thus have relevance not for an elite group of adults, but instead for the positive development of all adults; thus, my second concern is resolved. I would like to believe that the truck driver who helped us, now in his 60s, has lived much of his adult life in a postformal stage, even though he might not be able to solve the balance-beam problem when tested in isolation. Certainly on the occasion of our first meeting, when the college-educated survey team was involved in stealing fruit, the truck driver who helped us was functioning at a more advanced stage of moral development.

A third implication is that it might be possible for one to develop in a positive direction beyond concrete operations while minimizing the dangers of formal operations. From the social-mind perspective, these dangers arise primarily for those relatively isolated individuals who acquire the full power of formal operations in the absence of the supportive framework of interpersonal relations (Figure 9.1,b). It is likely that many who read this chapter—persons who have achieved high scores on individual performance tests, who have pursued graduate study in the social sciences, and similar accomplishments—are among those who have suffered the crises of epistemological loneliness and the skepticism and perhaps even the dogmatism to which Chandler (1987) referred. I am less confident that the truck driver in my story suffered through these states. Instead, he might very well have enjoyed a full, rich, balanced, and meaningful adulthood. Thus, my third concern, regarding the possibility of a more positive route through adolescence and adulthood, is eased.

A fourth implication is that formal operations is not an end in itself, as if the goal for each individual person is to "have it." Instead, formal operations is merely a tool—not a tool for individualistic reasoning, but a tool in the service of friendship, cooperation, and community. Thus, my fourth concern is resolved. In this larger, interpersonal context, the critical test of adulthood is not that a person demonstrate that he or she can, in isolation, solve formal operational problems. Rather, the critical test of adulthood is whether an individual can communicate and work together with other adults within a formal operational framework, which of course is what adults do in their daily work and family life. The truck driver in my story stopped his truck and joined us not to solve the balance-beam problem but for the sake of friendship and community or, in Furth's (1987) paraphrasing of Piaget, "the love and respect of others and the desire to coordinate [his] own with the other's viewpoint" (p. 133).

What I have proposed is consistent with the social-mind perspective of Vygotsky, Habermas, Harre, and others, thus resolving the fifth concern. Adopting the social-mind perspective permits a developmental theory without awkward transitions from social mind to single, isolated mind in adolescence and then back to social mind. This perspective further permits a figure-ground reversal in how we conceive of the relationship between formal operations and other positive features of adult development, so that the stage of formal operations is understood not as an unambiguously positive achievement and a necessary foundation for further development (Figure 9.1,c), but rather as an optional development (Figure 9.1,a) presenting some serious dangers that the individual must strive to negotiate successfully (Figure 9.1,b) as well as some opportunities for positive development in adulthood and old age (Figure 9.1,d). From the social-mind perspective, an adult apparently not reasoning in a formal operational manner in an individualized assessment might now be regarded not necessarily as having failed to achieve this particular developmental stage, but perhaps instead as someone who is successfully negotiating his or her way beyond the dangers of formal operations.

IMPLICATIONS FOR EDUCATION AND ASSESSMENT

Being stuck within a single-mind, individualistic mode of formal operations is deviant and potentially dangerous with respect to further development. Maintaining a firm foundation in interpersonal relations, communication, and cooperation is a recommendation for positive development during adolescence, adulthood, and aging. The developmental challenge is not how to restore relativity, values, and meaning to life at some stage "beyond formal operations," but rather how to maintain these in one's life from childhood through early adulthood as one strives to negotiate successfully the dangers of formal operations.

The importance of the preceding paragraph becomes more clear when we consider what should be prescribed in a program of education for positive development. The single-mind perspective implies that in our schools the teachers should strive to inculcate formal operational thinking into the minds of as many individual students as possible. The teaching and the system of examinations should have as their purposes, as the end point for instruction and development, that the students should be able to perform in isolation—and in competition with each other—so that as adults they will be think-alike workers, interchangeable and replaceable units (things, not persons) within the economic system. College students—the subjects for much research in psychology—are deviant not merely because they are bright, in late adolescence, living away from home, not working full-time, and so forth, but also because within the group of college students are those who have been most successfully socialized into the deviant developmental sequence of single-mind, individualized, formal operational thinking (Figure 9.1,b).

In contrast, the social-mind perspective leads to the suggestion that teachers should not strive to directly inculcate formal operational thinking, but should strive instead to promote an atmosphere conducive to communication, friendship, cooperation, and a sense of community. Within such a healthy context, as the desire to share knowledge and therefore the need for the tool of formal operational thought arise, adolescents and young adults can be trusted to develop these capabilities for themselves. Indeed, if the essence of formal operational thought is its basis in interpersonal relations, then an educational system that encourages deviant, individualistic thought might result in the development of less formal operational thinking within our society than would otherwise be the case.

From the social-mind perspective, procedures for the assessment of formal operational thinking need to be developed that are based not in individualized performance but rather in the performance of the group, in communication and cooperation (similar to the mock assessment of the party type described above). Briefly, individuals must be assessed while working together with other persons; if the group as a whole is able to solve formal operational tasks, then individuals who have contributed to the group process should be given credit as being formal operational. Is it conceivable that a person could be formal operational within the group context but not on his or her own? It is. A particular individual might have a "missing link"—a piece of understanding or an operation to contribute to the group—thus completing the structure and providing the solution (see Figure 9.1,d), while this same individual may lack other understandings or operations that would have been necessary for an individualized solution (Figure 9.1,b). Wechsler (1971) raised the same possibility, asking whether a group of individuals, through working together, might come up with a better solution than individually, and furthermore, whether they might have "acquired or made use of perceptions or insights not experienced or available to them when working or cogitating alone'' (p. 904). Thus, the whole is greater than the sum of the parts; the intelligent functioning of the group is greater than that of any individual person within the group. The notion that the performance of the group as a whole can be no better than the performance of the most intelligent group member must be rejected.

In our society, the historical image of the mature, adult thinker has been the isolated scientist, Thomas Edison, working alone in his laboratory (perhaps even late at night, so as to avoid the distraction of other people). However, I can close this chapter with the counterexample of Jean Piaget, a formal operational scientist who proclaimed the necessity of interpersonal relations in his work, as this quotation from an interview by the journalist J.-C. Bringuier (1980, p. 18) illustrates:

Bringuier: ''Do you think a researcher should work alone?''

Piaget: ''Oh no; you must have contacts, and you must, especially, have people who contradict you. You have to have a group'' (p. 18).

For Piaget (1971), the operations of intelligence and those of cooperation are the same operations, for actions can be collective as well as individual; the most general forms of thought are ''forms of cognitive exchange or of interindividual regulation'' (p. 361). What is required, as we move forward to a renewed consideration of positive development in adulthood and aging, is a bridging of the paradigms of individualistic cognition, on the one hand, and social interaction, motivation, and affect, on the other. I have attempted to show how such a bridge might be ''fruitfully'' constructed if we can relinquish our traditional individual-mind perspective and adopt a social-mind perspective instead, one in which the human mind is conceived as deriving its unique qualities and the strength it displays in adulthood and aging from its essential basis in the interpersonal relations of friendship and cooperation.

NOTE

I am grateful to John Broughton and David Moshman for their close reading of the manuscript and for their encouragement.

REFERENCES

Bringuier, J.-C. (1980). *Conversations with Jean Piaget* (B. M. Gulati, Trans.). Chicago: University of Chicago Press.

Broughton, J. M. (1981). Piaget's structural developmental psychology: IV. Knowledge without a self and without history. *Human Development, 24*, 320–346.

Chandler, M. J. (1987). The Othello effect: Essay on the emergence and eclipse of skeptical doubt. *Human Development, 30*, 137–159.

Commons, M. L., Richards, F. A., & Armon, C. (Eds.). (1984). *Beyond formal operations: Late adolescent and adult cognitive development*. New York: Praeger.

Elkind, D. (1967). Egocentrism in adolescence. *Child Development, 38*, 1025–1034.

Erikson, E. H. (1963). Childhood and society (2nd ed.). New York: Norton.

Ferretti, R. P., Butterfield, E. C., Cah, A., & Kerkman, D. (1985). The classification of children's knowledge: Development on the balance-scale and inclined-plane tasks. *Journal of Experimental Child Psychology, 39,* 131–160.

Fischer, K., Hand, H. H., & Russell, S. (1984). The development of abstractions in adolescence and adulthood. In M. L. Commons, F. A. Richards, & C. Armon (Eds.), *Beyond formal operations: Late adolescent and adult cognitive development* (pp. 43–73). New York: Praeger.

Furth, H. G. (1987). *Knowledge as desire: An essay on Freud and Piaget.* New York: Columbia University Press.

Habermas, J. (1984). *The theory of communicative action.* Boston: Beacon.

Harre, R. (1984). *Personal being.* Cambridge, MA: Harvard University Press.

Hooper, F. H., Hooper, J. O., & Colbert, K. K. (1984). *Personality and memory correlates of intellectual functioning: Young adulthood to old age.* Basel: Karger.

Inhelder, B., & Piaget, J. (1958). *The growth of logical thinking from childhood to adolescence.* New York: Basic Books.

Kaye, K. (1982). *The mental and social life of babies: How parents create persons.* London: Methuen.

Kivnick, H. Q. (1985). Intergenerational relations: Personal meaning in the life cycle. In J. A. Meacham (Ed.), *Family and individual development* (pp. 93–102). Basel: Karger.

Kramer, D. A. (1983). Post-formal operations? A need for further conceptualization. *Human Development, 26,* 91–105.

Labouvie-Vief, G. (1980). Beyond formal operations: Uses and limits of pure logic in life-span development. *Human Development, 23,* 141–161.

Lunzer, E. A. (1978). Formal reasoning: A reappraisal. In B. Z. Presseisen, D. Goldstein, & M. H. Appel (Eds.), *Topics in cognitive development: Vol. 2. Language and operational thought.* New York: Plenum.

McCarthy, T. (1978). *The critical theory of Jurgen Habermas.* Cambridge, MA: MIT Press.

Meacham, J. A. (1984). The social basis of intentional action. *Human Development, 27,* 119–124.

Meacham, J. A. (1989). Autonomy, despair, and generativity in Erikson's theory. In P. S. Fry (Ed.), *Psychology of helplessness and control in the aged* (pp. 63–98). Amsterdam: North-Holland.

Meacham, J. A. (1990). The loss of wisdom. In R. J. Sternberg (Ed.), *Wisdom: Its nature, origins, and development* (pp. 181–211). New York: Cambridge University Press.

Meacham, J. A., & Emont, N. C. (1988). The interpersonal basis of everyday problem-solving. In J. D. Sinnott (Ed.), *Everyday problem-solving: Theory and application* (pp. 7–23). New York: Praeger.

Nelson, K. (1985). *Making sense: The acquisition of shared meaning.* Orlando, FL: Academic.

Pepper, S. C. (1942). *World hypotheses.* Berkeley: University of California Press.

Piaget, J. (1971). *Biology and knowledge* (B. Walsh, Trans.). Chicago: University of Chicago Press.

Sampson, E. E. (1977). Psychology and the American ideal. *Journal of Personality and Social Psychology, 35,* 767–782.

Siegler, R. S. (1976). Three aspects of cognitive development. *Cognitive Psychology, 4,* 481–520.

Sinnott, J. D. (1984). Postformal reasoning: The relativistic stage. In M. Commons, F. Richards, & C. Armon (Eds.), *Beyond formal operations* (pp. 288–315). New York: Praeger.

Sinnott, J. D. (1989). Adult differences in the use of postformal operations. In M. Commons, J. Sinnott, F. Richards, & C. Armon (Eds.), *Beyond formal operations* (Vol. 2, pp. 239–278). New York: Praeger.

Vygotsky, L. S. (1978). *Mind in society.* Cambridge, MA: Harvard University Press.

Wechsler, D. (1971). Concept of collective intelligence. *American Psychologist, 26,* 904–907.

White, K. M., Speisman, J. C., Costos, D., & Smith, A. (1987). Relationship maturity: A conceptual and empirical approach. In J. A. Meacham (Ed.), *Interpersonal relations: Family, peers, friends* (pp. 81–101). Basel: Karger.

10

Age Differences versus Age Deficits in Laboratory Tasks: The Role of Research in Everyday Cognition

JAMES M. PUCKETT, HAYNE W. REESE,
STANLEY H. COHEN, AND LESLEE K. POLLINA

This chapter is addressed to the role of research on everyday or practical cognition within the larger domain of research on cognitive aging. Although a recent call has been made to essentially abandon research on everyday cognition (Banaji & Crowder, 1989), we believe that such research may yet be invaluable in investigating adult age differences in cognition when taken together with research on laboratory cognition. To explain this position, we first explore four possible research outcomes employing everyday and laboratory tasks and their theoretical interpretations. Next, a potentially fruitful postformal theory (Pascual-Leone, 1983, 1984) is reviewed, and we outline some general directions in which that theory might be enhanced in both depth and breadth in order to deal with the issues that we raise. A number of definitions of everyday processing are then reviewed in relation to this postformal theorizing. We conclude that none of the definitions at this time compels a differentiation between everyday and laboratory cognition as two distinct types, although this remains a possibility that we discuss in relation to the four possible research outcomes. Finally, we discuss methodological considerations, and we report a preliminary experiment that illustrates and tests some of the issues raised herein.

THE PROBLEM

For the most part in this chapter, we are discussing problem solving (conflict resolution, problem finding, induction, deduction, etc.), although other types of cognition may also be relevant (memory, perception, etc.). The terms "everyday," "real-world," and "practical" comprise one category of tasks, and will be used interchangeably. Similarly, the terms "laboratory" and "academic" will be used interchangeably and considered as one category. Although the first grouping seems internally valid, some doubt may exist as to whether laboratory and academic tasks should be grouped together. Certainly some laboratory tasks require mental operations far removed from traditional academic tasks, but the converse may not be true (that is, the category of academic tasks may be subsumed under the category of laboratory tasks). Nevertheless, both laboratory and academic tasks have been contrasted with the first grouping (e.g., Sternberg & Wagner, 1986); therefore, laboratory and academic tasks appear to be functionally equivalent for our present purposes. The basis for distinguishing between the two larger groupings is questionable, however, and will be considered in some depth later.

Although some cogent criticisms of research on everyday cognition have recently been proffered (Banaji & Crowder, 1989), research interest in the approach has been increasing (e.g., Cohen, 1989; Poon, Rubin, & Wilson, 1989; Sinnott, 1989a; Sternberg & Wagner 1986). The historical reasons for this increase have been traced by Sinnott (1989a), who pointed out that research on everyday cognition was initiated in part because of the observation that in the large literature on laboratory and academic cognitive tasks, old adults generally perform poorly compared to young adults (e.g., Kausler, 1982; Reese & Rodeheaver, 1985).

In response to the age-related difference in laboratory tasks, theorists such as Labouvie-Vief (1985) have argued that laboratory and academic tasks do not allow old adults to take advantage of their natural, possibly postformal, modes of cognition. In contrast, everyday tasks should engender a more reasonable index of cognitive performance in old age, because old adults' cognition is said to have developed to cope with the demands of everyday tasks. Rather than reflecting age deficits in performance on laboratory tasks, the poorer performance by old relative to young adults on laboratory tasks is said to be due merely to age differences in strategies or modes of thought.

This hypothesis is certainly viable, but so are other explanations for the widespread age-related differences on laboratory tasks. Labouvie-Vief and others appear to have assumed, for old adults at least, that the interface between the task type and the strategy chosen is better for everyday than for laboratory tasks. They clearly assumed that old adults perform better on everyday than laboratory tasks. However, without knowing the performance level and strategies used by the older group in each task domain, it is impossible to evaluate this and other positions.

A CONCEPTUAL FRAMEWORK

Four possible research outcomes and some possible associated theoretical positions will be defined in terms of two crossed variables. First, for a given set of everyday and laboratory tasks, or perhaps for all such tasks, old adults either

Figure 10.1
**Possible Research Outcomes, Based on Whether Old Adults Differ in Strategies
and Performance between Everyday and Laboratory Tasks, and Possible
Theoretical Interpretations of Age Differences in Laboratory Task Performance**

Performance of older adults
better or same in everyday tasks as
compared to laboratory tasks

		Performance Better	Performance Same
	Strategies Different	Context-dependent strategies; perhaps disuse of academic strategies in laboratory tasks	Global decrement position; strategies and processes deficient in old age
Strategies of old adults same or different in laboratory as compared to everyday tasks	Strategies Same	Context-dependent strategy effectiveness; perhaps processing-based	Processing-based strategy deficiency with no context effects

(a) use the same strategies across task domains or (b) use different strategies.
Second, for a given set of tasks, old adults either (a) perform better on the
everyday than on the laboratory tasks (perhaps resulting in an absence of age
differences between young and old adults on everyday tasks), or (b) do not
perform better on everyday than on laboratory tasks (age differences may persist).
These four possibilities involving performance and strategies are summarized in
Figure 10.1.

Definitions and Assumptions

Generally, poorer and better performance in this chapter are conceptualized
in terms of two aspects: (a) quality of the problem solution according to objective
considerations (given several equally desirable solutions, the subject's own criteria for success determine the best one), and (b) quantitative parameters such
as time to solution and number of errors.

Although anecdotes abound, we do not assume that elderly adults will perform
better on everyday than on laboratory tasks nor that strategies will differ across
task types, because not enough systematic data are available to permit any general
inferences. Whereas the performance and strategies used by old adults may or
may not differ between laboratory and everyday contexts, the efficiency of most

basic information processes (e.g., speed of processing, susceptibility to distractions, working memory capacity) clearly declines with age (e.g., Botwinick, 1984; Craik, 1977; Kausler, 1982; Poon, 1985; Salthouse, 1985). We further assume that basic processes are equally deficient for everyday and laboratory tasks. Even though the basic processes decline, however, compensatory strategies may be employed, or new styles of thinking may emerge, partially as a result of the decline in basic processes (e.g., Pascual-Leone, 1983). For example, Sinnott (1989c) proposed that old adults may use "strange loops" in solving problems while younger adults may not. A strange loop is an executive process exemplifying positive mental growth, and might be expected to facilitate everyday but not laboratory problem solving. However, strange loops may consist of recombinations of the basic mechanisms that decline with age and that underlie other executive processes that might be more likely than strange loops to be used in laboratory tasks (Anderson, 1983; Berg & Sternberg, 1985; Pascual-Leone 1983, 1984; Rybash, Hoyer, & Roodin, 1986). Thus, it is unclear whether old adults' performance will improve on everyday as opposed to laboratory tasks even if their strategies differ across the two task types.

For our present theoretical purposes, it does not appear necessary to distinguish between those cases in which the elderly may perform more poorly and those in which they may perform the same on everyday and laboratory tasks. Our purposes may require only distinguishing these two cases from the case in which the elderly perform better on everyday than laboratory tasks. Similarly, it may not be necessary to specify whether old adults use the same strategies as young adults in either task domain (laboratory or everyday) or whether young adults improve in performance on everyday tasks in comparison to laboratory tasks. However, the framework in Figure 10.1 may eventually need to be expanded to take into account these and other factors as it may ultimately prove inadequate for interpreting age differences in everyday and laboratory performance. In the meantime, it is serviceable for purposes of illustrating the present issues and approach.

Four Possible Research Outcomes

The first set of empirical outcomes to be considered is that old adults use different strategies in everyday and laboratory tasks, and that they perform better on everyday than laboratory tasks (Figure 10.1). This set of findings would be compatible with a contextual position in that the interface between task context and strategy would determine problem-solving efficacy. The reason for the poor performance of old adults in laboratory tasks would probably be due to factors other than the use of strategies that have developed to meet the demands of everyday tasks. Instead, the use by old adults of academic strategies that have become deficient due to disuse (Denney & Wright, 1976) is implicated as one possible explanation of their poor laboratory task performance.

A second set of findings is that different strategies are used by old adults in everyday and laboratory tasks, but that performance for old adults is the same on the two types of tasks. This case would suggest a general or global age-deficit position, with generally ineffective strategy implementation in old age (Kausler, 1970, 1982). Although elderly adults may have evolved strategies specifically for use in everyday as opposed to laboratory tasks, deficiencies in strategy derivation or strategy implementation in both task contexts are indicated (Kausler, 1970).

A third set of outcomes is that the same strategies are used by old adults across task domains, but that old adults perform better in the everyday than in the laboratory domain. This case would be compatible with the position of Labouvie-Vief (1985) and others to the extent that superior performance on everyday tasks reflected the use of strategies developed to cope with everyday tasks, provided that these strategies are not appropriate for laboratory tasks (the strategies that were presumably once available for use in laboratory tasks are apparently no longer employed or perhaps no longer available). Alternatively, because strategies are the same in this scenario, a processing explanation of the differential effectiveness of strategies might be suggested. For example, old adults might perform better on everyday tasks because the task materials are more familiar and the processing of these materials is more automatized than that of materials in laboratory tasks (cf. Rybash et al., 1986), leading to a greater functional capacity of working memory (Anderson, 1983; Case, 1985). Greater capacity of working memory might in turn allow more efficient problem solving wherein, for example, goals and subgoals could be stacked and retrieved more reliably (e.g., Anderson, 1983), leading to better performance on everyday than laboratory tasks.

The fourth set of outcomes is that the same strategies are used by old adults across task types, and old adults perform the same in everyday as in laboratory tasks. Because strategies are constant across task domains in this case, age differences in laboratory tasks would probably be attributable to age deficits in processing or strategy effectiveness (e.g., Kausler, 1970; Salthouse, 1985) or both; in other words, a processing-based strategy deficiency. Because performance is also constant across task domains, this explanation would probably apply equally to everyday task performance.

Thus, the difference/deficit question regarding traditional laboratory tests can be addressed by using information from performance on everyday tasks, but it appears necessary to know whether the strategies used by old adults are the same across the two domains and whether performance varies across domains. However, the particular set of outcomes obtained may vary with the dimensions of the specific everyday and laboratory tasks that are studied (discussed below). That is, rather than a universal explanation for age differences in laboratory performance, the explanations will probably vary as a function of particular laboratory tasks and their defining characteristics.

We now address additional considerations in successfully answering the question of performance and strategy differences between laboratory and everyday tasks.

A THEORETICAL BASIS FOR ANALYZING STRATEGIES AND PERFORMANCE

A theoretical foundation that can aid in analyzing the commonality of processes and strategies across task domains is needed in this area of research. This foundation should be comprehensive enough to model the potentially extremely wide array of processes and strategies that may be tapped across age groups and task domains. We have chosen Pascual-Leone's (1983, 1984) theory as a starting point because it makes predictions about specific age periods and because it is not only based on research and theory in adult cognition but is also strongly tied to the extensive body of research and theory in child cognition (e.g., Case, 1985; Pascual-Leone, 1970). Our theorizing has also been informed, however, by the comprehensive and extremely detailed theory of Anderson (1983), and the less detailed but extremely comprehensive theories of Sternberg (1985; Berg & Sternberg, 1985) and Rybash and colleagues (1986). In addition to a purely theoretical base, task contents need to be analyzed in a coherent and fairly detailed manner, suggesting an integration of a modified Pascual-Leone approach with a task-analysis framework such as that of Case (1985).

Pascual-Leone's Postformal Theory

Pascual-Leone (1983) predicted that older adolescents and young adults (approximately ages 17–25 years) view personal and interpersonal problems such as identity and intimacy (Erikson, 1963) as being of utmost importance, and that they use abstract, superordinate reasoning in attempting to solve these tasks. Adults in this "late-formal" stage and in the next ("predialectical") stage are at the peak of their information-processing abilities. Our theoretical integration predicts that late-formal adults' strategies are suited for laboratory tasks. Older adults may no longer prefer these strategies, as new modes of thinking come to predominate in later stages (e.g., "dialectical," discussed below). Nevertheless, the late-formal strategies may continue to be used by older adults in laboratory tasks, whereas the newer strategies may be used in everyday tasks.

Somewhat older young adults (roughly 25–35 years old), who, according to Pascual-Leone, are in a "predialectical" stage, are said to attempt to avoid conflicts and contradictions in personal and employment situations by using defense mechanisms such as denial. They can meet the attentional demands of both defense mechanisms and normal momentary processing because they are at the peak of the trade-off between available attentional capacity and the automatization of the materials being processed (Case, 1985; Pascual-Leone, 1983).

However, the use of defense mechanisms to avoid conflicts results in immediate but ineffective conflict resolution as compared to adults in Pascual-Leone's next stage.

Individuals in the "dialectical" stage (ages 35–55) decline in attentional capacity, leading to an inability to divide attention effectively, and therefore they cannot meet the simultaneous attentional demands of defense mechanisms and more routine cognitive chores. Consequently, they eventually abandon the defense mechanisms and finally confront contradictions rather than attempting to avoid them (Pascual-Leone, 1983). Those individuals who have declined the most in attentional ability should develop the strongest tendency to confront contradictions, and presumably should successfully solve them. Simultaneously, the declining attentional capacity of these individuals may have an overall negative effect on problem solving in terms of, for example, stacking goals and subgoals. The net effect for these individuals may be an increase in ability to solve problems involving contradictions but a decrease in ability to solve other types of problems. The leading problems in this stage are predicted to include balancing personal and generative needs (Erikson, 1963).

In the "transcendental" or young-old stage (ages 55–75), personal stress management (Cummings, Greene, & Karraker, in press), integrity (Erikson, 1963), and life review (Butler, 1963) are thought to be the predominant everyday problems. Effortful memory processes are thought to decline (e.g., Craik, 1977) in this stage, resulting in greater reliance on abstracted, automatized personal experience (Pascual-Leone, 1984) and reliance on encapsulated skills and knowledge (Rybash et al., 1986) in dealing with problems. Thus, adults in this stage are expected to exhibit sophisticated intuitive thinking based on personal experience. This thinking may appear to be concrete in the Piagetian sense (Case, 1985), but may also have the characteristics of wisdom (Pascual-Leone, 1983). Old adults are predicted to display this thinking particularly in everyday tasks, whereas earlier (late-formal) modes of thinking may continue to be used in laboratory tasks. If so, one of the two sets of outcomes in the upper half of Figure 10.1 should be obtained.

"Posttranscendental" or old-old adults (ages 75 and over) are expected to have declined in the ability to access automatized knowledge and in the operation of even elementary automatic processes. Some evidence for this outcome is seen in longitudinal studies where even presumably automatized abilities such as lexical access show reliable declines by age 75 (Schaie & Hertzog, 1983). Old-old adults should therefore exhibit less elegant solutions than young-old adults, even for the most salient everyday concerns of the old-old, which are predicted to include loneliness and coping with loss.

Our theoretical integration is meant to facilitate the process of task analysis for the purposes of identifying strategies and assessing performance. Although this theoretical integration is based most closely on Pascual-Leone's theory, it is not constrained by that theory, and any of several alternative theoretical frameworks would suffice. The present theory has been chosen for the sake of convenience in analyzing age differences in strategy and performance in both everyday and laboratory tests.

WHAT IS EVERYDAY COGNITION?

Internal and External Validity Considerations

One problem confronting an analysis of strategies used in solving everyday and laboratory tasks is that of certifying that a task is truly "everyday." It can be argued that the distinction between everyday and laboratory tasks is ill-defined or "fuzzy" (Zadeh, 1982). Numerous definitions of everyday cognition have been proposed, but none is entirely compelling as delineating two distinct types of cognition. Indeed, theorists such as Anderson (1983) and Sternberg (1985) appear to lean toward the view that everyday cognition is merely one manifestation of an integrated cognitive system. We agree with this view. Whether the single- or dual-domain view of cognition eventually predominates, we can proceed on the assumption that the two types of tasks are at least superficially different in some ways.

Perhaps contributing to the fuzziness of the concept of everyday cognition, many different definitions of what distinguishes an everyday task from a laboratory task have been proposed. Because of the multiple definitions, it might be very difficult, and perhaps even unwise (Banaji & Crowder, 1989), to devise a single task for research purposes that meets all the criteria that have been proposed. Rather than attempt to create such a task, a more practicable long-range research strategy can be adopted. For each definition and corresponding dimension of an everyday task, a pair of tasks might be devised that vary along that dimension while holding constant as many other factors as possible. Thus, a laboratory version of the task and an everyday version defined by a given dimension should result (we provide below a preliminary report on one such experiment). Over several such sets of tasks, we should be able to determine whether old adults use the same or different strategies and whether their performance differs as a function of the task dimensions said to reflect everyday cognition.

Although most or all of the extant criteria should be tested, no one definition of everyday tasks need be satisfied in every test of everyday cognition, and it is not necessary to achieve ecological validity in any task (although ecological validity is desirable as a secondary goal). For the purposes of the particular research objectives outlined in this chapter, we agree with the position of Banaji and Crowder (1989). Namely, at this stage of empirical and theoretical development in the field, generalizable principles are more likely to result from the control and isolation of determining variables than from ecologically valid methods, and the latter may well yield uninterpretable and ungeneralizable results.

Definitions of Everyday Tasks

Two definitions of everyday tasks (Sinnott, 1989b) are that (a) the tasks are in fact likely to be encountered in the real world and (b) the tasks would be regarded as important if encountered. These criteria should not be difficult to implement as one test of differences in strategies and performance, but they need not be implemented in every study of everyday processing, as pointed out above. Like all the criteria reviewed below, Sinnott's (1989b) two-part criterion appears somewhat fuzzy. Specifically, some problems are rarely actually encountered (e.g., a plane crash in one's front yard), and some problems might not be viewed as very significant if they did occur (e.g., a wart on the forearm). Nevertheless, these problems might be viewed by most people as being everyday problems, and certainly not as academic or laboratory problems. Conversely, academic and laboratory tasks can be taken seriously even by old people, perhaps explaining why test anxiety has received so much attention in laboratory research with old adults. Also, the frequency of occurrence of academic and academic-like tasks is high for students (young and old), professors, and other segments of the population (e.g., crossword puzzle enthusiasts), for whom such tasks probably matter a great deal. Although Sinnott's conception may be correlational or fuzzy rather than logically necessary or absolute, it is testable.

Another conceptualization of everyday tasks is that they involve tacit knowledge (Wagner & Sternberg, 1986). Tacit knowledge refers to the rules and elements of knowledge in a task domain that are unwritten, perhaps unspoken, and perhaps even unconscious, but that are nevertheless necessary to perform well in the domain. An example would be setting professional priorities for a novice business manager or an untenured assistant professor (Wagner & Sternberg, 1986; an instructive point is that in the latter example, everyday and academic concerns are identical, further calling into question the distinction between the two). However, this criterion, like Sinnott's (1989b), is also neither logically necessary nor absolute, in that good performance on academic and laboratory tasks also depends in part on tacit knowledge. As examples, tacit strategies are associated with good performance on multiple-choice academic examinations, and frequent anecdotes are heard about the intelligence testee who gives an answer that is correct but that must be scored as wrong because it does not reflect a congruence of tacit assumptions between the examiner and the testee (Examiner: "Name two days of the week that begin with a t"; Testee: "Today and tomorrow"). In fact, tacit knowledge is so ubiquitous that it may be difficult, although perhaps not impossible, to devise tasks that vary in the extent to which tacit knowledge is involved.

Scribner (1986) argued that everyday tasks are embedded in the higher level goals of real life rather than being ends in and of themselves. However, any academic or laboratory task is also embedded within the higher level goals of real life. For instance, the elderly adult's goal of participating in an experiment may be nested within the goal of aiding science and the community, which may be nested within the goal of feeling good about oneself, and so forth. The position taken here is that all goals (except the highest) are nested hierarchically within higher level goals. Although the capacity of working memory imposes practical limitations on the number of goals that can be hierarchically stacked and reliably retrieved (Anderson, 1983), this limitation is equally a property of everyday and laboratory goals. Manipulating Scribner's (1986) dimension of everyday tasks, according to one interpretation of this criterion, seems tantamount to manipulating working memory requirements in terms of the number of subgoals to be tracked (Anderson, 1983). However, the *type* of higher level goal rather than the number of such goals may be more important in determining the motivation of old adults to solve problems, and consequently the strategies they use and their resulting performance.

A common theme in definitions of everyday tasks is that they are essentially social (cf. Ford, 1986) rather than logico-mathematical in nature. Walters and Gardner (1986; J. M. Walters, personal communication, 1989) extended this criterion by saying that everyday tasks employ various combinations of all types of intelligence (social, musical, kinesthetic, spatial, linguistic, and analytical in Gardner and colleagues' framework), whereas laboratory and academic tasks emphasize linguistic and analytical abilities. This hypothesis appears to be experimentally implementable in a fairly straightforward manner. However, this definition is correlational rather than absolute, insofar as academic and laboratory-like tasks can be found for every type of intelligence that Gardner and colleagues identify, and insofar as many everyday tasks involve primarily linguistic and analytical intelligence (e.g., writing letters, balancing checkbooks).

Arlin (1989) reviewed a number of dimensions of everyday tasks, some of which are redundant with those already covered here. An additional dimension proposed by Arlin is that everyday tasks are more familiar than laboratory tasks. Like several of the other criteria reviewed above, this one should be easily manipulable experimentally. This factor fits well with our emphasis and that of Case (1985) on the importance of the familiarity of materials and the resulting automaticity of processing, but like other criteria discussed above, it does not appear to be absolute. For example, some tasks such as the ''20-Questions'' task that appear to be reasonably well known in everyday contexts also appear in the laboratory, and familiarity of words is often manipulated in laboratory tasks. Conversely, some everyday tasks may be unfamiliar (e.g., preparing for an audit by the Internal Revenue Service).

Another distinction discussed by Arlin (1989) is that between problem definition and problem structure. Problems may be ill-defined versus well-defined, with the former descriptor applicable to everyday tasks. Arlin collapsed this dimension with that of ill-structured versus well-structured, since she could find no meaningful distinction between the concepts. Ill-defined tasks are poorly defined in terms of the initial problem state, the goal state, the steps required to proceed from the initial state to the goal state, or some combination. Again, this demarcation between the real word and the laboratory is fuzzy. Some academic and laboratory tasks are ill-defined (e.g., pleasing the experimenter or getting a good letter of recommendation from a professor) and some everyday and practical tasks are well-defined (e.g., playing a lottery). Nevertheless, this conception seems to be close to the heart of much theorizing about what comprises old adults' postformal cognition. Fortunately, the criterion should be translatable into operational definitions by varying the clarity of the initial problem state, the clarity of the goal state, or the clarity of allowable strategies for progressing from the initial state to the goal state.

Rybash and colleagues (1986) characterized everyday cognition as being encapsulated within domains of expertise, a conceptualization not unlike that of Ceci and Liker (1986). The mechanisms of encapsulation may be the same as the mechanism described in intricate detail by Anderson (1983) that are responsible for the development of automaticity with practice. In any case, everyday cognition is, according to Rybash and colleagues, an expert activity. Pitting automatized performance against nonautomatized performance would be meaningless, as the conclusion would be forgone. Moreover, this distinction between everyday and laboratory cognition, like the other definitions above, is fuzzy. Some laboratory-like and academically based skills are automatized even for most old adults (e.g., vocabulary, spelling) while some everyday performances may not be encapsulated or automatized (e.g., repairing a toaster). The definition of Rybash and colleagues (1986) appears to differ from Arlin's (1989) familiarity criterion only in the degree of familiarity and automatization that each definition assumes.

Conclusions Regarding the Nature of Everyday Cognition

In light of the assessment of the preceding criteria, our position is that there may be no fundamental differences between everyday and laboratory tasks other than the fact that the parameter values of many everyday tasks are inherently more variable than those of laboratory tasks from one occasion to the next (Banaji & Crowder, 1989). Any dimension that is said to distinguish between everyday and laboratory task domains is equally valid as a task dimension within each domain. On the average, a given parameter value (e.g., *ill-defined* or *unfamiliar*) may tend to appear more so in one task domain than in the other, but the proper research focus in our opinion is not on task domains but on task dimensions that are said to define the domains. A corollary of this assumption is that no universal explanation of age differences in laboratory tasks will be found, but rather that the explanation among the alternatives in Figure 10.1 will vary as a function of the particular parameter varied.

We further assert that the cognitive mechanisms underlying everyday and laboratory tasks are probably the same, and that these mechanisms are better studied in controlled experimental situations than in uncontrolled situations (Banaji & Crowder, 1989). However, as delineated above, we believe that research on the dimensions of everyday versus laboratory cognition will prove to be extremely useful for investigating the issue of age deficits versus age differences in cognition as outlined in Figure 10.1.

MISCELLANEOUS METHODOLOGICAL CONSIDERATIONS

If a given dimension indeed distinguishes between everyday and laboratory tasks, then variations in the dimension should operate across task domains unless otherwise specified. As suggested earlier, each dimension of everyday tasks or practical cognition should be operationalized individually if possible. A specific operationalization might entail a task in an actual everyday setting, a simulation of an everyday task such as Frederiksen's (1986) "in-basket" technique for business managers, or a remote analogue of a real-world task; however, in each case a laboratory isomorph of the everyday task would need to be devised that varies from the everyday task only in terms of the studied dimension(s).

Even though the tasks need not be ecologically valid, they should nevertheless be selected in terms of age-graded interest in order to obtain maximal performance in each age group. Otherwise, the problem of age differences in motivation will continue to plague this area as it has plagued research involving traditional laboratory tasks. An approach such as that of Sternberg and Berg (1987) is desirable, in which the interest value of tasks is determined for each age group, independently of the probability of actually encountering the tasks in the real world.

Perhaps equally important in investigating everyday cognition is the need to include sample sizes adequate for the analysis of individual differences within each age group. Whether a large battery of tasks is given to subjects and followed by a factor analysis, or a small set of tasks is administered and followed by simple correlations or multiple regressions, valuable information would be provided in explaining why strategies and performance in old adults do or do not differ across everyday and laboratory domains.

In order to analyze strategies, a framework for systematic protocol analysis such as that of Ericsson and Simon (1984) can also be used, as advocated by Giambra and Arenberg (1980). Ericsson and Simon found that when certain guidelines are followed, talking aloud while solving problems does not interfere with ongoing processing, and unambiguous and replicable conclusions can be drawn regarding the use of the same or different strategies and processes across everyday and laboratory tasks.

A PRELIMINARY EXPERIMENTAL REPORT

Rationale

In this section, we summarize our first approximation toward realizing our suggested research methodology in everyday cognition. A study begun in one of our laboratories involves analogues of Arenberg's (1968) poisoned meals task, in which subjects must determine, by questioning the experimenter, which of several foods is poisoned. We chose not to use the format of poisoned meals per se because the task we developed was meant to satisfy Sinnott's (1989) criterion that the problem should be likely to be encountered in the real world. Rather, we devised a lost keys task, wherein the subject must determine in which of several locations the keys can be found. In some ways, this task represents a simulation of an everyday task (cf. Frederiksen, 1986). Although it falls short of complete ecological validity as a simulation, in that some artificial constraints and artificial opportunities for locating the keys are provided (i.e., the subject can rule out up to half but no more than half the locations in a single guess), it provides a simulation with reasonable validity vis-à-vis Sinnott's (1989b) frequency and motivation criteria. It also meets Arlin's (1989) familiarity criterion.

The choice of an Arenberg-like task was based on its original development as an isomorph of concept-formation tasks involving abstract dimensions of stimuli (Arenberg, 1968). Although our tasks superficially resemble Arenberg's concept-formation task, functionally it is an analogue of the 20-Questions task (see Reese & Rodeheaver, 1985) and thus allows various problem-solving strategies to be used.

Method

In the present abstract version of the task, letters define groupings of binary choices consisting of individual numbers (e.g., A: 1, 2; B: 3, 4; etc.), analogous, respectively, to courses in a poisoned meal and binary choices of particular foods within each course. In the present everyday version of the task, corresponding to courses and foods, respectively, were rooms and locations (e.g., living room: top of television, under couch cushion; kitchen: counter, stove).

Thus, everyday and laboratory isomorphs of the task were readily available in which the formal task characteristics, including such factors as instructions and task difficulty, were constant across tasks. This pair of tasks also appears to hold constant the other dimensions of everyday cognition reviewed above. Specifically, the two tasks may be equated in that they appear to be relatively well defined (Arlin, 1989), to be embedded within the same number of higher level goals (Scribner, 1986), to involve the same amount of tacit knowledge (Wagner & Sternberg, 1986), and to involve only analytical intelligence as opposed to social and other intelligences (Walters & Gardner, 1986).

Briefly, other details of the study included the elimination of memory requirements by providing subjects with a visual record of the choices they made while talking out loud and a visual record of the feedback regarding those choices. This procedure was intended to isolate strategy differences from memory-processing differences, although ultimately, simultaneous manipulation of memory requirements might be desirable in order to determine whether memory load influences the strategy adopted. Subjects were given eight initial locations and three opportunities to narrow the available choices to the correct location. Therefore, the optimal strategy was to eliminate half the remaining locations with each question. After the three questions, as a check on the dimensions being manipulated, subjects were asked whether they viewed each task as familiar, whether it was likely to happen to them in the real world, and whether it would matter to them if it did happen. As an anchor item, we also asked them to describe the most significant everyday problem they had encountered in the last month and how much they were concerned about that problem, in order to compare the latter response (concern) with their response to how much the experimental tasks would matter.

The preliminary results reported here are based on samples of 12 young (age 18–35) and 12 old (age 65–82) adults. Half of each age group received the laboratory version of the task, and half received the everyday version. We grouped subject's strategies into two categories. The first consisted of questions about single items, regarded as a "primitive" strategy (Denney & Wright, 1976). The second category included eliminating pairs of items with each question (e.g., rooms that included two locations) and eliminating half the remaining items on each trial, regarded as more "sophisticated" strategies.

Results

The preliminary results are shown in Table 10.1. Half the young adults given the laboratory task used primitive strategies and half used better strategies. All young adults given the everyday task used the more sophisticated strategies. Half the older adults given the laboratory task used primitive strategies, and half used better strategies. All older adults given the everyday task used the primitive strategy. The use of the relatively primitive item-checking strategy by older adults in the everyday task may reflect their reliance on this strategy in real life when keys are lost. Old adults might not use this primitive strategy in the abstract laboratory version of the task because they do not see any connection with such real-world situations.

Discussion

This experiment was not designed to assess performance level. It did not yield separable measures of performance and strategy, and the current designations of "primitive" and "advanced" were somewhat arbitrarily assigned by the experimenter. Instead, the experiment was designed to test whether the same or different strategies are used in everyday and laboratory contexts. The preliminary data suggest that different strategies are used in laboratory and everyday tasks by both age groups. If further data and analyses in this experiment continue to suggest that older adults use different strategies in everyday and laboratory tasks, some position in one of the two upper cells in Figure 10.1 might be supported.

Table 10.1
Preliminary Results for Everyday and Laboratory Isomorphs of a "Lost Keys" Task: Percentage of Strategies Used

Age	Strategy	"laboratory"	"everyday"
young	primitive	50	0
	advanced	50	100
old	primitive	50	100
	advanced	50	0

Plans for Future Research

We intend to supplement this experiment with another study in which the same task dimensions are varied but in which the assessment of performance is emphasized rather than assessment of strategy. Conjointly, the two experiments will determine which of the cells in Figure 10.1 applies to the dimensions based on the criteria of Sinnott and Arlin that were varied in these two experiments. That is, depending on the reasons for any strategy differences that are confirmed, and depending on whether the performance of old adults is found to differ between everyday and laboratory tasks, Denney and Wright's (1976), Kausler's (1970), or some other theoretical interpretation may be supported.

This set of experiments investigating Arlin's and Sinnott's criteria is not intended to stand alone but rather to be supplemented with others that will collectively explore all the dimensions of everyday cognition and determine age differences in strategies and performance. Perhaps one of the outcomes in Figure 10.1 and its associated explanation for age differences in laboratory tasks will be obtained for all task dimensions. More likely, the outcomes and explanations for age differences in laboratory tasks will vary as a function of task dimensions.

Conclusion

Although more ecologically valid approaches to everyday cognition may prove useful for uncovering new phenomena or emergent properties of behavior that cannot be observed in the laboratory, the presently endorsed approach would ultimately be necessary for isolating the causal variables even for those phenomena or properties. In the meantime, the present approach to everyday cognition promises rapid progress toward understanding adult age differences in everyday and laboratory cognition.

SUMMARY

In summary, a framework has been proposed whereby various research outcomes regarding strategies and performance of old adults in everyday and laboratory tasks can be used to interpret whether poor performance by old adults relative to young adults in laboratory tasks can be accounted for by age differences in strategies or by age deficits in strategies or processes. The theory of Pascual-Leone (1983), together with other theoretical notions and various methodological techniques, can aid in identifying strategies and in assessing performance in this research enterprise. A review of the literature on everyday cognition leads to the conclusion that existing definitions and corresponding dimensions of everyday cognition are fuzzy. It is recommended that these dimensions of everyday cognition be investigated individually by creating everyday and laboratory task isomorphs. It is suggested that the explanation of poor performance of older compared to young adults in laboratory tasks will vary as a function of the task dimension investigated. A final interpretation of the data from an initial experiment manipulating familiarity and motivational criteria will occur within the current framework and within the context of further experiments.

REFERENCES

Anderson, J. R. (1983). *The architecture of cognition*. Cambridge, MA: Harvard University Press.

Arenberg, D. (1968). Concept problem solving in young and old adults. *Journal of Gerontology, 23*, 279–282.

Arlin, P. K. (1989). The problem of the problem. In J. D. Sinnott (Ed.), *Everyday problem solving: Theory and applications* (pp. 229–237). New York: Praeger.

Banaji, M. R., & Crowder, R. G. (1989). The bankruptcy of everyday memory. *American Psychologist, 44*, 1185–1193.

Berg, C. A., & Sternberg, R. J. (1985). A triarchic theory of intellectual development in adulthood. *Developmental Review, 5*, 334–370.

Botwinick, J. (1984). *Aging and behavior*. New York: Springer.

Butler, R. N. (1963). The life review: An interpretation of reminiscence in the aged. *Psychiatry, 26*, 65–76.

Case, R. (1985). *Intellectual development: Birth to adulthood* (pp. 25–56). Orlando, FL: Academic.

Ceci, S. J., & Liker, J. (1986). Academic and nonacademic intelligence: An experimental separation. In R. J. Sternberg & R. K. Wagner (Eds.), *Practical intelligence* (pp. 119–142). New York: Cambridge University Press.

Cohen, G. (1989). *Memory in the real world*. Hillsdale, NJ: Erlbaum.

Craik, F. I. M. (1977). Age differences in human memory. In J. E. Birren & K. W.

Schaie (Eds.), *Handboook of the psychology of aging* (1st ed., pp. 384–420). New York: Van Nostrand Reinhold.

Cummings, E. M., Greene, A. L., & Karraker, K. H. (Eds.). (in press). *Life-Span Developmental Psychology: Life-Span perspectives on stress and coping*. Hillsdale, NJ: Lawrence Erlbaum.

Denney, N. W., & Wright, J. C. (1976). Cognitive changes during the adult years: Implications for developmental theory and research. In H. W. Reese (Ed.), *Advances in child development and behavior* (Vol. 11, pp. 213–224). New York: Academic.

Ericsson, K. A., & Simon, H. A. (1984). *Protocol analysis: Verbal reports as data*. Cambridge, MA: MIT Press.

Erikson, E. (1963). *Childhood and society* (2nd ed.). New York: Norton.

Ford, M. E. (1986). For all practical purposes: Criteria for defining and evaluating practical intelligence. In R. J. Sternberg & R. K. Wagner (Eds.), *Practical intelligence* (pp. 183–202). New York: Cambridge University Press.

Frederiksen, N. (1986). Toward a broader conception of human intelligence. In R. J. Sternberg & R. K. Wanger (Eds.), *Practical intelligence* (pp. 84–118). New York: Cambridge University Press.

Giambra, L. M., & Arenberg, D. (1980). Problem-solving, concept learning, and aging. In L. W. Poon (Ed.), *Aging in the 1980's: Psychological issues* (pp. 253–259). Washington, DC: American Psychological Association.

Kausler, D. H. (1970). Retention-forgetting as a nomological network for developmental research. In L. R. Goulet & P. B. Baltes (Eds.), *Life-span developmental psychology: Research and theory* (pp. 305–353). New York: Academic.

Kausler, D. H. (1982). *Experimental psychology and human aging*. New York: Wiley.

Labouvie-Vief, G. (1985). Intelligence and cognition. In J. E. Birren & K. W. Schaie (Eds.), *Handbook of the psychology of aging* (pp. 500–530). New York: Van Nostrand Reinhold.

Pascual-Leone, J. (1970). A mathematical model for the transition rule in Piaget's development stages. *Acta Psychologica, 32*, 301–345.

Pascual-Leone, J. (1983). Growing into human maturity: Toward a meta-subjective theory of adulthood stages. In P. B. Baltes & O. G. Brim (Eds.), *Life-span development and behavior* (Vol. 5, pp. 117–156). New York: Academic.

Pascual-Leone, J. (1984). Attentional, dialectic, and mental effort: Toward an organismic theory of life stages. In M. L. Commons, F. A. Richards, & C. Armon (Eds.), *Beyond formal operations: Late adolescent and adult cognitive development* (pp. 182–215). New York: Praeger.

Poon, L. W. (1985). Differences in human memory with aging: Nature, causes, and clinical implications. In J. E. Birren & K. W. Schaie (Eds.), *Handbook of the psychology of aging* (2nd ed., pp. 427–462). New York: Van Nostrand Reinhold.

Poon, L. W., Rubin, D. C., & Wilson, B. C. (1989). *Everyday cognition in adulthood and late life*. New York: Cambridge University Press.

Reese, H. W., & Rodeheaver, D. (1985). Problem solving and complex decision making. In J. E. Birren & K. W. Schaie (Eds.), *Handbook of the psychology of aging* (2nd ed., pp. 474–499). New York: Van Nostrand Reinhold.

Rybash, J. M., Hoyer, W. J., & Roodin, P. A. (1986). *Adult cognition and aging*. New York: Pergamon.

Salthouse, T. A. (1985). Speed of behavior and its implications for cognition. In J. E.

Birren & K. W. Schaie (Eds.), *Handbook of the psychology of aging* (2nd ed., pp. 400–426). New York: Van Nostrand Reinhold.

Schaie, K. W., & Hertzog, C. (1983). Fourteen-year cohort-sequential analyses of adult intellectual development. *Developmental Psychology, 19*, 531–543.

Scribner, S. (1986). Thinking in action: Some characteristics of practical thought. In R. J. Sternberg & R. K. Wagner (Eds.), *Practical intelligence* (pp. 13–30). New York: Cambridge University Press.

Sinnott, J. D. (1989a). Background: About this book and the field of everyday problem solving. In J. D. Sinnott (Ed.), *Everyday problem solving: Theory and applications* (pp. 1–6). New York: Praeger.

Sinnott, J. D. (1989b). An overview—if not a taxonomy—of "everyday problems" used in research. In J. D. Sinnott (Ed.), *Everyday problem solving: Theory and applications*. New York: Praeger.

Sinnott, J. D. (1989c). A model for solution of ill-structured problems: Implications for everyday and abstract problem solving. In J. D. Sinnott (Ed.), *Everyday problem solving: Theory and applications* (pp. 72–99). New York: Praeger.

Sternberg, R. J. (1985). *Beyond IQ: A triarchic theory of human intelligence*. New York: Cambridge University Press.

Sternberg, R. J., & Berg, C. A. (1987). What are theories of adult development theories of? In C. Schooler & K. W. Schaie (Eds.), *Cognitive functioning and social structure over the life course* (pp. 3–23). Norwood, NJ: Ablex.

Sternberg, R. J., & Wagner, R. K. (1986). *Practical intelligence: Nature and origins of competence in the everyday world*. Cambridge: Cambridge University Press.

Wagner, R. K., & Sternberg, R. J. (1986). Tacit knowledge and intelligence in the everyday world. In R. J. Sternberg & R. K. Wagner (Eds.), *Practical intelligence: Nature and origins of competence in the everyday world.* (pp. 51–83). New York: Cambridge University Press.

Walters, J. M., & Gardner, H. E. (1986). The theory of multiple intelligences: Some issues and answers. In R. J. Sternberg & R. K. Wagner (Eds.), *Practical intelligence: Nature and origins of competence in the everyday world.* (pp. 163–182). New York: Cambridge University Press.

Zadeh, L. (1982). A note on prototype theory and fuzzy sets. *Cognition, 12*, 291–297.

11

Investigating the Relationship between Cognition and Social Thinking in Adulthood: Stereotyping and Attributional Processes

JANE L. RANKIN AND JUDITH L. ALLEN

The search continues for effective ways of representing the myriad of changes that occur during adulthood and separating what is situationally bound or momentary from what endures. The range of available conceptualizations can be depicted by geographic metaphors: To the layperson, adulthood commonly appears as a broad, largely undifferentiated plateau rising up above adolescence and dropping sharply into old age. Postformal theorists have moved beyond this representation to conceptually reorganize adult cognitive development as a terraced hillside of stages and transitions. The number and the content of the terraces differ, as does the means by which individuals might move from one terrace to another, but the notions of order, progression, and hierarchy are always salient. For example, this description applies to the work by Perry (1970), who articulated a transition in young adults during their college careers from dualism, to relativism, and finally to commitment in relativism. Another such shift "upward" within adulthood is reported by Commons and Richards (1984), who used the concept of metasystematic thinking to describe cognitive development that succeeds formal thought. Yet another example is provided by Basseches's (1984) use of the term *dialectical thinking*, which captures adults' integration of continuously changing systems in a changing world. Finally, Kramer (1989) has argued that Pepper's (1942) four world hypotheses (formism, mechanism, contextualism, and organicism) constitute a developmental sequence which she captures with three basic concepts: absolutism, relativism, and dialecticism.

The image of a sequence of changes becomes too limiting, however, when attempting to model the interaction among psychological, social, and biological factors. In order to depict this more complex conceptualization of adulthood, there is a need for a metaphor such as the epigenetic landscape described by Waddington (1957), who presented adult developmental paths affected by biological (including genetic) factors, environmental opportunities, social forces, and their interplay. The image here is of a landscape formed into pathways that direct the movement of objects moving across it. This account suggests the possibility that the cognitive styles of adulthood represent not the fruits of experience nor signs of mature wisdom, but merely cognitive economies enforced by an information-processing system with a biologically diminished capacity. This account need not emphasize biological factors, however, as the broader social environment (e.g., work and institutional structures, social policies discouraging paid employment after retirement) also contributes to the paths that adult development may take, as do psychological factors (e.g., particular expertise, role perceptions) when they shape social/societal participation and biological outcomes, including courses of illnesses and recoveries. Sometimes the environment sharply constrains the range of outcomes—for example, where there is widespread famine, war, or periods of generalized prosperity—but more typically, there is a range of possible outcomes, and individual factors may vary greatly in potency and saturation.

The strength of the epigenetic account is that it incorporates the greater number of significant factors influencing change within adulthood, and does so in a manner consistent with the extensive literature on psychological, social, and biological factors. The value of this approach can be highlighted by contrasting it with the current research literature in which investigations of adult cognitive stages are largely independent of those concerning social and biological aspects of aging. The epigenetic account also is limited, however, in that it does not easily incorporate qualitative changes identified by stage theorists. Such one-dimensional approaches have been tremendously useful in the study of adult development, but inevitably suffer when exported to account for behaviors in a broader environment. There is a need, then, for research programs that can test epigenetic approaches while also including specific attention to the stage-related changes occurring across adulthood. Furthermore, to expand this area of study, theorists of adult development need to consider how stage-related evolutions in cognition, biological factors, and social/societal factors intertwine to determine the course of development.

In order to begin to meet these objectives, we have identified three models for capturing causal links between cognition and other domains of adult development:

1. Biologically influenced changes (e.g., in memory capacity) shape the evolution of adult cognitive stages and cognition in general. For example, the recent research of Clarkson-Smith and Hartley (1989) documents the effects of healthy physiological functioning (obtained through exercise) on elderly adult reasoning, working memory, and reaction time. This model suggests that biological factors exert a pervasive,

systematic, and continuing influence on cognition through the adult years, and not just during the aging years.

2. External social/societal forces influence adult cognitive changes. This model would emphasize the impact of such factors as life-style (e.g., Gribben, Schaie, & Parham, 1980), institutional settings (Langer & Rodin, 1976), and occupational factors, whereby the complexity of the job contributes to intellectual flexibility (Schooler, 1987). Meacham (ch. 9, this volume) emphasizes the parsimony of interpersonal relations as a continuing basis for developmental progress.

3. Cognitive development during the adult years shapes social perceptions and social behavior and, by influencing coping strategies, can affect health. For example, the acquisition of particular occupationally related expertise leads to social recognition and enhances social opportunities. There is little research on the social impact of adult cognitive development, but significant research on the effect of cognitive coping strategies on health (e.g., Rodin, 1983).

Obviously, no one research program can address the many interaction patterns derived from the three models described above. However, there are some particularly useful points for addressing the causal relations among the biological, cognitive/psychological, and social/societal systems. For example, Langer, Rodin, and colleagues, have contributed compelling research on the cognitive (and health) effects of institutional settings on frail elderly adults that would best be described by the second model (e.g., Langer & Rodin, 1976; Langer, Rodin, Beck, Weinmann, & Spitzer, 1979). However, there are other points of interface as well. One such interface is where cognitive structures meet well-established social forces. This chapter addresses that interface by summarizing a recent study consistent with a model of diminished processing capacity (the first of our three models) and by presenting two pieces of research investigating the social consequences of postformal thinking (addressing the third model).

MEMORY CAPACITY AND STEREOTYPING

There is ample evidence that changes in memory in older adults have broad effects on psychometric test scores (Cohen, 1957), language complexity (Kemper, 1988), and a variety of other aspects of cognition. In recent years, social psychologists, notably Myron Rothbart, have documented the impact of memory limitations on young adults' formation of stereotypes about groups. As memory load increased, Rothbart and colleagues (Rothbart, Fulero, Jensen, Howard, & Birrell, 1978) found that young adults combined information about individuals to form inaccurate group impressions. Subsequently, Rothbart, Evans, and Fulero (1978) demonstrated that the presentation of stereotypic expectancies before, but not after, the presentation of stimulus groups altered social judgments and the type of information remembered in the direction of provided expectancies.

Given that elderly adults typically perform less well on working-memory tasks than young adults (Hultsch & Dixon, 1989), it might be expected that they would be even more reductive than young adults in their processing of information, and more reliant on stereotypes. Rankin, Schulenburg, and Seal (1990) examined adult age-related differences in social judgments and memory, hypothesizing that reliance on provided expectancies would be more pronounced at higher memory loads and in elderly adults.

Forty-eight young adults, mean age 19.5 years, and 48 elderly adults, mean age 73.3 years, were presented stimulus sets that were preceded or followed by either a positive expectancy, describing the stimulus group as candidates for a citizenship award, or by a negative expectancy, describing them as candidates for a prison half-way house. To examine the impact of memory load, subjects were presented both with small (12-sentence) and large (36-sentence) stimulus groups (lists) of three-word declarative sentences; for example, "Keith is friendly." To assess the processing bias introduced by expectancies each stimulus group actually contained an equal number of individuals described by positive, negative, and neutral trait adjectives drawn from Anderson's (1968) list. Memory was tested with surprise recall and forced-choice recognition tests for the trait adjectives.

Young adults who received the positive expectancy estimated that there was a somewhat higher percentage of group members with desirable traits than those who received the negative expectancy, whereas older adults showed the opposite pattern. Thus, elderly adults were definitely not more influenced by provided expectancies, and were apparently more willing than young adults to report the discrepancy between provided expectancies and the actual stimulus groups they saw (an equal mixture of positive, neutral, and negative traits).

Expectancies influenced recognition memory in both age groups: More hits for positive traits occurred following the positive expectancy, and more hits for negative traits followed the negative expectancy. However, expectancy effects anticipated at high memory loads occurred at low memory levels also, indicating that even the smaller, 12-item stimulus group exceeded demands on memory capacity. Furthermore, elderly adults had significantly more hits for positive and negative than for neutral traits regardless of whether expectancies preceded or followed the stimulus group. Young adults' hit rates were higher for positive and negative traits when expectancies preceded the stimulus groups, but not otherwise, a pattern consistent with the findings of Rothbart and colleagues (Rothbart et al., 1978; Rothbart, Evans, & Fulero, 1979) for young adults. On the d' measure, the age-by-word type interaction evident for hits did not attain significance.

These findings did not provide evidence that older adults were more influenced by provided expectancies because of memory limitations. Interestingly, however, older adults recognized more traits that were clearly consistent *or* clearly inconsistent with the direction of stereotypic expectancies and relatively fewer of the neutral words than did young adults. The results suggested a sharpening in the processing of social information with age, such that information that did not aid in social judgments was more likely to be disregarded and subsequently forgotten.

All the information in the long and short list was relevant, but some was clearly congruent and some was clearly incongruent.

This pattern is reminiscent of that seen with the development of expertise (Glaser, 1987) in that older adults' memory for individual traits was organized around an abstraction (judgment relevance) that was not apparent in the surface presentation of the task, whereas young adults' memory was less discriminative, more closely reflecting the literal trait statements themselves. Sinnott (1989) has discussed the role of memory in developing person/environment interaction as limiting the perceptual filter and thereby decreasing risks of overstimulation. In this research those traits that did not provide information relevant to the expectancies (that were neither strongly positive or strongly negative) were seemingly most likely to be filtered out and lost to subsequent retention.

THE EFFECTS OF POSTFORMAL THOUGHT ON SOCIAL COGNITION

The third model described above suggests that cognition plays a leading role in development and can shape the individual's social world and influence his or her biological functioning. One point of interface concerns the social implications of formal and postformal thinking. Do postformal patterns of thought affect basic understandings of self and others? Does the acquisition of relativistic and dialectical concepts lead to a reorganization of the social world, to enhanced or diminished social perception? Currently, there are few studies where the implications of postformal thinking for social behaviors have been investigated (e.g., Benack, 1984; Kramer, 1989; Murphy & Gilligan, 1980). Furthermore, there is relatively little guidance on how age-related developmental stages affect social thinking because adult age differences in social cognition, even apart from differences as a function of level of adult development, remain largely unexplored (but see Abeles, 1987; Blank, 1982).

Exploring the implications of postformal thinking for social attitudes and behaviors offers many advantages. One is the prospect of a social psychology of adulthood where the search for explanation can supplement description, and more truly causal factors (e.g., patterns of thinking) can replace the index of chronological age in marking change. It is important for the evolution of postformal theory to examine how the hypothesized structures contribute to social judgments and social behaviors. The viability of postformal thought will ultimately depend on whether formal and postformal thinkers differ apart from how they solve problems (Cavanaugh & Stafford, 1989). For example, how much of the variance in social decision making can be accounted for by knowing a person's level of cognitive development? Does the development of postformal thinking mean there is a change in basic attribution processes such that individuals are more likely to see the choices of others being affected by their context and situation? This suggestion, first made by Blanchard-Fields (1986), was addressed by our first experiment.

EXPERIMENT 1: POSTFORMAL THINKING AND SOCIAL ATTRIBUTIONS

If postformal thinkers do endorse more relativistic thinking, then they may be more likely to take the context of a behavior into account when forming attributions. This suggestion that postformal observers would perceive contextual or situational factors as important in causing others' social behavior runs contrary to typical conceptual and empirical findings in studies of social perception. In the typical pattern, termed the *actor-observer effect*, perceivers are believed to see situational causes as responsible for their own behavior, and to overemphasize the role of dispositional factors as the cause of others' social behavior (Jones & Nisbett, 1972; Nisbett, Caputo, Legant, & Maracek, 1973). Therefore, Experiment 1 was conducted in order to determine whether postformal observers would be more likely to perceive situational factors as more responsible for the behavior of an actor, compared to formal observers, who would be more likely to perceive dispositional factors as more responsible. In order to assess the effect of postformal thinking on the actor-observer effect, Studies 2 and 3 by Nisbett and colleagues (1973) were replicated after participants were assessed for level of cognitive development.

Research in adult cognition has been slowed by the requirements of the lengthy interviews used by investigators (e.g., Basseches, 1984; Perry, 1970; Sinnott, 1984) to determine the level of thinking. The different content areas represented, the variety of interview techniques employed, difficulties obtaining reliable scoring across investigators, and the sheer length of time required for interviewing makes it difficult to explore the implications of formal thought for other areas. Recently Kramer, Goldston, and Kahlbaugh (1990) developed a paper-and-pencil instrument investigating three forms of thinking (absolutism, relativism, and dialecticism) relevant to the formal/postformal transition. Obviously, the use of such an instrument greatly facilitates research on implications of postformal thinking, and one of the purposes of the current research was to explore this technique for measuring postformal thought and ascertaining the relationship between postformal thought thus measured and social attributions.

Method—Experiment 1

Participants in this study were 38 undergraduates (17 males, 21 females) at a midwestern private university who participated for extra credit points for their introductory psychology class. Enrollment at this institution is drawn predominately from the middle and upper-middle class. Participants were run in small groups, first completing the Social Paradigm Belief Inventory (SPBI) in order to assess level of cognitive development. The SPBI (Kramer, Goldston, & Kahlbaugh, 1990) is an objective, forced-choice measure of beliefs derived from Pepper's (1942) worldview philosophy. Three content domains are represented in the instrument: the intrapersonal domain (i.e., person perception), the interpersonal domain, and the societal domain. Three subscales comprise it: The absolutism subscale encompasses Pepper's formistic and mechanistic world-views, the relativism subscale encompasses his contextual worldview, and the dialectical subscale is derived from his organismic worldview. Thus, for each of 27 items, subjects are asked to choose which of three statements (absolute, relativistic, or dialectical) most closely approximates their own thinking. Subjects are given 1 point for an absolute response, 2 points for a relativistic response, and 3 points for a dialectical response, consistent with the sequence of development of these forms of thought (see Kramer & Woodruff, 1986). Each of the three statements within each item are comparable in format and approximate length, and the order of statements within an item were randomized across the 27 items. Cronbach alpha internal consistencies for the absolute, relativistic, and dialectical items were .60, .83, and .84, respectively, and the test-retest correlation was .77 (Kramer, Kahlbaugh, & Goldston, 1990). The correlation between the SPBI and the mean response level of subjects interviewed about their worldview beliefs was .62.

Kramer and colleagues (Kramer, Kahlbaugh, & Goldston, 1990) report that the SPBI is moderately related to other paradigm scales: .33 with the Organicism-Mechanism Paradigm Inventory (Johnson, Germer, Efran & Overton, 1988), and −.31 with the Formism Scale, −.35 with the Mechanism Scale, .40 with the Contextualism scale, and .16 with the Organicism Scale of the World Hypothesis Scale (Harris, Fontana, & Dowds, 1977). However, SPBI scores are not significantly related to scores on a social dogmatism scale (Troldahl & Powell, 1965), the Budner (1962) Intolerance of Ambiguity Scale, the Crowne and Marlowe (1960) Social Desirability Scale, and the second half of the Wechsler Adult Intelligence Scale (WAIS) Vocabulary subtest.

The first part of the experiment replicated Study 3 of Nisbett and colleagues in which participants were asked to fill out questionnaires indicating for themselves and three other stimulus persons which of three descriptions best fit the stimulus person: a trait term, its polar opposite, or the phrase "depends on the situation." There were 20 such 3-choice items for each of the stimulus persons, with the presentation order of the stimulus persons counterbalanced. The trait terms used were taken from Nisbett and colleagues (1973, p. 161). The number of trait terms or situational causes chosen out of a total of 20 possible was counted for each participant.

In the second part of the experiment, which replicated Study 2 of Nisbett and colleagues (1973), participants were asked to write four brief paragraphs describing why they liked the person they had dated most often during the past year, why they had chosen their major field of study, why their best friend liked the person he or she had dated most often, and why their best friend had chosen his or her major field of study. The participants' paragraphs were coded for the degree to which they stressed "entity" versus "dispositional" reasons, following the coding procedures described as follows by Nisbett and colleagues:

The subject's paragraphs were scored for the degree to which they stressed "entity" versus "dispositional" reasons. Each reason was coded as being either a pure entity

Table 11.1

Mean Number of Situational Ascriptions of Self (out of 20) to Each Stimulus Person for Individuals Low and High in Postformal Thinking

Level of Cognitive Development	Stimulus Person			
	Self	Acquaintance	Parent	Dan Rather
Low Post-formal	6.40	4.35	5.00	3.28
High Post-formal	4.61	3.28	3.94	4.30

reason . . . or as invoking some dispositional property of the actor. . . . Reasons were coded as being dispositional if they referred in any way to the person doing the choosing. Reasons coded as dispositional therefore included many which could be described as Entity X Disposition interaction reasons. (1973, p. 160)

Coding was performed by the experimenters and one investigator.

Results—Experiment 1

Scores on the SPBI ranged from 41 to 71, with a mean score of 60.08. Participants were divided into two groups on the basis of SPBI scores: individuals scoring greater than or equal to 63 ($N = 18$), and individuals scoring less than 63 ($N = 20$).

Overall, it was predicted that all participants would tend to express or choose more entity or situational causes for their own behaviors, while expressing or choosing more dispositional causes for the behaviors of others, replicating Nisbett and colleagues' (1973) actor-observer effect. However, we also predicted an interaction with level of cognitive development, such that observers who scored higher on relativism and dialecticism might show less extreme differences in judgments of self and others by expressing or choosing more situational or entity causes for others' behaviors than would observers who scored higher on absolutism. Whether or not they scored high in postformal thought, participants were expected to express or choose more situational or entity-based causes when judging their own behaviors.

In order to assess attributions from the first part of the experiment (questionnaire data), subjects' choices of either trait terms or situational descriptions were simply counted for descriptions of self, an acquaintance, a parent, and Dan Rather (a news correspondent). It was predicted that subjects who scored higher on relativism and dialecticism would be more likely to choose more situational descriptions for an acquaintance, a parent, or Dan Rather than would subjects who scored low on these concepts. As can be seen from Table 11.1, that was not the case. An analysis of variance was conducted to assess the effect of level

Table 11.2
Number of Entity Reasons and Dispositional Reasons Given by Subjects as Explanations of Their Own and Their Best Friend's Choices of Girlfriend/ Boyfriend and Major for Individuals Low and High in Postformal Thought

Level of Cognitive Development

Low in Post formal Thought

	Girlfriend/Boyfriend		Major	
Explanation	Entity	Dispositional	Entity	Dispositional
Self	5.11	1.56	1.50	2.56
Friend	2.70	1.70	.78	2.33

High in Post formal Thought

	Girlfriend/Boyfriend		Major	
Explanation	Entity	Dispositional	Entity	Dispositional
Self	4.16	1.32	1.18	1.82
Friend	1.76	2.06	.33	2.41

of cognitive development on dispositional versus situational choices. When describing friends, subjects with relatively higher postformal thinking scores were no more likely to choose situational descriptors than subjects who showed less postformal thinking ($F = .424$, $n.s.$). Similarly, there were no significant differences between groups in choosing situational descriptors for parents ($F = .682$, $n.s.$), or for Dan Rather ($F = 1.26$, $n.s.$). Although no specific predictions were made concerning the choice of dispositional versus situational descriptions for self, an analysis of high-scoring versus low-scoring subjects' choices showed no differences ($F = 1.27$, $n.s.$).

In the second part of the study, subjects were asked to write reasons for their own or their friends' choices of a girlfriend/boyfriend and a major. It may be seen from Table 11.2 that, regardless of their postformal thinking score, observers were more likely to describe their own choices of a boyfriend/girlfriend and a major as being due to properties of the entity, while seeing their friends' choices of a boyfriend/girlfriend and a major as being due to dispositional properties of their friends.

When explaining why they liked their girlfriend/boyfriend, subjects were much more likely to use explanations referring to the other person than their own traits, needs, and interests ($t = 4.37$, $p < .0001$). In contrast, when explaining why their friend liked their boyfriend/girlfriend, subjects gave the same number of entity and dispositional reasons ($t = 1.11$, $p = .28$). When explaining why they had chosen their major, subjects gave equal numbers of entity and dispositional causes ($t = 1.64$, $p = .122$). Finally, when subjects explained why their friends chose a major, they gave substantially more dispositional causes for their friends' choices ($t = 3.29$, $p < .004$). These data provide a very close replication of the original findings of Nisbett and colleagues (1973).

Subjects who scored lower on postformal thinking also demonstrated the actor-observer bias in the patterns of their paragraphs. Subjects were more likely to explain their own choices of a girlfriend/boyfriend as being due to something about that person ($t = 3.38$, $p < .003$), while explaining their friends' choices as equally due to entity and dispositional causes ($t = .36$, $p = .724$). In explaining their own choice of a major, subjects believed that both entity and dispositional causes were equally important ($t = 1.14$, $p = .272$), while believing that their friends' choices of a major was due to their disposition ($t = 5.17$, $p < .0001$).

A comparison of observers' explanations for friends' choices of a girlfriend/boyfriend showed a tendency for observers who scored higher on postformal thinking to use more entity explanations as predicted, but the differences were not significant ($t = 1.17$, $p = .12$, one-tailed). Similarly, when comparing individuals' explanations of why their friends chose a major, those who scored above the median in postformal thought tended to choose more entity explanations as predicted, although again the difference was not significant ($t = 1.38$, $p = .09$, one-tailed).

Discussion—Experiment 1

We predicted that observers who scored high on postformal thinking would show a diminished actor-observer effect as compared to those who scored low; that is, that postformal thinkers would tend to choose or offer more situational or entity items as explanations for the behavior of others than would their lower-scoring counterparts. The obtained pattern of results does not support these predictions, although there were trends in the predicted direction in the written explanations. Both low- and high-scoring postformal observers tended to demonstrate the actor-observer effect, replicating previous work (Jones & Nisbett, 1972; Nisbett et al., 1973). In these particular tasks, context or situational factors did not appear to be more important to those who scored high on postformal thinking.

EXPERIMENT 2: POSTFORMAL THOUGHT AND STEREOTYPING

Experiment 2 examines the effects of postformal thought on a social judgment task where stereotypes could be used. It examines a more applied situation—judgments of transgressors—in order to test whether postformal thinkers' judgments would be less reliant on personal characteristics and more affected by circumstances surrounding the transition. The procedures are based on a study by Bodenhausen and Wyer (1985) in which college students' willingness to parole a criminal, judgments of the likelihood of recidivism, and sentence recommendations on second offense differed systematically as a function of the stereotyped group. Furthermore, Bodenhausen and Wyer (1985) demonstrated that when a transgression was stereotypic of the target's ethnic group, other relevant information was less likely to be considered. Subjects' pattern of recall suggested that they reviewed other available information in an attempt to confirm the implications of this impression; that is, they recalled more stereotype-consistent than stereotype-inconsistent information.

The question to be addressed was whether subjects who are relativistic and dialectical thinkers would be less likely to have their judgments swayed by stable, personal characteristics, (e.g., race) and the extent to which they would be influenced by mitigating circumstances surrounding a crime. One would expect that relativistic and dialectical thinkers would be more sensitive to situational factors and that when there were mitigating circumstances for a crime, they might be more lenient in parole recommendations, foresee a lower probability of recidivism, and be less punitive after a second offense.

Method—Experiment 2

Participants in this research were 111 undergraduate psychology students (47 men and 64 women) drawn from the same source identified in Experiment 1. The sample was overwhelmingly white. Subjects were tested in small groups: they first completed the three case files of the social judgment task, and then took the Social Paradigm Belief Inventory (SPBI) and the Logical Reasoning Test (LRT). After the Logical Reasoning Test they were probed for their memory of the case files. The session concluded with administration of the 10-item Need for Cognition Scale and the subjects' completion of questions about their age, sex, and years of schooling.

Stimulus Case Files. Participants were given three case files pertaining to prisoners eligible for parole. Roughly half the subjects read the case files of three males with stereotypically black names (Tyrone Washington, Roosevelt Jones, and Leroy Jackson) and the other half read the case files of males with stereotypically white names (Allen Baker, Jim Johnson, and Scott Fuller). In all three cases, single incidents of theft were described, but the three cases varied in the number of mitigating circumstances associated with the crime. Pilot testing with subjects drawn from the same student population as the final sample revealed that theft was a crime stereotypically associated with blacks. An additional pilot sample of college students provided the mitigating circumstances used in the research. Thus, each case file contained:

1. Six pieces of *background* information including the name, hometown, age, marital status, number of dependents, and identifying marks.

2. Five pieces of *crime-relevant* information, including how the crime was committed, the original plea entered in the trial, the length of the sentence and the amount of time already served, and ratings of the target's behavior since imprisonment.

3. Either zero, two, or four *mitigating circumstances*; that is, factors in the target's life that might have led him to commit the theft (e.g., unemployment, ill family members, lack of job skills).

To minimize the chances that participants would detect experimental manipulations, they were shown files with names stereotypic of one racial group only, and mitigating circumstances were presented in narrative form. Finally, only on the last page of the protocol were subjects asked what they thought the purpose of the study was. None of them guessed correctly.

Social Judgment Task. Following each case file, there were three questions. The first two ("How strongly do you feel that the man should be paroled at this time?" "If he is released, how likely is it that he will commit another crime?") were answered on an 11-point scale ranging from zero (not at all) to 10 (extremely). The third question was, "If he did commit the same crime again, to how many years (from zero to 30) would you sentence him if you were the judge?"

Social Paradigm Belief Inventory. The SPBI (Kramer, Goldston, & Kahlbaugh, 1990) was administered (see Experiment 1 methods).

The Logical Reasoning Test. The Logical Reasoning Test was developed by Burney (1974), and attempts to translate the interview tasks described by Piaget (1937/1952) into an objective, paper-and-pencil test for determining an individual's level of cognitive development (see Sund, 1976, pp. 165–173, for presentation of test items). The Logical Reasoning Test has reasonably good internal reliability ($r_{tt} = +.83$), and classifications using this test agree well (85%) with the classification of subjects' level of cognitive development on the traditional set of Piagetian interview tasks (Burney, 1974).

Need for Cognition Scale. The Need for Cognition Scale (Cacioppo & Petty, 1982) was administered to determine each individual's motivation to engage in cognitive reasoning. The test appears to have good reliability, convergent, discriminative, and content validity, as the populations selected to develop the scale were thought to fall near the extremes on the dimension of need for cognition.

Results—Experiment 2

Scores on the SPBI were somewhat skewed toward the high end of the possible range (from 27 to 81) with a mean score of 60.64 and SD of 5.52. As expected, raw scores on the absolutism scale were low ($M = 4.12$, $SD = 2.64$), but surprisingly for a college sample, raw scores on the relativism scale ($M = 11.35$, $SD = 2.81$) were roughly equivalent to those for dialecticism scale ($M = 11.53$, $SD = 2.82$).

Because of the quasi-experimental nature of the research, multivariate and univariate analyses of variance were the primary modes of statistical analysis. There were three between-subjects variables: race of case file (black, white); gender (male, female); and SPBI score (below or above the median). Additionally, there was one within-subjects variable, the number of mitigating circumstances described in the case file. Dependent measures included both social judgments and memory measures.

A multivariate analysis of variance was conducted on the three social judgment measures: parole recommendation, perceived likelihood of recidivism, and the length of prison sentence recommended following a second offense. The only significant effect was that of SPBI score, $F(3, 100) = 2.87$, $p < .05$. Subsequent univariate analyses revealed that the effect was significant only on the parole recommendation measure, with subjects who scored higher on the SPBI being more willing to parole ($M = 6.68$) than those low on the SPBI, $M = 5.73$, $F(1, 103) = 6.95$, $p < .01$.

A multivariate analysis of variance was conducted to measure the retention of six background facts and five pieces of crime-relevant information. All scores were converted to proportions since the number of items differed for the two categories. None of the main effects was significant, but there were significant interactions between race and gender, $F(2, 101) = 4.90$, $p < .01$, and between SPBI scores and race, $F(2, 101) = 3.50$, $p < .05$. Subsequent univariate analyses of variance revealed that better memory for background information in the group with higher SPBI scores, $F(1, 102) = 4.83$, $p < .05$, and a significant interaction between SPBI scores and race, $F(1, 102) = 6.67$, $p < .01$ (Figure 11.1). Separate post-hoc analyses on this interaction revealed that the group with scores below the median on the SPBI remembered significantly more about black targets than white targets, $F(1, 44) = 9.26$, $p < .01$, but the high SPBI group showed no significant differences in memory for the background information of blacks and whites.

A separate analysis of variance on memory for crime-relevant information found that the overwhelmingly white sample remembered more crime-relevant information for black targets, $F(1, 102) = 4.20$, $p < .05$, but that effect was qualified by an interaction between race and gender of the subject, $F(1, 102) = 9.84$, $p < .01$ (Figure 11.2). Post-hoc analyses with the sexes separated revealed that women showed no significant differences in their memory as a function of race, but men remembered significantly more when a black target was described,

Figure 11.1
Retention of Background Information about Black and White Targets as a
Function of Postformal Thinking Patterns

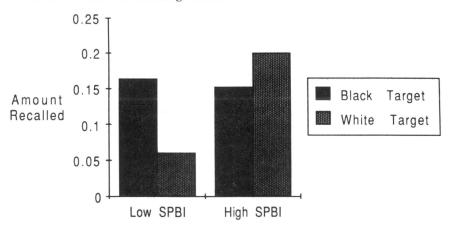

Figure 11.2
Retention of Crime-Relevant Information as a Function of Target Race and Sex
of Subject

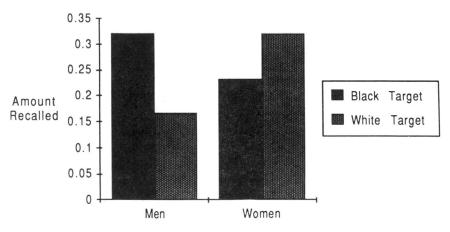

$F(1, 43) = 9.60$, $p < .01$. The interaction between SPBI scores, race, and gender was not significant. Proportional memory for mitigating circumstances was tested for the two stories that included mitigators, but revealed no significant effects or interactions.

Discussion—Experiment 2

Experiment 2 failed to replicate Bodenhausen and Wyer's (1985, Exp. 1) finding that members of stereotyped racial groups were treated more severely than were those who were not members. There was no difference for black and white targets in parole judgments, perceived likelihood of recidivism, and recommendations for punishment following a second offense. However, subjects who endorsed postformal thinking patterns showed significantly stronger tendencies to recommend parole for both blacks and whites. Surprisingly, stories in which there were mitigating circumstances (e.g., unemployment, family illness) that might have diminished blame on the target did not increase recommendations for parole or decrease perceptions of the likelihood of future crime. It may be that extenuating circumstances, if they reflect relatively enduring aspects of the target's situation, are seen not only as precipitants for the previous criminal act, but as factors that might lead to future crime as well.

Whereas the effect of race did not emerge on the immediate social judgments that people made, it was evident on memory measures. Subjects who scored at the lower (absolutism) end of the SPBI showed a significantly better memory for the background of criminal perpetrators who were members of the stereotyped out-group, in this case blacks, than for whites, which suggests that their memories reflected the absolutist assumption that people, things, and events are grouped into fixed, stable categories.

Similarly, in this overwhelmingly white sample, white males remembered more about the circumstances of crimes committed by blacks, reflecting outgroup derogation, than they did about crimes committed by members of their own race and gender group. According to this analysis, women evaluate both white and black males as out-group members, and therefore showed less difference in their memory as a function of race. Thus, memory is affected not only by cognitive development but also by subject attributes that determine social distance from the targets to be evaluated.

One purpose of this research was to investigate the properties of the newly developed Social Paradigm Belief Inventory. Perhaps the most surprising finding was that a sample of typical college student subjects actually scored slightly higher on the dialectical subscale of the SPBI than they did on the relativism subscale, and far higher than they did on the absolutism subscale. This contrasts with a previous study using the SPBI (Kramer, Goldston, & Kahlbaugh, 1990), which found somewhat higher relativistic than dialectical scores among college students, and with previous interview studies, (e.g., Kramer & Woodruff, 1986), which found that dialectical concepts emerged in people's thinking during the middle years. Across various samples, the SPBI may prove to be a less conservative measure of postformal thinking than the traditional interview format. Individuals may be able to recognize and endorse dialectical concepts presented in a multiple-choice format before they produce them spontaneously in interviews.

GENERAL DISCUSSION

The experiments described in this chapter illustrate only a fraction of the methods by which the intertwining systems involving adult cognitive development can be addressed. Their contribution lies in adding some initial links between the cognitive and social/societal domains. We found that older adults were differentially likely to retain information that was relevant to provided expectancies, a form of selective processing that is likely to shape social perception. The two experiments described in this chapter also provide evidence of connections between cognitive stage and social judgment: Those who scored higher on a test of postformal reasoning were more likely to recommend parole, indicating the potential spread of a basic cognitive change to applied social judgments. However, there was also compelling evidence of the impact of social information (race of target and social distance from target) on memory. Thus, aspects of cognition appear to be organized by level of thinking and by the social (in this case, racial) attributes of the task.

These findings suggest that characterizations of adult cognitive development as a terraced hillside of self-contained stages or as biologically driven decremental change will inevitably fail to capture the multidimensional nature of the influences on adult thought. Emphasis on such models, with their implicit reductionism, blinds observers to the interplay of different domains (biological, psychological/cognitive, and social) in shaping thought and particularly to the ofttimes determinative role of social factors on cognition. More successful depictions must capture the multidimensional nature of the forces shaping adult cognition, not merely asserting that the domains are interconnected but attempting to capture causal relationships among them.

Experiments 1 and 2 pertained to social implications of postformal thinking and examined worldviews among a relatively homogeneous college student sample. Thus, the possibility exists that a broader range of scores from a more heterogeneous sample might have produced more potent social effects. Further, since postformal thinking was assessed as a difference between same-age individuals on an instrument designed to measure developmental change, this research might underestimate the potential social impact of postformal thought. These two factors may account for the lack of significant effects in the experiment on attributions. Significant differences were obtained between college students who scored high and those who scored low on the Social Paradigm Belief Inventory, both on a social judgment (parole recommendation) and on memory for attributes of the criminal, indicating that even for a homogenous sample, level of cognitive development impacts social judgment and social memory.

The fact that postformal thought had some significant effects in some social judgments but not others provides some preliminary indications of its likely scope and limitations, and merits further investigation. Such investigation offers the promise of a potential explanation for the wide individual differences in adulthood attributed to age which may actually reflect different levels of cognitive development. This research is also likely to be helpful in understanding the organization of social cognition in that tasks that show similar patterns of developmental change are more likely to be structurally related than those that show disparate patterns.

In future research it will be particularly important to see how age and cognitive stage interact with the processing requirements of social tasks and the social ecology of the broader environment. Is it the case that when age and stage groups are compared there will be a grading of developmental differences in terms of the social processing the task requires, its complexity, and the type of judgment required (e.g., impression formation versus judging attractiveness)? This would suggest a prominent causative role of the social-processing system. Will the social inputs and social consequences in the broader environment be determinative such that the processing of most social information will be age- and stage-invariant but relatively cultural-specific, or will it be possible to adequately predict the social tasks that will be age- and stage-dependent simply by examining the cognitive requirements of the tasks: the demands on working memory, requirements for deep versus shallow processing, for example? If this turns out to be the case, it would suggest a central role for basic cognitive processing.

One promising line of investigation would involve the type of social cognitive task that the perceiver is performing; cognitive development may differentially influence some tasks but not others. For example, our data would suggest that level of cognitive development may not differentially influence perceivers' initial perceptions of which stimuli of a given situation they will attend to, such as the salience of the target person versus the social situation. Salience has been found to be the most important factor influencing causal attributions (Strack, Erber, & Wicklund, 1982), and has been used as a primary explanation for the actor-observer bias (Taylor & Fiske, 1975, 1978). According to Taylor and Fiske, "Observers will perceive situations as causally important to the extent that situations are made salient; observers will perceive dispositions of actors as more important to the extent that actors are made salient" (1978, p. 253). Our findings in the attribution study suggest that level of cognitive development did not lead to differential perceptions of the salience of the target person versus the situation; all perceivers saw the target as more salient, and therefore, more causal. Consequently, the actor-observer effect was not diminished in postformal thinkers.

However, social judgment tasks performed where situational factors are perceived as salient should reveal differences according to level of cognitive development. For example, in Experiment 2, participants were asked to read narratives about perpetrators and the circumstances surrounding their criminal acts, and to consider relevant factors in making a decision about parole. Results of this study suggest that level of cognitive development was predictive of participants' willingness to parole: individuals who scored high on postformal concepts were more likely to recommend parole than those who scored low. It may be the case that the social judgments of formal operators are consistently organized around stable collections of traits. With the transition to more post-formal concepts, social judgment would still reflect actor attribution when actors are salient, but would reflect the person-situation interaction when specific context is introduced.

Alternatively, changes in the social-processing system itself might account for the age-differentiated and stage-differentiated judgments and memory shown in Rankin, Schulenburg, and Seal (1990) and in Experiment 2. There has been much attention to human expertise in the cognitive domain on tasks as diverse as playing chess, reading x-rays, and solving physics problems. Glaser (1987) suggested that expertise is acquired over long periods of learning and experience, and describes it as the acquisition of prototypes in memory of frequently experienced situations that individuals use to integrate and interpret instances of related knowledge. Such representational capacity reduces the role of, and the demands on, general processing. Among its other attributes, Glaser (1987) noted that expertise enables individuals to revise problem representations and to access multiple possible interpretations of a situation.

As in the cognitive domain, the frequent application of skills in interpersonal situations may lead to the development of different levels of social expertise which could account for the age and cognitive-stage differences in this research. A possible example of development of social expertise occurred in the revision of problem representation in the study by Rankin, Schulenburg, and Seal (1990): older adults' judgments were modified more significantly than those of young adults when the actual stimuli presented were discrepant from provided expectancies. The fact that their memories were more selective than those of younger adults, with more frequent forgetting of traits that were not relevant to provided expectancies, might serve as another example of the ability to revise problem representations that characterizes social expertise. Individual differences in the acquisition of a social expertise that accesses multiple possible interpretations of a situation may account for the fact that individuals in Experiment 2 who endorsed more postformal concepts were more lenient in their parole judgments. Further, their memories were not as influenced by personal attributes (in this instance, race) as those of adults who endorsed fewer postformal concepts. In summary, the present data suggest that increasing tendencies to postformal thought reduce the use of one social heuristic, namely stereotyping, and replace it with consideration of the person-environment interaction.

REFERENCES

Abeles, R. P. (Ed.). (1987). *Life-span perspectives and social psychology*. Hillsdale, NJ: Erlbaum.

Anderson, N. H. (1968). Likableness ratings of 555 personality-trait words. *Journal of Personality and Social Psychology, 9*(3), 272–279.

Basseches, M. (1984). Dialectical thinking as metasystematic form of cognitive organization. In M. L. Commons, F. A. Richards, & C. Armon (Eds.), *Beyond formal operations: Late adolescent and adult cognitive development* (pp. 216–238). New York: Praeger.

Basseches, M. (1984). *Dialectical thinking and adult development*. Norwood, NJ: Ablex Publishing Corporation.

Benack, S. (1984). Postformal epistemologies and the growth of empathy. In M. L.

Commons, F. A. Richards, & C. Armon (Eds.), *Beyond formal operations: Late adolescent and adult cognitive development* (pp. 340–356). New York: Praeger.

Blanchard-Fields, F. (1986). Attributional processes in adult development. *Educational Gerontology, 12*, 291–300.

Blank, T. O. (1982). *A social psychology of developing adults*. New York: John Wiley & Sons.

Bodenhausen, G. V., & Wyer, R. S. (1985). Effects of stereotypes on decision making and information-processing strategies. *Journal of Personality and Social Psychology, 48*, 267–282.

Budner, S. (1962). Intolerance of ambiguity as a personality variable. *Journal of Personality, 30*, 29–50.

Burney, G. M. (1974). *The construction and validation of an objective formal reasoning instrument*. Unpublished doctoral dissertation, University of Northern Colorado, Greeley.

Cacioppo, J. T., & Petty, R. E. (1982). The need for cognition. *Journal of Personality and Social Psychology, 42*(1), 116–131.

Cavanaugh, J. C., & Stafford, H. (1989). Being aware of issues and biases: Directions for research on postformal thought. In M. Commons, J. D. Sinnott, F. A. Richards, & C. Armon (Eds.), *Adult development: Comparisons and applications of developmental models* (pp. 279–292). New York: Praeger.

Clarkson-Smith, L., & Hartley, A. A. (1989). Relationships between physical exercise and cognitive abilities in older adults. *Psychology and Aging, 4*, 183–189.

Cohen, J. (1957). The factorial structure of the WAIS between early adulthood and old age. *Journal of Consulting Psychology, 21*, 283–290.

Commons, M. L., & Richards, F. A. (1984). A general model of stage theory. In M. L. Commons, F. A. Richards, & C. Armon (Eds.), *Beyond formal operations: Late adolescent and adult cognitive development*. New York: Praeger.

Crowne, D. P., & Marlowe, D. (1960). A new scale of social desirability independent of pathology. *Journal of Consulting Psychology, 24*, 349–354.

Glaser, R. (1987). Thoughts on expertise. In C. Schooler & K. W. Schaie (Eds.), *Cognitive functioning and social structure over the life course* (pp. 81–94). Norwood, NJ: Ablex.

Gribben, K., Schaie, K. W., & Parham, I. A. (1980). Complexities of life style and maintenance of intellectual abilities. *Journal of Social Issues, 36*, 47–61.

Harris, M., Fontana, A. F., & Dowds, B. N. (1977). The world hypothesis scale: Rationale, reliability, and validity. *Journal of Personality Assessment, 41*, 537–547.

Hultsch, D. F., & Dixon, R. A. (1989). Learning and memory and aging. In J. E. Birren & K. W. Schaie (Eds.), *Handbook of the psychology of aging* (3d ed.). San Diego: Academic.

Johnson, J. A., Germer, C. K., Efran, J. S., & Overton, W. F. (1988). Personality as the basis for theoretical predilections. *Journal of Personality and Social Psychology, 55*, 824–835.

Jones, E. E., & Nisbett, R. E. (1972). The actor and the observer: Divergent perceptions of the causes of behavior. In E. Jones, D. Kanouse, H. Kelley, R. Nisbett, S. Valins, & B. Weiner (Eds.), *Attribution: Perceiving the causes of behavior*. Morristown, NJ: General Learning Press.

Kemper, S. (1988). Geriatric psycholinguistics: Syntactic limitations of oral and written language. In L. L. Light & D. M. Burke (Eds.), *Language, memory, and aging* (pp. 58–76). New York: Cambridge University Press.

Kramer, D. A. (1989). A developmental framework for understanding conflict resolution processes. In J. D. Sinnott (Ed.), *Everyday problem solving in adulthood* (pp. 133–152). New York: Praeger.

Kramer, D. A., Goldston, R. B., & Kahlbaugh, P. E. (1990). *Age differences in paradigm beliefs, personality/attitudinal measures, and affect intensity.* Manuscript submitted for publication.

Kramer, D. A., Kahlbaugh, P. E., Goldston, R. B. (1990). *A measure of paradigm beliefs about the social world.* Manuscript submitted for publication.

Kramer, D. A., & Woodruff, D. S. (1986). Relativistic and dialectical thought in three adult age groups. *Human Development, 29,* 280–290.

Langer, E. J., & Rodin, J. (1976). The effects of choice and enhanced personal responsibility for the aged: A field experiment in an institutional setting. *Journal of Personality and Social Psychology, 34,* 191–198.

Langer, E. J., Rodin, J., Beck, P., Weinmann, C., & Spitzer, L. (1979). Environmental determinants of memory improvement in later adulthood. *Journal of Personality and Social Psychology, 37,* 2003–2013.

Murphy, J. M., & Gilligan, C. (1980). Moral development in later adolescence and adulthood: A critique and reconstruction of Kohlberg's theory. *Human Development, 23,* 77–104.

Nisbett, R. E., Caputo, C., Legant, P., & Maracek, J. (1973). Behavior as seen by the actor and as seen by the observer. *Journal of Personality and Social Psychology, 27,* 154–164.

Nisbett, R. E., & Ross, L. (1980). *Human inference: Strategies and shortcomings of social judgment.* Englewood Cliffs, NJ: Prentice-Hall.

Pepper, S. C. (1942). *World hypothesis: A study in evidence.* Berkeley, CA: University of California Press.

Perry, W. B. (1970). *Forms of intellectual and ethical development in the college years: A scheme.* New York: Holt, Rinehart & Winston.

Piaget, J. (1952). *The origins of intelligence in children.* New York: Harcourt, Brace. (Original work published 1937).

Rankin, J. L., Schulenburg, J. G., & Seal, J. D. (1990). *Social cognition in young and elderly adults: Effects of stereotypic expectancies.* Manuscript submitted for publication.

Rodin, J. (1983). Behavioral medicine: Beneficial effects of self-control training in aging. *International Review of Applied Psychology, 32,* 153–181.

Rothbart, M., Evans, M., & Fulero, S. (1979). Recall for confirming events: Memory processes and the maintenance of social stereotypes. *Journal of Experimental Social Psychology, 15,* 343–355.

Rothbart, M., Fulero, S., Jensen, C., Howard, J., & Birrell, P. (1978). From individual to group impressions: Availability heuristics in stereotype formation. *Journal of Experimental Social Psychology, 14,* 237–255.

Schooler, C. (1987). Psychological effects of complex environments during the life span: A review and theory. In C. Schooler & K. W. Schaie (Eds.), *Cognitive functioning and social structure over the life course.* Norwood, NJ: Ablex.

Sinnott, J. D. (1984). Postformal reasoning: The relativistic stage. In M. L. Commons,

F. A. Richards, & C. Armon (Eds.), *Beyond formal operations: Late adolescent and adult cognitive development* (pp. 298–325). New York: Praeger.

Sinnott, J. D. (1989). Changing the known; knowing the changing: General systems theory paradigms as ways to study complex change and complex thoughts. In D. A. Kramer & M. Bopp (Eds.), *Transformation in clinical and developmental psychology* (pp. 51–69). New York: Springer.

Strack, F., Erber, R., & Wicklund, R. A. (1982). Effects of salience and time pressure on ratings of social causality. *Journal of Experimental Social Psychology, 18*, 581–594.

Sund, R. B. (1976). *Piaget for educators: A multimedia program.* Columbus, OH: Merrill.

Taylor, S. E., & Fiske, S. T. (1975). Point of view and perceptions of causality. *Journal of Personality and Social Psychology, 32*, 439–445.

Taylor, S. E., & Fiske, S. T. (1978). Salience attention and attribution: Top of the Head Phenomena. In L. Berkowitz (Ed.), *Advances in experimental social psychology* (Vol. 11, pp. 249–288). New York: Academic Press.

Troldahl, V., & Powell, F. (1965). Short dogmatism scale. *Social Forces, 44*, 211–214.

Waddington, C. H. (1957). *The strategy of the genes.* London: Allen & Unwin.

12

Perceived Problem Relevancy and Its Relationship to Reasoning on Everyday Problems

RICKARD A. SEBBY AND DENNIS R. PAPINI

As Sinnott (1989a) has observed, one of the significant issues to be further explored and clarified in the field of everyday problem solving involves the specification of contextual factors, factors that relate to the nature of the subject's experience (both past and present) and to the nature of the problems presented to the subject. More realistic appraisals of the cognitive and intellectual functioning of adults (e.g., Adams, Labouvie-Vief, Hakim-Larson, DeVoe, & Hayden, 1989; Blanchard-Fields, 1986; Capon & Kuhn, 1979; Denney & Pearce, 1989; Denney, Pearce, & Palmer, 1982; Sinnott, 1975, 1989b) have been facilitated by the development of supposedly more relevant, familiar, and ecologically valid problem contexts.

Two observations are offered relative to this research. The investigators in these studies assumed that the problems were relevant or familiar to their subjects without assessing these factors. In addition, because a direct measurement of the relevancy or familiarity of the problems was not made, the specific relationship between problem relevancy and problem-solving performance also could not be examined. Several studies (e.g., Arenberg, 1968; Demming & Pressey, 1957; Hulicka, 1967) have indicated that the cognitive performance of older adults is negatively affected by the presentation of problems viewed by older adult subjects as irrelevant and nonmeaningful. However, as Labouvie-Vief (1980) has observed, only through indirect means (e.g., noncompliance with instructions, refusal to participate) have subjects indicated their evaluation of the research strategy or the tasks employed.

Thus, while research in the area of adult cognitive development indicates that the relationship between task relevancy and problem-solving performance is an important one, the perceptions of individuals who are asked to respond to the problems presented have typically not been assessed. One recent exception is a study conducted by Cornelius and Caspi (1987). These authors did attempt to examine the potential effect of familiarity on problem-solving performance. Young, middle-aged, and older adults rated how frequently they experienced the situations described in the Everyday Problem Solving Inventory on a 5-point scale. Correlational analyses failed to find a significant relationship between familiarity and performance on the multiple-choice inventory. With respect to subject differences in familiarity, younger age groups (i.e., the young and middle-aged) were more familiar with problems involving family, friends, or work issues than were older adults. When the problem-solving performance of the three age groups was examined, the performance of the older adult group was superior to the other two groups. Cornelius and Caspi suggested that familiarity (or experience) alone does not have a direct effort on problem-solving performance.

While familiarity may not exert a direct effect on problem-solving performance, the question of the effect of problem relevancy remains to be resolved. Undoubtedly, familiarity and relevancy are related concepts, but what may be familiar may not necessarily be relevant. According to *Webster's New World Dictionary* (1986), a familiar problem would be one that is well known, often encountered, or common to the individual. The operational definition of problem familiarity provided by Cornelius and Caspi (1987) conformed to this meaning in that familiarity consisted of the frequency with which individuals experienced various situations. Conversely, a relevant problem would be one that is perceived to be pertinent, to the point, or related to the matter in hand by the individual. Following this definition it is possible that a commonly occurring problem (i.e., familiar) may not be perceived by an individual as being particularly pertinent or very directly related to one's own life. Another distinction that can be drawn between familiarity and relevancy can be related to the degree of emotional importance subjects attach to the issues on which a problem is based. A problem may be quite familiar (i.e., commonly occurring) but may not provoke much emotional reaction. Research by Blanchard-Fields (1986) indicated that a problem's emotional saliency is related to problem-solving performance. It seems possible that an assessment of problem relevancy may yield a different pattern of results if its relationship to problem-solving performance was assessed. In addition, it should be pointed out that the method employed by Cornelius and Caspi did not allow the direct examination of the effect of familiarity on problem-solving performance on a problem-by-problem basis. Specifically, no examination of the relationship between a particular subject's familiarity rating of a problem and the type of reasoning evidenced on that problem was made.

This type of individualized analysis of the relationship between a problem's relevancy (or familiarity) and the problem-solving performance evidenced on that problem would seem to be especially important in light of the advance of recent theoretical models of adult cognitive development (e.g., Baltes, Dittmann-Kohli, & Dixon, 1985; Berg & Sternberg, 1985; Denney, 1984; Labouvie-Vief,

1982, 1985) that stress individual adaptation to the demands imposed by the social-cultural milieu. For example, Baltes and colleagues suggested that as individuals grow older, they select particular domains within which cognitive functions are selectively optimized. Denney pointed out that certain cognitive abilities, as limited by age-related biological factors, may be optimally exercised by the environment to the detriment of other unexercised abilities. Labouvie-Vief argued that cognitive functioning comes to be regulated by an increasing reference to one's own desires and attitudes, and an increasing awareness of one's own personal situation. More specifically, Labouvie-Vief and her colleagues (Labouvie-Vief, DeVoe, & Bulka, 1989; Labouvie-Vief, Hakim-Larson, DeVoe, & Schoeberlein, 1989; Labouvie-Vief, Hakim-Larson, & Hobart, 1987) have found that a transition in thinking occurs during adulthood that entails the increased integration of thinking with personal experience and perspective. Adults increasingly regulate their thinking and behavior in relation to the emotional saliency of the problem situation (Blanchard-Fields, 1986) and, accordingly, show a more direct relationship between reasoning and the emotional saliency of a problem.

According to Labouvie-Vief's theoretical model (1982, 1985), cognitive development is conceptualized as a multifaceted process that depends on each individual's experiential base. Four primary levels of reasoning are postulated: the presystemic, the intrasystemic, the intersystemic, and the integrated. At the presystemic level, the individual functions concretely, and actions and events are thought to be determined by external causes. Intrasystemic and intersystemic levels can be generally described as a progressive internalization of external events and an increasing sensitivity to pragmatic concerns. The integrated level reflects the individual's acceptance of the inevitability of conflict and a recognition of the inseparability of logical and emotional issues. Considered from this theoretical vantage point, problem relevancy can be understood to reflect a process whereby an individualized definition of relevancy is constructed with the resulting definition requiring the examination of problem relevancy on an individual and problem-by-problem basis.

Previous research by Adams and colleagues (1989) presented a preliminary examination of the explanatory usefulness of the theory as it generally related to adult cognitive development. Adams and colleagues investigated the reasoning ability of five groups ranging from 9-year-olds to subjects in their 30s. Problems were created in which a logical syllogism (if/then) was embedded in either a context relevant to an adult or a context not specific to a particular developmental period. With the exception of the nature of the embedding context, the logical structure and difficulty of the problems were identical. A scoring scheme based on Labouvie-Vief's (1982) model of adult cognitive development was employed. Three scoring levels corresponding to the intrasystemic, the intersystemic, and the integrated cognitive levels of her theory were established. Situated between each of these three levels were two transitional levels, resulting in a 5-point rating scale. Assignment of a subject's problem-solving response was generally based on an individual's increasing awareness of the self's role in interpreting the premises of a problem and evaluating each potential solution in terms of pragmatic, social, cultural, and personal relevance. Importantly, perceptions of problem relevancy were not assessed in this study.

The findings of the study indicated that adult age groups reasoned at higher levels (i.e., intersystemic and integrated reasoning), relative to preadolescent and adolescent groups. These younger age groups tended to give solutions that were logical but exhibited little or no self-awareness of pragmatic or personal constraints. In addition, subjects' reasoning on syllogisms embedded in adult contexts was significantly higher than that observed on the decontextualized (or formal) problems.

Sebby and Papini (1985) conducted an extension of the previously described study. The extension was achieved through two modifications. First, the age groups sampled were broadened to include middle-adult (26–44 years) and older-adult age groups (59–78 years) as well as including an adolescent/young adult group (18–25 years). Second, subjects were presented with syllogisms embedded in formal, adult-, and older-adult–relevant contexts. The form of the syllogistic problems was identical to those developed by Adams and colleagues, except that the contexts were delineated into specific situations thought to affect middle-aged adults (e.g., marital conflict, career concerns) and older adults (e.g., retirement, relocation, grandparenting). This delineation was empirically validated in a pilot study in which 300 volunteers of all ages rated whether particular contexts were more applicable to young, middle, or older adults. Only problem contexts that were rated as appropriate to a particular age group by 75% of the raters were included in the subsequent study. Sebby and Papini found that the middle- and older-adult age groups were more likely to use intersystemic- and integrated-level reasoning, relative to the younger age group. Moreover, the two older age groups' superiority to the younger group was particularly evident on the syllogisms embedded in middle-adult and older-adult problem contexts.

Taken as a whole, the findings reported by Adams and colleagues (1989) and by Sebby and Papini (1985) implied that problem relevancy (i.e., relation of problem content to issues affecting individuals) influences the nature of the reasoning process. Further specification of the role of relevancy as it may influence the reasoning of older-adult and elderly subjects remains to be explored. Thus, the present study was designed to more completely specify the influence of problem relevancy as it affects the reasoning performance of young, middle, and older adults.

A methodology similar to that employed by Sebby and Papini (1985) was used in this study with one significant addition. Problem relevancy was assessed by requiring subjects to rate (on a 5-point scale) the degree to which they thought particular problems were relevant to their life experience. Based on the results of previous research (Adams et al., 1989; Blanchard-Fields, 1986; Sebby & Papini, 1985), we predicted that adolescents and young adults would exhibit more intrasystemic reasoning than the other two age groups, regardless of the perceived relevancy of the problems. As observed by Blanchard-Fields (1986), subjects in the youngest age groups may be limited by a more immature cognitive system that is less able to integrate information from an emotionally salient (i.e., relevant) problem context. Conversely, we expected that reasoning and problem relevancy would be more directly related among subjects in the two older age groups. Problems perceived as being more relevant should allow these subjects to utilize more of their experiences as they attempt to solve these problems, resulting in the more extensive use of intersystemic- and integrated-level reasoning because these two types of reasoning depend on the interpretation of problems in light of personal experiences and perspectives. It is important to point out that Labouvie-Vief (1982) did not postulate a strict age-graded progression in the acquisition of intersystemic or integrated reasoning. Although age is correlated with the progression in reasoning, individual differences based on one's particular life context are important to note. Such differences were expected in the present study.

METHOD

Subjects

One hundred fourteen subjects (51 males and 63 females) between the ages of 18 and 83 years agreed to participate in this study. Following Birren (1964), the participants in this study were assigned to one of three age groups (early maturity, maturity, and later maturity) for analytical purposes. The early-maturity group consisted of 38 subjects (23 males and 15 females) between the ages of 18 and 24 (M age = 19.4 years, SD = 2.5). The maturity group was comprised of 39 subjects (13 males and 26 females) between the ages of 25 and 50 (M age = 30.9 years, SD = 4.5). The later-maturity group included 37 subjects (15 males and 22 females) between the ages of 51 and 83 years of age (M age 68.5 years, SD = 4.1). Subjects assigned to the later-maturity group resided in their own homes and were in relatively good health.

A two-way analysis of variance of subjects' educational status across the age and gender groups described above indicated that this variable was comparable for the subjects (all F's > .05). This variable was assessed on a 5-point scale (with elementary school, high school, technical/vocational school, college, and graduate school being points 1 through 5, respectively). Subjects indicated the level of educational achievement they had reached. Means for the males in the early-maturity, maturity, and later-maturity age groups were 3.61, 3.73, and 3.77, while the corresponding means for females in the three age groups were 4.00, 4.13, and 3.82, respectively. More variability (SD = 1.20) was observed for the later-maturity than for the maturity (SD = .53) or the early-maturity groups (SD = .74). More subjects in the oldest group were widows or widowers than were subjects in the other two age groups.

Procedure

Subjects were asked to engage in two types of activities as part of this investigation. First, subjects were asked to solve problems that were embedded in contexts designed to be more or less relevant to individuals using a "thinking aloud" strategy. Second, subjects were asked to rate the relevancy of each problem to their life using a 5-point scale. This scale ranged from "very relevant to my life" to "not at all relevant to my life." Following these two phases, subjects were administered a demographic questionnaire.

Each of the subjects was individually interviewed by a trained experimenter in a quiet laboratory room. Subjects were asked to verbally report thought processes as they solved problems (Giambra & Arenberg, 1980). A review of the thinking aloud strategy (Ericsson & Simon, 1980) has suggested that it is an appropriate means of maximizing the report of mental processes involved in problem solving. The experimenters were trained to probe the subject's statements in order to ascertain the level of reasoning involved in the solution of problems. Specific attention was given during the training of the experimenters to methods by which subjects' thoughts could be elicited without biasing them toward particular answers. For example, experimenters were trained to encourage the thinking aloud process by using open-ended statements (e.g., "Tell me more about what you're thinking").

Each participant responded to a total of 16 verbal syllogisms that were purposely embedded in four different contexts thought to differ in relevancy. These syllogisms were constructed using if-then statements, with the only difference between types of problems being the personal relevancy of the context in which they were embedded. Formal syllogisms (4 problems were presented) were designed to minimize the potential relevance of the problem's embedding context. Conversely, contextual syllogisms thought to maximize the potential relevance of the problem's embedding context were constructed. Three different types of contextual syllogisms (with each type composed of 4 problems) were presented: adult-relevant (family/marital relations), adolescent-relevant (parent-adolescent relations), and older-adult–relevant (retirement, relocation). Three hundred individuals who ranged in age from 18 to 62 had previously rated the relevancy of each of the problems used in this study for particular age groups. Only syllogisms embedded in contexts rated as relevant for young, middle-aged or older-adult cohorts or not relevant to any age group (formal) by 75% of these volunteers were used in this study. Table 12.1 provides examples of the different types of embedding contexts employed in the verbal syllogisms.

Each participant's verbalizations were tape-recorded and later were independently scored by one male and one female rater using a scheme developed by Adams and colleagues (1989) and described in Sebby and Papini (1989). In brief, the scoring scheme allowed the identification of the following three levels of reasoning specified by Labouvie-Vief's (1982) theory: intrasystemic, intersystemic, and integrated. The raters were unaware of specific characteristics of

Table 12.1
Examples of Four Syllogistic Problem Contexts

Problem Context	Example
Formal Syllogism	Nancy shows Tom a stack of cards with numbers printed on both sides of each card. Nancy tells Tom that if there is a number 2 printed on one side of a card, then the number 9 and the number 4 are printed on the other side of the same card. Nancy hands Tom a card with the number 2 printed on one side. Is there a 9 and a 4 on the other side of the card? How certain are you of your answer
Adolescent Syllogism	Jean does not keep her room clean, and it is especially messy by Friday. Sara, Jean's mother, warns her that if her room is not clean by the time she gets home from work, she will not be allowed to go to the basketball game at school that night. Jean does not clean her room. Sara arrives home from work. Does Jean get to attend the basketball game? How certain are you of your answer?
Adult Syllogism	John is known to be a heavy drinker, especially when he goes to parties. Mary, John's wife, warns him that if he comes home drunk one more time, she will leave him and take the children. Tonight John is out late at an office party. John comes home drunk. Does Mary leave John? How certain are you of your answer
Older Adult Syllogism	Ellen, who has lived in the same house for the last 25 years, has almost fallen down the stairs on at least a half-dozen occasions. After her last near-fall, Ellen promised that if it ever happened again she would sell her house and move into another that had only one floor. Yesterday, Ellen had another near-fall but avoided it by catching herself on the handrailing. Does Ellen move into a new house? How certain are you of your answer?

the subjects (e.g., their age or education) when the ratings were performed. The average level of agreement reached by the two raters was 86%. When conflicts between the two raters arose, a third rater evaluated the problem and a discussion of the difference in the ratings resolved the conflict.

RESULTS

Three sets of analyses were conducted in order to examine subjects' problem-solving performance, the degree to which the problems were perceived as relevant, and the relationship between problem-solving performance and the perceived relevancy of the problems.

Problem-Solving Performance

Separate sums corresponding to the frequency with which subjects engaged in intrasystemic-, intersystemic-, and integrated-level reasoning were computed across the 16 problems. For the intrasystemic scores, a two-factor analysis of variance (age group by gender) indicated that the three age groups significantly differed, $F(2, 108) = 6.20$, $p < .01$, with the following means (3.24, 1.29, 1.43) corresponding to the early-maturity, maturity, and later-maturity groups, respectively. Bonferroni t tests indicated that the middle and oldest age groups differed significantly from the young group of subjects. Although no significant effects were indicated for intersystemic scores, a significant age effect, $F(2, 108) = 22.88$, $p < .01$, was observed for integrated reasoning. Subjects in the oldest age group had a significantly higher frequency of integrated reasoning ($M = 5.40$), relative to the middle ($M = 2.02$) or the youngest age group ($M = .56$).

The effect of problems being embedded in particular problem contexts (e.g., adolescent-relevant, adult-relevant, older-adult–relevant, and formal contexts) was also examined. This analysis was conducted based on the hypothesis that different problem contexts may be differentially relevant at particular stages of the life cycle. This potential effect was examined by summing the problem-solving scores for each of the four problems composing each problem context and analyzing each context separately. In each case, a two-factor ANOVA was employed. For the adolescent-relevant problems, a significant age effect was indicated, $F(2, 108) = 24.09$, $p < .01$. All the means were found to differ significantly, with subjects in the later-maturity group having the highest mean scores (3.63), followed by subjects in the maturity group (3.15), and subjects in the early-maturity group (2.56). A similar age effect was obtained when the adult-relevant problems, $F(2, 108 = 19.10$, $p < .01$), the older-adult–relevant problems, $F(2, 108) = 21.10$, $p < .01$, and the formal problems, $F(2, 108) = 8.56$, $p < .01$, were examined. These data, as represented in Figure 12.1, indicate that the three age groups did evidence different levels of performance on the four types of problems, with the later-maturity age group performing at the highest level, regardless of the problem context. Although overall performance declined on the formal problems, the same relative relationship between the three age groups was maintained.

Relevancy Rating of Problems

Subjects were asked to rate the relevancy of each of the problems on a 5-point scale (with higher ratings reflecting greater perceived relevancy of each problem to their own lives). A total of 187 problems were rated by subjects as being highly relevant, while 297 problems were rated as having the lowest relevancy. Two separate 2×3 analyses of variance were conducted to examine whether the number of problems rated as having high or low relevancy varied

Figure 12.1
**Average Problem-Solving Scores as a Function of Age Group and Problem
Context**

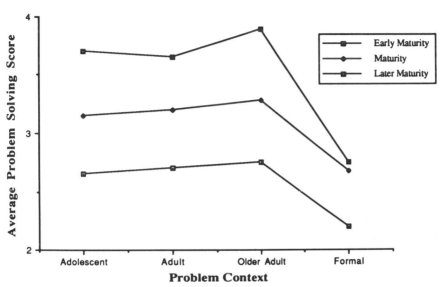

by age group and gender. The only effect found to be significant, age group,
$F(2, 108) = 7.00$, $p < .05$, occurred when high-relevancy problems were
examined. More problems were reported as being highly relevant among the
later-maturity age group ($M = 7.05$) than among the maturity ($M = 4.96$) or
the early-maturity age group ($M = 4.55$), with the differences between the latter
two groups failing to reach significance.

Relevancy ratings were then examined by summing across all 16 problems to
derive an overall score for each subject and by separately examining sums of
ratings computed for each of the four types of problem contexts. A two-way
ANOVA (age group by gender) indicated that the three age groups differed in
their overall ratings of the relevancy of the problem, $F(2, 108) = 4.44$, $p <
.05$, with subjects in the later maturity group having the lowest relevancy ratings
($M = 2.43$), relative to the maturity group ($M = 2.86$) and the early-maturity
group ($M = 2.73$). Tukey HDSs indicated that only the maturity and the later-
maturity age groups differed significantly.

Similar two-way analyses conducted on the relevancy ratings for each of the
four problem contexts generally indicated that the three age groups differed in
their ratings of the problems in each context. Means and standard deviations
relevant to these analyses are presented in Table 12.2. The significant age group
effect on the adolescent-relevant problems, $F(2, 108) = 28.76$, $p < .01$, indicated that subjects in the maturity age group saw these problems as being more
relevant than did the younger or the older age groups, with mean differences

Table 12.2
Means and Standard Deviations (in parentheses) of Relevancy Ratings by Subjects in Each Age Group on Each Task Type

Task Type

Age Group	Formal	Adolescent	Adult	Older Adult
Young	2.10 (0.73)	3.32 (0.80)	2.77 (0.43)	2.45 (0.71)
Middle	1.96 (1.07)	3.53 (0.91)	2.91 (0.87)	3.17 (0.73)
Older	2.16 (0.97)	2.33 (0.94)	2.11 (0.49)	3.09 (0.79)

between the early- and later-maturity, and the maturity and later-maturity groups, being significant. Similar findings were obtained for the adult-relevant problems, $F(2, 108) = 13.03$, $p < .01$. On the older-adult–relevant problem type, the significant age group effect, $F(2, 108) = 11.05$, $p < .01$, was due to the fact that the youngest subjects saw these problems as being less relevant to their lives than did either of the two older age groups. The relevancy ratings of the two older groups were not found to differ significantly. No significant differences were observed for the formal problem context.

Relationship between Reasoning and Problem Relevancy

In order to examine whether reasoning performance was affected by the subject's perception of the relevancy of a problem, the number of problems on which intrasystemic, intersystemic, and integrated reasoning was evidenced was determined for each subject within each age group. Subjects in the early-maturity group utilized intrasystemic, intersystemic, and integrated reasoning on 60%, 33%, and 7% of the problems, respectively. The corresponding percentages for the maturity group were 20%, 49%, and 31% for intrasystemic, intersystemic, and integrated reasoning, respectively. Subjects in the later maturity group used intrasystemic, intersystemic, and integrated reasoning on 10%, 35%, and 55% of the problems, respectively.

After the type of reasoning used on each problem was identified, average relevancy ratings for each subject were computed by summing across problems displaying each type of reasoning. This sum was then divided by the number of problems found to exhibit that particular type of reasoning. For example, if a particular subject utilized integrated reasoning on four problems, the relevancy ratings provided by that subject for those four problems would be summed and divided by 4 (the number of problems displaying integrated reasoning). Similar averages were computed for intersystemic and intrasystemic reasoning for each subject.

Figure 12.2
Average Relevancy Ratings as a Function of Age Group and Type of Reasoning

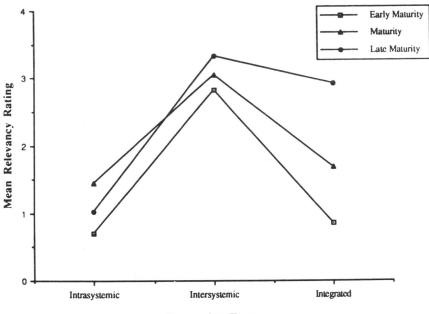

In order to compare ratings by type of reasoning, a three-factor analysis of variance with two between-subject factors (age and gender) and one within-subject factor (level of reasoning) was conducted. Ratings were found to differ in relation to level of reasoning, $F(2, 216) = 47.22$, $p < .001$, and an age by level of reasoning interaction was indicated, $F(4, 126) = 3.25$, $p < .01$. The interaction is depicted in Figure 12.2.

Subjects in the early-maturity age group had the highest perceived relevancy ratings of problems on which they used intersystemic reasoning. Relevancy ratings or problems on which intrasystemic and integrated reasoning was used were low, and did not differ from one another significantly. For subjects in the maturity age group, the highest perceived relevancy ratings of problems were related to the use of intersystemic reasoning. Although the early-maturity and maturity age groups did not significantly differ when the relevancy ratings related to the use of integrated reasoning were compared, subjects in the maturity age group did tend to evidence higher ratings on problems in which that type of reasoning was used. Examination of the results obtained for the later-maturity age group revealed that the highest relevancy ratings were associated with problems on which integrated and intersystemic reasoning was used. Moreover, the relevancy ratings associated with problems on which integrated reasoning was used by this age group differed significantly from those ratings observed for the other two age groups.

DISCUSSION

Overall, the pattern of findings obtained in this study indicate that despite the lower overall relevancy ratings of the problems provided by the oldest subjects, this age group (later-maturity) had the strongest perceptions of the relevancy of selected problems. This age group also had the greatest propensity to use integrated reasoning strategies (integrated reasoning increased in frequency from 7% among the early-maturity group, to 31% among the maturity group, to 55% among the later-maturity group). Finally, the relationship between perceived relevancy and problem-solving performance was significantly stronger among the oldest age group relative to the other two age groups.

The findings of lower overall perceived relevancy and greater problem-solving performance among the oldest age group are similar to those obtained by Cornelius and Caspi (1987), who examined subjects' perceptions of problem familiarity and problem-solving performance. In the present study, subjects in the middle (maturity) age group had the highest average overall relevancy ratings of the problems, although subjects in the oldest (later-maturity) age group gave more problems the highest possible relevancy rating (a rating of 5). Varying the problem context (adolescent-relevant, adult-relevant, or older-adult–relevant) did not seem to exert a salient influence on subjects' perception of problem relevancy. Additional research is necessary to investigate the manner in which relevancy can be further defined and manipulated in order to examine its effects on problem-solving performance. It may be that problem relevancy functions as an *interface* variable (Lachman, 1986; Lachman, Baltes, Nesselroade, & Willis, 1982) which serves to mediate the relationship between personality and cognition. Specific features of problems (the emotionality or vividness of the situation depicted) may be important to consider, perhaps in relation to the past and present living experiences of the subject.

Such perceptions of problem relevancy may be expected to differ among subjects with respect to particular problems. This individualized relevancy results from each one having increasingly accumulated different experiences and evolved various personal characteristics (e.g., cognitive, personality). As several current theories of adult cognitive development suggest (e.g., Baltes et al., 1985; Berg & Sternberg, 1985; Labouvie-Vief, 1982), adults are expected to increasingly personalize the world in terms of their own particular niche and the personal characteristics and abilities they possess. One would also expect that the perceived relevancy of a problem would affect a subject's tendency to exert the effort necessary to integrate experience, cognitive factors, and other attributes. This tendency would also be expected to be influenced by age-related factors (cognitive ability, experience, and personality characteristics).

The most significant finding of this study provides some tentative support for the direct relationship between the perceived relevancy of a problem and the type of reasoning used by a subject on that problem, although this relationship seems to be mediated by the developmental level of the individual. For example, following Labouvie-Vief (1982), young adults in this study were less likely to reason at the intersystemic level and more likely to use intrasystemic styles of reasoning when solving problems. When these young adults did use intersystemic reasoning, their perception of the relevancy of those problems was significantly higher. Moreover, subjects in the maturity group demonstrated that intersystemic reasoning was related to the perception of greater problem relevancy. This age group also evidenced greater perceived problem relevancy when integrated reasoning was used, relative to the youngest age group. The strongest support for the relationship between perceived relevancy affecting problem-solving performance was observed in the performance of the later-maturity age group. In this group, both integrated reasoning and intersystemic reasoning were related to higher perceived problem relevancy. What seems to be implied by these results is that only when subjects have reached a certain point in development is problem relevancy related to the manifestation of the highest level of reasoning (i.e., integrated reasoning).

Other researchers (Blanchard-Fields, 1986; Labouvie-Vief, Hakim-Larson, et al., 1989) have observed that with increasing age, subjects are more able to integrate personality, cognitive, and stimulus characteristics (e.g., a problem's emotional saliency). The pattern of findings observed for the subjects in the later-maturity age group in this study are consistent with these previously obtained results. Moreover, the effect of relevancy observed here indicates that among subjects of the most advanced developmental level, problems perceived as being more highly relevant prompted such integration, while problems having little perceived relevancy did not.

According to the coding scheme used in this study, the age-related effects that were observed here can be interpreted as reflecting the tendency of individuals with greater experience to embed solutions to problems in their own experience and to recognize the self's role as an integrator of pragmatic, social, and personal concerns. According to various investigators (Arlin, 1984; Armon, 1984; Blanchard-Fields, 1986; Labouvie-Vief, 1982; Sinnott, 1989b), "mature reasoning" entails the recognition of an inherent interpretation of multiple perspectives. More specifically, mutually contradictory interpretations of the same issue may be produced and reconciled by the same interpreter. In our study, this tendency was found to dramatically increase among the oldest subjects, and was influenced by the perceived relevancy of individual problems. Current theories of adult cognitive development (e.g., Denney, 1984; Labouvie-Vief, 1982) support the notion that everyday problem-solving abilities may be affected by sensitivity to or experience with particular individualized problem contexts.

Several significant issues remain to be more fully explored as a result of the findings of this study. First, a more in-depth analysis of the features that define relevancy for subjects would seem to be mandated. Perhaps a more detailed analysis of the particular characteristics that subjects find relevant in the embedding context of particular problems could serve to provide further information regarding the nature of the stimulus materials needed to construct relevant, meaningful problems. Second, further explication of the nature of the relationship between problem relevancy and problem-solving performance undoubtedly depends on expanding the scope of the experiential, cognitive, and personality characteristics of the problem solvers that are examined. The possibility that this effect is directly and solely mediated by age is quite remote. More expansive and naturalistic investigations of the nature of problem solving as it occurs in everyday contexts such as marriage (see Kramer, 1989) or care giving may provide additional insight into the nature of the factors and forces at work when individuals attempt to solve everyday problems.

REFERENCES

Adams, C., Labouvie-Vief, G., Hakim-Larson, J., DeVoe, M., & Hayden, M. (1989). *Modes of thinking and problem solving: Developmental transitions from pre-adolescence to middle adulthood.* Paper under review.

Arenberg, D. (1968). Concept problem solving in young and old adults. *Journal of Gerontology, 23,* 279–282.

Arlin, P. (1984). Adolescent and adult thought: A structural interpretation. In M. L. Commons, F. A. Richards, & C. Armon (Eds.), *Beyond formal operations* (pp. 258–271). New York: Praeger.

Armon, C. (1984). Ideals of the good life and moral judgment: Ethical reasoning across the lifespan. In M. L. Commons, F. A. Richards, & C. Armon (Eds.), *Beyond formal operations* (pp. 357–380). New York: Praeger.

Baltes, P. B., Dittmann-Kohli, F., & Dixon, R. A. (1985). New perspectives on the development of intelligence in adulthood: Toward a dual-process conception and a model of selective optimization with compensation. In P. B. Baltes & O. G. Brim, Jr. (Eds.), *Life-span development and behavior* (Vol. 6, pp. 33–76). New York: Academic.

Berg, C. A., & Sternberg, R. J. (1985). A triarchic theory of intellectual development during adulthood. *Developmental Review, 5,* 334–370.

Birren, J. E. (1964). *The psychology of aging.* Englewood Cliffs, NJ: Prentice-Hall.

Blanchard-Fields, F. (1986). Reasonings on social dilemmas varying in emotional saliency: An adult developmental perspective. *Psychology and Aging, 1,* 325–333.

Capon, N., & Kuhn, D. (1979). Logical reasoning in the supermarket: Adult females' use of proportional reasoning strategy in an everyday context. *Developmental Psychology, 15,* 450–452.

Cornelius, S. W., & Caspi, A. (1987). Everyday problem solving in adulthood and old age. *Psychology and Aging, 2,* 144–153.

Demming, J. A., & Pressey, S. L. (1957). Tests "indigenous" to adult and older years. *Journal of Counseling Psychology, 4,* 144–148.

Denney, N. W. (1984). A model of cognitive development across the life span. *Developmental Review, 4,* 171–191.

Denney, N. W., & Pearce, K. A. (1989). A developmental study of practical problem solving in adults. *Psychology and Aging, 4*, 438–442.

Denney, N. W., Pearce, K. A., & Palmer, A. M. (1982). A developmental study of adults' performance on traditional and practical problem-solving tasks. *Experimental Aging Research, 8*, 115–118.

Ericsson, K. A., & Simon, H. A. (1980). Verbal reports as data. *Psychological Review, 87*, 215–251.

Giambra, L. M., & Arenberg, D. (1980). Problem solving, concept learning, and aging. In L. Poon (Ed.), *Aging in the 1980's*, Washington, DC: Gerontological Society.

Hulicka, I. (1967). Age differences in retention as a function of interference. *Journal of Gerontology, 22*, 180–184.

Kramer, D. A. (1989). A developmental framework for understanding conflict resolution processes. In J. D. Sinnott (Ed.), *Everyday problem solving* (pp. 133–152). New York: Praeger.

Labouvie-Vief, G. (1980). Adaptive dimensions in adult cognition. In N. Datan & W. Lohman (Eds.), *Transitions in aging* (pp. 3–26). New York: Academic.

Labouvie-Vief, G. (1982). Dynamic development and mature autonomy. *Human Development, 25*, 161–191.

Labouvie-Vief, G. (1985). Intelligence and cognition. In J. E. Birren & K. W. Schaie (Eds.), *Handbook of the psychology of aging* (2nd Ed., pp. 500–530). New York: Van Nostrand Reinhold.

Labouvie-Vief, G., Hakim-Larson, J., DeVoe, M., & Schoeberlein, S. (1989). Emotions and self-regulation: A life span view. *Human Development, 32*, 279–299.

Labouvie-Vief, G., Hakim-Larson, J., & Hobart, C. (1987). Age, ego level, and the life-span development of coping and defense processes. *Psychology and Aging, 2*, 286–293.

Labouvie-Vief, G., DeVoe, M., & Bulka, D. (1989). Speaking about feelings: Conceptions of emotion across the life span. *Psychology and Aging, 4*, 425–437.

Lachman, M. E. (1986). The role of personality and social factors in intellectual aging. *Educational Gerontology, 12*, 339–344.

Lachman, M. E., Baltes, P. B., Nesselroade, J. R., & Willis, S. L. (1982). Examination of personality-ability relationships in the elderly: The role of the contextual (interface) assessment mode. *Journal of Research in Personality, 16*, 485–501.

Sebby, R. A., & Papini, D. R. (1985, November). *The influence of contextual variation on adult cognition.* Paper presented at the meeting of the Gerontological Society of America, New Orleans.

Sebby, R. A., & Papini, D. R. (1989). Problems in everyday problem solving. In J. D. Sinnott (Ed.), *Everyday problem solving: Theory and applications* (pp. 55–71). New York: Praeger.

Sinnott, J. D. (1975). Everyday thinking and Piagetian operativity in adults. *Human Development, 18*, 430–443.

Sinnott, J. D. (1989). Summary: Issues and directions for everyday problem solving research. In J. D. Sinnott (Ed.), *Everyday problem solving: Theory and application* (pp. 300–306). New York: Praeger.

Sinnott, J. D. (1989b). A model for solution of ill-structured problems: Implications for everyday and abstract problem solving. In J. D. Sinnott (Ed.), *Everyday problem solving: Theory and applications* (pp. 72–99). New York: Praeger.

13

Limits to Problem Solving: Emotion, Intention, Goal Clarity, Health, and Other Factors in Postformal Thought

Ideas and theories in science pass through predictable stages of development as they are refined (e.g., Bateson, 1979). Brainstorming or intuitive "hunches," often based on a real-life question, are followed by descriptive data collection and correlational analyses of variables that seem to be related, perhaps causally, in a process-oriented way, to the phenomena of interest. Only then are experimental studies worthwhile, because enough has become known about the phenomenon as a whole to allow investigators to choose wisely in selecting independent variables to manipulate as potential causes. The experimental studies may appear at first to trivialize the original real-life question because, by controlling, they omit so many nuances of the real situation. However, without taking the steps of experimentation *and* interpretation of results in a real context, we may omit important pieces of the puzzle of complex events. As experimental work begins, the new theory is often related to other models or variables about which information and processes are known.

The study of postformal thought is entering the correlational/experimental phase of scientific inquiry. It is important that we now do correlational studies and experiments rather than simply spending more time in theorizing. Theories already exist (Commons, Richards, Armon, 1984), and to some extent have empirical support (Commons, Armon, Kohlberg, Richards, Grotzer, Sinnott, 1989; Commons, Sinnott, Richards, Armon, 1989). This is also true for the theory of relativistic self-referential postformal thought (Sinnott, 1984; 1989a, 1989b; 1989c). The purpose of this chapter is to describe how this next scientific step (i.e., experimentation) was taken to test Sinnott's theory, how a few probable parameters of self-referential postformal thought were manipulated, and what the results of those manipulations were. A second purpose of this chapter is to begin relating the data on self-referential postformal thought to other cognitive and physical variables already used in the field.

This chapter presents five studies, the description of results from the first part of a major research program. Very little space in this chapter will be devoted to explaining the theory itself; interested readers who are not familiar with this literature are urged to read Sinnott (1981, 1984, 1989a, 1989b, 1989c) for an introduction.

The main characteristics of relativistic postformal operations (Sinnott, 1984) are (a) self-reference and (b) the ordering of formal operations. Self-reference is a general term for the ideas inherent in the new physics (Wolf, 1981) and alluded to by Hofstadter (1979) using the terms "self-referential games," "jumping out of the system," and "strange loops." The essential notions are that we can never be completely free of the built-in limits of our system of knowing, and that we come to know that this very fact is true. This means that we take into account, in all our decisions about truth, the fact that all knowledge has a subjective component and therefore is, of necessity, incomplete. Therefore, any logic we use is self-referential logic. Nonetheless, we must *act*, and do so by making a lower-level decision about the higher-level "rules of the game" (nature of truth); then play the game by those rules. Sooner or later we come to *realize* that this is what we are doing. We then can consciously use self-referential thought.

The second characteristic of postformal operations is the ordering of formal operations. The higher level postformal system of self-referential truth decisions orders formal truth systems and logic systems, one of which is somewhat subjectively chosen and imposed on data. Perhaps there are 16 or 27 levels interposed between formal and relativistic operations, but the number of levels above formal and below relativistic is not important. The approach is linked to Piaget's theory, *and* is a logical extension of it.

Now this is the logic of the "new" physics (relativity theory and quantum mechanics, Sinnott, 1981). New physics is, oddly enough, the next step beyond Newtonian physics, and is built on the logic of self-reference. Is it unthinkable that the development of logical processes themselves would follow that ladder to increasing complexity? Some characteristics that separate new physics thinking from earlier forms can be found in Sinnott (1984).

A new type of cognitive coordination occurs at the postformal level. Another kind of coordination of perspectives also seems to happen on an *emotional* level, over developmental time. This coordination parallels the cognitive one, and is probably in a circular interaction with it.

RESEARCH QUESTIONS

The data presented in this chapter address five research questions drawn from the theory of relativistic postformal self-referential thought.

1. Is there evidence for the model and the relativistic self-referential operations proposed by Sinnott (1981, 1984)? This is a continuing effort to provide descriptive evidence.

2. Do physical variables such as health or other cognitive variables such as memory relate to self-referential thought? This is one of many possible correlational questions.

3. Do the presence or absence of goal clarity and heuristic availability influence self-referential thought as hypothesized (Sinnott, 1983, 1989a, 1989c)? This is the first experimental question to be addressed in this chapter.

4. Does manipulation of *emotion, intention, mind wandering, problem realism*, and *directness of instruction to produce* that sort of thought influence the presence and quality of relativistic self-referential thought? This is the second experimental question to be addressed in this chapter.

5. Are there age differences in performance? This is a quasi-experimental question.

It was hypothesized that operations would be found, would support earlier hypotheses, and would be influenced by the manipulations. If the hypotheses are supported, it would provide more evidence for positive cognitive development in mature adults, would indicate that the "whole" person is involved in the cognitive task (Sinnott, 1989b), and would suggest that such complex thinking could be fostered or retarded by interpersonal, motivational, problem-context, and attentional factors. The information gained would once again directly address the real-life issues that were an original interest. This chapter is organized to address methodology and then the research questions in the order in which they appear above.

GENERAL METHODOLOGY

Subjects and General Procedure

Respondents were volunteers in the Baltimore Longitudinal Study of Aging (BLSA; Shock et al., 1985). They were well-educated, highly motivated men and women in good enough health to come to the Gerontology Research Center for 2–3 days of testing. Two hundred ten respondents participated in the "Standard Administration" of problem solving which followed the clinical interview method of Piaget (Sinnott, 1984). Forty respondents took part in the "Thinking Aloud" administration, in which respondents spoke without interruption and then answered standard questions (Sinnott, 1989c). The number of respondents in any analysis sometimes differed from the total number of subjects, however, since not every protocol was complete and some other variables of interest in some analyses (variables already on record) had not been given to all the problem solvers.

Respondents received many psychological and physical tests during each visit (every 2 years) to the BLSA. These data are on file for 30 years of visits and are the source of data for some analyses using memory or blood pressure measures (Shock et al., 1985). In each case they received six of Sinnott's logical problems, shown in Table 13.1. When a respondent was scheduled to be tested with

Table 13.1
Problems

ABC

Six letters of the twenty-six letters of the alphabet appear below. Imagine that you are making pairs of the letters. writing down all the possible ways of putting two different letters together. How many pairs will you have when you make all possible pairs of the six letters?

(Remember, although any letter will appear several times in different pairs, the same letter should not appear twice in the same pair:
(AB BC BD). Use these letters: A B C D E F

VC

Six foods appear in the list below. All six are good sources of Vitamin C. Your doctor asked you to eat two different foods which are good sources of Vitamin C everyday. 1). How many different pairs of goods might you eat when you make all possible pairs of the six foods? In other words, how many possible pairs are there? 2). In each pair you make, how many portions of each food must you eat to get at least 2 units of Vitamin C from that pair?

Vitamin C Sources

1 portion	No. of units of Vitamin C in portion
1 orange	1 unit
1 grapefruit	2 units
8 oz. tomato juice	1 unit
1/2 cup cabbage	1 unit
20 grapes	1/2 unit
1 cup greens	1 unit

Find: 1) _____ possible pairs of different foods.   2) In each pair, how many portions of each to get at least 2 units of Vitamin C ?

CAMP

You have six children who love to go camping. You have patience enough to take two children, but no more, with you on each trip. Each child wants a chance to camp with each of the other brothers and sisters during the summer. How many trips would be necessary to give each child a chance to camp with every brother and sister if you take only two children each trip? How do you know?

172

POW

A family consisting of a father in his 40's and a 15-year-old child live in the suburbs. They learn that a 70-year-old grandmother (the father's mother) will need to live with them due to her failing health. Right now the family members have this "power relationship": the father runs the house and the child follows his rules (father dominant; child dominated). The grandmother has made it clear that when she comes she may not want anyone, including the father telling her what to do. If the grandmother moves in, what are all the possible "power relationships" that might develop among pairs of individuals in the household? (The possible power relationships are 1) dominant-dominated; 2) or equal-equal).

WK

You are supervising the assembly of a magazine that comes out monthly. Several workers are putting pages in order; others are binding the pages. The binders finish 20 magazines every half hour. However, those putting pages together in order, finish 40 in two hours. Some of your workers are idle part of the time. Equal numbers of workers are performing each task, and there are more than enough supplies in each area. All the workers can handle both jobs. What can you do to keep all the workers equally busy?

CAKE

A friend is having a birthday, and you are making a cake for the party. The cake recipe calls for 2 cups of flour, 1 cup of milk, and 1 cup of sugar, among other things. You have measured all the flour into a bowl and have added the sugar when the doorbell rings. You leave to answer it. When you return to the kitchen you forget that the sugar is in the bowl and add 1 more cup of sugar, plus the milk. Suddenly you realize your mistake; your cake will be too sweet. What can you do to solve the problem? (substituted for CAMP in Standard Administration)

BR

A family consisting of a mother in her 40's, a father in his 40's, a ten-year-old girl, a 12-year-old girl and a 15-year-old boy live in a small two-bedroom house in Detroit. One of the bedrooms is large and well-decorated, and has a single bed; the other bedroom also has a single bed. This summer the family learns that a grandfather who lives alone in a one-bedroom apartment two blocks away can no longer live alone. He might move in with the family. What are all the possible ways that the six persons can use the two bedrooms in the house?

173

Table 13.2
Criteria for Relativistic, Self-Referential Postformal Operations

1. **Metatheory shift:** There is the production of abstract and practical (real-life) solutions as well as a shift between conflicting abstract a priori and real a priori. This shift is stated by the subject. The solution always includes problem definitions. For example, the subject might ask whether we want the hypothetical solution that is logical on paper or the solution that would really be viable. (The respondent may or may not then proceed to give both solutions.)

2. **Problem definition:** There is a statement of the meaning and demands of the problem for the subject. There is also the decision to define problems in a certain, chosen way. The subject indicates a change in the types of parameters from solution to solution. Defining the problem is the first concern, but the subject need not give alternative solutions since these solutions might be precluded by the problem definition. The problem definition may include a metatheory shift. For example, the subject might wonder what the real problem is, whether it is the need to have peace in the family or to use all the space. The subject might then decide to treat it like an algebra problem.

3. **Process/product shift:** There is a description of a process as one answer and an outcome as another answer. Or there may be a description of two processes that achieve the same outcome. Often there is a statement by a subject that there is a solution and that finding the solution is actually a never-ending process.

4. **Parameter setting:** The subject names key variables to be combined or made proportional in the problem other than those given in the written demands of the problem. Often the subject explicitly writes out key variables. Alternatively she or he may change the variables that limit the problem from solution 1 to solution 2. Parameter setting differs from problem definition in that it is less inclusive and more concrete.

5. **Pragmatism:** One can choose a best solution among several, or, one can choose the best variant of a solution that has two processes. For example, the subject might say that if you want the most practical solution, it's number 2, but if you want the quickest, easiest solution, it's number 1. This is the only operation that cannot be given a passing score unless the subject actually gives more than one solution.

6. **Multiple solutions:** There is a direct statement that there are many correct solutions intrinsic to a problem with several causes, or that no problem has only one solution. Also, the subject may create several solutions. For example, the subject might respond that he or she sees four solutions that could be termed correct, or that there are limitless arrangements that would be correct if you change the constraints.

7. **Multiple causality:** There is a statement that multiple causes exist for any event or that some solutions are more probable than others. For example, some subjects state that the solution depends on all past relations of the persons in the problem. As such, when the three persons in the problem get together anything could happen, depending on personalities and on how each reacts.

8. **Paradox:** The subject gives a direct statement or question about perceived, inherently conflicting demands that are integral to the problem, not simply two solutions with different parameters. For example, the Bedroom Problem can be read in two conflicting ways. The subject notices that two different things are being said at once, both of which could change the way the problem should be solved.

9. **Self-referential thought:** Awareness that the subject must be the ultimate judge of which belief system dominated his/her thinking, i.e., of what is "True". For example, the subject might say that she, a therapist, can never be free of a bias but can only be aware of which bias is coloring her view of a client. But all the views are "true", and she must choose one and go on with the treatment sessions.

175

Sinnott's own tests, he or she first took problem solving, either the standard administration or the thinking aloud administration form. Standard administration subjects then went on to an Everyday Memory test (Sinnott, 1986) and a laboratory memory-response time test. Thinking aloud subjects only sometimes went on to the same laboratory memory test. All respondents had blood pressure taken in a seated position during a physical at each visit. Additional details about measures and procedure are given in the context of each section below.

RESEARCH QUESTIONS ADDRESSED

Study 1: Is There Evidence for Self-Referential Operations?

This question has been addressed in earlier studies. To continue addressing this question, descriptive data from both the standard administration and the thinking aloud administration of six logical problems were used. Protocols were scored by two raters for reliability purposes. The operations are defined in Table 13.2, taken for the most part from Sinnott (1984). For the standard administration, a large proportion of respondents—from 26% to 85%, depending on the problem—displayed a crucial operation, that of creating more than one complete, logical solution (Table 13.3). For the thinking aloud sample (Table 13.3) the proportion of respondents expressing self-referential thought aloud (i.e., making the statement that "Truth" is, of necessity, based on one's *choice* of a standard or a logic such that two mutually contradictory solutions may both be "True" solutions) ranged from 2% to 27%, depending on the problem. The proportion stating multiple goals toward which they were working while solving the problem ranged from 10% to 45%, depending on the problem. For comparison purposes the proportion showing formal operations is in Table 13.3: 2% to 60%, depending on the problem. Looking at evidence for self-referential thought, multiple goals, and multiple solutions, from 2% to 85.3% of adult subjects showed *some* evidence of postformal thought, and 2% to 60% showed formal operational thought.

We concluded that the operations considered part of self-referential, relativistic postformal thought were present to some extent in these analyses based on two independent subject samples and both nomothetic and ideographic (Sinnott, 1989c) analyses. (In addition, self-referential operations were also evident in a third sample of teachers interviewed by Lee, 1987.) Because of this consistency of results, this research question will not be given any more attention in this chapter. It appears that there is evidence for the existence of self-referential Piagetian postformal operations in adults, although individual differences are large and operations do not appear to represent a "stage" in the traditional Piagetian sense (Kramer, 1983).

Table 13.3
Evidence for Postformal Operations during Thinking Aloud and Standard Administration

Thinking Aloud *

	ABC	CAMP	BR	WK	VC
Have formal operations:	60%	57%	2%	30%	37%
Use self-referential thought:	10%	2%	27%	15%	7%
State multiple goals:	10%	12%	45%	15%	30%

Standard Administration

	ABC	VC	WK	CAKE	BR	POW
One solution	68.4%	29.2%	28.3%	11.3%	20.8%	27.4%
More than one solution	25.9%	68.4%	65.4%	85.3%	75.5%	64.3%

*before probe

Table 13.4
Simple Correlations between Blood Pressure and Problem Solving*

Systolic pressure level (N = 54)	
Time to complete ABC	.37
Passing WK	-.22
Use a formal solution for CAKE	-.32
Systolic change (12 years) (N = 15)	
Time to complete WK	.45
Passing VC	.46
Diastolic pressure level (N = 54)	
Time to complete BR	-.29
Importance of ABC	.26
BR	.27
POW	.32
Diastolic change (12 years) (N = 54)	
Time to complete BR	-.45
Passing BR	-.28
POW	-.28
Importance of WK	.36
BR	.29

* standard administration, significant at .05 level

Study 2: Do Physical Variables Such as Health or Other Cognitive Variables Such as Memory Relate to Self-Referential Thought?

To address the first part of this question, a correlational model was used to relate data on file for blood pressure (our chosen first attempt at a concrete operationalization of a physical health variable) to problem-solving data. To address the second part of this question, a correlational model was used to relate data on file from laboratory-type memory tasks and naturalistic-type memory tasks to problem-solving data. Problem solving was assessed with six problems during standard administration procedures only (and not during thinking aloud) in analyses reported here; the complete memory and blood pressure data of thinking aloud administration respondents were not available at the time of analysis, so the N in these analyses is smaller (see Table 13.4).

Measures

Casual systolic and diastolic blood pressure was measured during the respondents' general physical examination, given each visit, and before venipuncture or any other invasive procedure. Pressure was measured in both arms at the level of the brachial artery by physicians using mercury sphygmomanometers with standard-sized cuffs (14 cm × 52 cm). This took place on the morning of the first day of testing during each visit while participants were in a seated position. The right arm pressure was used for analyses. Right-left pressures were very highly correlated.

Problem-solving variables included the following: time to first solution (nearest minute); number of logical solutions, passing in a formal operational sense, scored P/F (Inhelder & Piaget, 1958); perceived importance of the problem, scored on a 1 (unimportant) to 5 (very important) scale; and whether the respondent created both a practical/naturalistic and an abstract sort of solution (scored yes-no). Number of solutions, practical versus abstract paradigm shift, and passing formally are the scorable variables in this standard administration format that are relevant to postformal operations.

Analyses

Blood Pressure and Problem Solving. Systolic and diastolic levels at three points about 6 years apart and the changes in pressure from the first of the three times to another were available for analysis. It was expected that higher blood pressure, as one index of poor health, would be positively related to time spent in solving a problem (due to health and stress factors) and perceived problem importance (stress factors), and negatively related to performance (health factor). The blood pressure variables were correlated with each problem-solving variable for each of the six problems.

For most of the variables there was no significant relation, partly due to the seriously reduced *n* (see Table 13.4). However, there were some significant relations that suggested that the overall question should be pursued in future work. These results were not always as hypothesized (see Table 13.4). High or increasing systolic pressure was positively related to time to complete certain problems of a more abstract type, while high or increasing diastolic pressure was negatively related to time to complete a problem of an everyday type. Systolic pressure was negatively related to formally passing two of the problems, but systolic pressure *change* was positively related to formally passing a third problem. Diastolic pressure change was negatively related to formally passing the everyday forms of the two problems. Both diastolic pressure and diastolic change were positively related to the perceived importance of problem. The number of significant simple correlations was above a chance level. However, when multiple regressions were performed with age entered first and blood pressure second, only two results remained significant. Therefore, it was concluded that there was no evidence for a blood pressure parameter for these performance variables. Other operational definitions of health may lead to different results, however.

Memory and Problem Solving. Two types of memory tests were given to problem-solving respondents: a naturalistic memory test (Sinnott, 1986) and a laboratory-type memory/response time test. In addition, a Wechsler Adult Intelligence Scale Vocabulary test (WAIS-V) and a Benton Visual Retention Test were given. A metamemory test was also included in Sinnott's test. The naturalistic memory component included 13 pencil-and-paper test items typed in random order, which required recall or recognition of events of the test experience. Subjects were randomly assigned to Set A items or Set B items (similar in purpose but differing in content). There was no time limit. Respondents spent from about 10 to 20 minutes alone in the room and answered the memory questions. The second test session (Time 2) was given from 7 to 10 days later by telephone. The experimenter called the respondents at a location and, sometimes, at a time selected by the respondent. Virtually all the respondents participated at Time 2, which indicated to us that dropouts would not create a problem. At Time 2, respondents received both A and B items in counterbalanced order. At Time 2, the item set that had been given the first time was repeated, augmented by a second 13-item set of the same type as the first. The metamemory items asked for an absolute rating of memory ability, a rating of age-comparative ability, and a rating of recent change in ability, all scored on a 5-point scale. The naturalistic test yielded a total score, and five subscale scores of interest measuring recall, recognition, prospective memory, action memory, and incidental memory. A similar set of scores was obtained a week to 10 days later.

The laboratory memory test included a measure of *immediate free recall* (IMFR), consisting of a demand to report as many nouns as possible on paced lists previously viewed. After the immediate recall task and an interpolated task, *delayed free recall* ("report as many words as possible from the previous IMFR list") was given. Finally, for *delayed recognition*, the IMFR list words and 12 distractor words were shown, one at a time, The task was to state whether each word had already been presented. The laboratory test therefore gave scores for immediate free recall, delayed free recall (measures were total words and words correct), and a measure of delayed recognition.

WAIS vocabulary subtest (WAIS-V) is part of the Wechsler Adult Intelligence Scale (WAIS; Wechsler, 1955), and involves defining 40 words. The resulting raw score of 0–2 for each word reflects the respondent's understanding of the words. The second cognitive test, the Benton Visual Retention Test (BVRT; Benton, 1963) is a nonverbal memory test made up of 10 designs each having one or more figures. The respondent inspects each design for 10 seconds and then reproduces it from memory. The measure is the total errors on all 10 designs. The WAIS-V and BVRT in various forms were administered individually during a single session, and were repeated approximately every 6 years.

Table 13.5 is a summary of the numerous significant correlations between

Table 13.5

Summary of Significant Results: Correlations between Problem Solving and Memory*

1. The more illustrated the problem the more it related to everyday memory.

2. Memory was most often related to importance, time to solve, and number of solutions.

3. Number of solutions was positively related to memory performance, most often for BR and VC, least often for ABC and CAKE.

4. Time to solve was positively related to memory especially for WK, least for ABC and VC.

5. The strongest relations were at Time 1.

6. Metamemory related positively to problem solving on the few occasions when relations were found.

7. Action memory was the scale most positively related to problem solving.

8. The worse the everyday memory, and the better the lab memory, the more important solving problems was judged to be, especially for ill structured ones.

9. Total (delayed) word recall (lab task) related positively to number of solutions for VC, POW.

10. WAIS vocabulary and BVRT performance related positively to solving logically and creatively.

*.01 level, standard administration

memory and problem-solving variables in this sample of 210 respondents reflecting the full adult age spectrum. The first seven entries relate to naturalistic memory, number 9 relates to lab memory, and number 10 relates to the WAIS and Benton tests. It was concluded that memory of all sorts played a major role in postformal self-referential thought. More work is needed to determine the memory components and the problem contexts most related to performance.

Study 3: How Do Goal Clarity and Heuristic Availability Relate to Self-Referential Problem-Solving Performance?

In earlier work (Sinnott, 1985, 1989c), based on the thinking of Sweller (1983) and Sweller and Levine (1982), I described the relationships one might logically find between *goal clarity* and *heuristic availability*, in various combinations, and problem-solving variables of the sort I measured. These combinations and hypothesized relations are in Table 13.6 taken from Sinnott (1985). The idea was to begin to clarify the role of self-referential postformal operations in problem solving using traditional problem-solving terms.

The reader might keep in mind that goal clarity and heuristic availability are analog rather than digital constructions in real life. Goals are more or less clear; heuristics are more or less available. Here they have been artifically dichotomized for purposes of preliminary experimental tests. In retrospect this may not be a good strategy since it is not clear, for example, where on the continuum of clarity individuals cross the line between what for them is a "clear" goal and what for them is a "not clear" goal. However, due to practical constraints, we compromised in the solution of this metaproblem, and decided on the temporary use of a dichotomy.

Two hypotheses from Table 13.6 were selected for the first tests of the overall relations in Question 3. The data from standard administration respondents (a sample balanced for age) were used.

Hypothesis 1: If a respondent has an available heuristic (clear algorithm or method of moving toward a particular goal) and uses it to successfully move toward a clear goal, he or she will use *that* heuristic for every problem at hand that can be construed to be remotely similar; that is, he or she will give them *all* clear goals. This tests one prediction for situation 1 in Table 13.6.

One way of addressing this question was to see if respondents did see the problems as similar to one another, and then to see if they used the same heuristic to work out each of them. From the taped thinking aloud interviews we saw that the great majority of respondents saw a pattern of similarity to the problems, namely that four of six standard administration problems were combinatorial problems. Those respondents who got more abstract, well-structured (Churchman, 1971) combinatorial problems first (like ABC) had virtually only one way to reach a solution (and the only goal), namely combinatorial logic. If they passed, they used it. Consequently, the operationalization of the independent variable for situation 1 in Table 13.6 (condition 1 of the independent variable

Table 13.6
Expected Relations of Perceived Goal Clarity and Availability of Heuristic to Some Dimensions of Strategy, Problem Space, and Performance on Well-Structured Problems, and Skills Needed

Clarity of Any One Goal*	Availability of Learned Heuristic/Algorithm	Probable Strategy
1) Clear	Available	Use learned heuristic or algorithm. Performance on well-structured problems should be good if persons prefer this approach. Seeing problems this way is related to youth and good skills. Small problem space.
2) Clear	Unavailable	Use Means-end analysis. Medium problem space. If performance is poor on well-structured problems by solvers who prefer this strategy, it is due to time-consuming nature of strategy to find a heuristic. Seeing problems this way is related to poor skills. Train for skills to improve performance.
3) Unclear	Available	Use learned heuristic/algorithm and assume that goal is "whatever is yielded by that process". Small problem space. If performance is poor on well-structured problems by solvers who prefer this strategy, error probably due to "not having the concept"; performance may be rapid. Seeing problems this way may be related to aging-related decline. Train for flexibility to improve performance.
4) Unclear	Unavailable	Trial and error responding and search for positive feedback, or decision about nature of problem; hypothesis testing for positive feedback from system to verify rules/goal; problem "solved" when an elected goal produces usable results within an accepted belief system. Very large problem space. Solvers capable of these strategies may make errors on well-structured problems because: 1) they see more options than the task designer did; and 2) they take too long. Seeing problems this way is related to maturity. Those who can reach a logical solution under these conditions can also do so under any of the other conditions in the Table.

*May be examined in terms of subgoals or overall problem goal.

= "clear goal, available heuristic") was "formally passed ABC when given first," or "formally pass VC (the next most well-structured problem) first." Performance of "ABC first, pass" versus "ABC first, fail" groups on the other problems was compared using Age × Group Status ANOVAs. "ABC first, pass" groups were more likely to pass VC later, but no other results were significant. In contrasting "VC first, pass" with "VC first, fail" groups on performance on later problems, the "VC first, pass" respondents proved more likely to pass BR and POW.

Results were interpreted to mean that the hypothesis was supported to some minimal extent. Seeing ABC or VC, given first, as "clear goal/available heuristic" problems led to other problems being solved using the same heuristic, even if they were naturalistic problems. (However, this learning mechanism seemed to have its limits. The BR problem, which made the most naturalistic, ill-structured (Churchman, 1971) demands, usually was not solved spontaneously using the abstract combinatorial strategy, even if that strategy was well entrenched.) A single, simple, abstract approach became the dominant problem-solving style, and there were few postformal operations, and (by definition) a small problem space (Newell & Simon, 1972). How quickly we "get in a rut" even in a set of six problems, and what a tribute this is to the efficiency of our processing. Of course, more *complex postformal* processing is not often seen under such conditions.

Parenthetically, it quickly became clear that those who received a more naturalistic (ill-structured) problem first (by randomized partial counterbalancing) focused on the *practical* aspects and the *uniqueness* of the situation in subsequent problems. This supported the hypothesis in a general way, but was not very amenable to quantification. "Did they do something similar?" became too much of a judgment call. These respondents were more likely to appear deficient in formal logical skills and to "fail" Piagetian logical problems. Since everyday adult life presents a learning experience that teaches us to expect ill-structured naturalistic problems, it does not seem surprising that older adults then do "less well" on well-structured laboratory problem solving than younger adults, who are learning to view problems abstractly in schools. In summary, there is some limited evidence that strategies predicted for situation 1 in Table 13.6 were found in these respondents' transcripts.

Hypothesis 2. If a respondent can use an abstract combinatorial logic on the BR problem (the most ill-structured one) presented first in the set of six problems, then he or she can use that strategy on all the other (less ill-structured) problems. This tests the last strategy prediction for situation 4 in Table 13.6. A series of Age × Pass BR status ANOVAs did not support this hypothesis. As noted above, almost all respondents who got BR first, even those who chose to use abstract combinatorial logic to solve it, tended to focus on the uniqueness of subsequent problem situations. This did not lend itself to the consistent *use* of formal combinatorial logic, whatever the respondent *could* have done. Probes could demonstrate whether respondents *could* use such logic if requested to do so. Such data are being gathered. If they *could* indeed do so, it would support the "large problem space" prediction in Table 13.6, situation 4.

For this section we attempted to test two of the many predictions made about the effects of goal clarity and heuristic availability on strategy and use of postformal operations. Further work is needed, of course, to clarify the role of postformal operations in problem solving using traditional problem-solving terms. Goal clarity and heuristic availability had a limited effect on strategy and the use of Sinnott's self-referential, relativistic postformal operations.

Study 4: How Do Manipulations of (a) Problem Context, (b) Probe Questions, and (c) Emotion, Intention, and Mindwandering Relate to Problem-Solving Performance, Especially Postformal Problem-Solving Performance?

This study was an attempt to vary several parameters that seemed likely to influence the extent to which respondents used self-referential operations.

Problem context. Six formal operational problems were given to each respondent. In the thinking aloud administration, for five of those, the structure of the problem demanded (on a logical level) that respondents make combinations. However, as seen in Table 13.1, the context of problems differed, ranging from very well-structured and abstract to very ill-structured and naturalistic. It was hypothesized, within subjects, that postformal operations would be produced more often for the naturalistic, ill-structured combinatorial problems.

Sinnott (1984) showed the influence of context on individual postformal operations in a preliminary study. Context was also influential in the current data from both standard administration (Table 13.7) and thinking aloud administration (Tables 13.8 and 13.9, before probe; also see Table 13.3). The more naturalistic the context, the less respondents passed formally and the more they showed postformal thoughts, operationalized as self-referential thought, multiple goals, multiple solutions, and multiple methods.

Respondents very often made use of "noncognitive" processes to solve problems, as seen in Table 13.10. As many as 84% used processes not usually included in (and generally *excluded* from) problem-solving models. Context, in thinking aloud data, also influenced the presence or absence in protocols of descriptors of visual versus verbal representation, mindwandering statements (i.e., not related specifically to the task at hand), evaluative statements, emotional expressions, and respondents' use of their own personal history to shed light on the problem at hand. These were all elements that had been found in earlier work to be used in solving naturalistic logic-based problems. Table 13.10 has these data and the correlations between noncognitive processes and passing formally, number of goals, and number of methods. The later subsection on age effects has additional context × age effects.

We concluded that the manipulation of context strongly influences the occur-

Table 13.7
Context Effects: Percent of Age Subsamples Using Multiple Solutions for WK, BR, and POW, Standard Administration

	WK	**BR**	**POW**
One Solution			
20's, 30's (n = 37)	40.5	13.8	16.2
40's, 50's, 60's (n = 109)	24.5	18.2	32.1
70's, 80's (n = 52)	31.4	32.7	32.6
More than one solution			
20's, 30's	59.4	86.1	83.7
40's, 50's, 60's	71.9	81.7	65.1
70's, 80's	61.1	63.6	59.6

rence of formal and postformal thought. Problem context manipulations also are related to changes in the style of problem solving in ways that impact on variables as diverse as creativity, emotionality, and logical correctness.

Probes. In the thinking aloud administration, three of the six problems (ABC, BR, and POW) were followed by several structured probing statements. These probes were designed to: (a) make explicit demands for postformal thinking by asking for several solutions, several goals, and several ways of seeing the problem; (b) offering formal operational and nonformal operational solutions based on smaller and larger problem spaces and asking respondents to judge the truth and logical correctness of solutions; (c) demonstrating the possibility of self-referential statements in order to prime respondents to use some of their own; and (d) getting respondents to reflect on their thinking processes. Products for any one problem could therefore be scored *before* the probes when, so far, the respondent had been the only speaker and thinker, and *after* the probe, when the respondent had had more input. Table 13.9 has the results of probing. Probing increased the rate of formally passing to some extent. Depending on problem context, probes increased the use of multiple methods and self-referential thought greatly. We concluded that probes are valuable in bringing out more postformal thought than would normally appear. However, it would be interesting to know what militates against the spontaneous expression of postformal ideas so that probes are necessary for so many respondents.

Influence of emotion, intuition, attention. During thinking aloud administration, equal numbers of respondents were given one of four sorts of experiences in addition to the general task of thinking aloud while solving problems. One group was offered a free candy bar (which was to be eaten later), an action that led to a more positive mood (Isen & Shalker, 1982); another group was asked to "create as many good solutions as possible"; a third group was told it was acceptable to "let your mind wander, get off the topic, if you feel it will help you solve the problems"; and a control group was not told anything else. These

Table 13.8
Summary of Significant Effects of Problem Context MANOVAs, Thinking Aloud
Data

Formal operational response: Most often on ABC, CAMP, least on BR

Number of goals: Most on BR, least on ABC, CAMP, WK

Postformal, self-referential statements (spontaneous):   Most on BR, least on CAMP, VC

Visual representation: Most on ABC, POW, least on CAMP, WK, VC

Verbal representation: Most on BR, POW, least on CAMP, VC

Mindwandering: Most on BR, POW, least on CAMP, VC

Evaluative statement: Most on BR, POW, least on CAMP, VC

Emotional statements: Most on BR, least on ABC

Mention of other related personal history: Most on BR, POW, least on VC

Table 13.9
Evidence for the Utility of Probing for Postformal Operations, Thinking Aloud Data

	ABC	BR	POW
Percent Passing			
(formally)			
Before probe	60%	2%	30%
After probe	77%	20%	52%
Multiple Methods			
Before probe	20%	27%	30%
After probe	82%	62%	55%
Self-Referential Statements			
Before probe	10%	27%	17%
After probe	67%	80%	85%

slightly varying comments were made like ordinary conversation prior to the start of the task. We reasoned that in a test situation, people might need a little permission to loosen up and be themselves, and that the statements, if intensified significantly by graded steps, might at *some* point be intense enough to enrich the general process of problem solving by suggesting to respondents that they use the helpful process components found in earlier studies (Sinnott, 1983).

These changes had some effect on some elements of the problem-solving process for certain problems as demonstrated by ANCOVA analyses controlling for age. Five effects reached significance and six effects were marginal (p = .06 to .10; Table 13.11). Generally, BR, POW, and WK were the most likely problems to be influenced. The processes most likely to be influenced were passing formally, number of goals, and number of methods to goal, although use of self-referential thought, emotion, and personal experience were also influenced. For the first three processes, improving mood by giving a gift of candy generally led to better scores, and encouraging more production led to poorer scores. The mindwandering condition was related to more self-referential thought, but not to more daydreaming. (Parenthetically, respondents never seemed aware that they were mindwandering, and insisted they did not do so.) The most emotion was generated by the control condition. The most reflection on personal history was in the productivity group. The instructions did not affect representational style or self-evaluation.

The fact that these manipulations had any effect at all was surprising to us. The effect of positive mood was similar to that found by Isen and Shalker (1982). It makes intuitive sense that focusing attention (even focusing on mindwandering or on being productive) would increase tension and lead to paradoxically opposite effects, as happens in the analog condition of being told to "Quick! Relax!" This suggests that the greatest number of solutions might be created by those who were told to "do nothing," who then relaxed attention. Focusing attention on producing a lot apparently leads to reaching back into personal history, perhaps for ideas. More work in this area of preconditions for self-referential postformal thought and for the use of various processes in ill-structured, naturalistic problem solving would help us to understand the parameters of using certain strategies, as well as what we might do to improve an individual's processing along some particular dimension. It is an interesting thought that, if these results are supported by replications, we may need to provide less intense demands and more time and rewards for quiet reflection to problem solvers engaged in complex decision making if we want complex thought to occur. This knowledge would have consequences for social policy, parent-child relations, organizational administration, and world peace.

Study 5: Are There Life-Span Age Differences in Performance?

There usually are two reasons for asking this question: to study decline, and to study style of processing. Age differences also might be seen as negative or positive differences; one group could be seen as worse than another, or both groups might be shown to be adaptive to different demands. The question was posed here to examine both style and decline; that is, to look at both positive and negative differences. Earlier work found the middle-aged respondents to be the most creative and productive overall (Sinnott, 1984, 1989c), but with wide variations from problem to problem (Sinnott, 1989c). Subjects giving the most self-referential truth statements were age 41, 68, 71, 26, 61, and 78 in descending order (Sinnott, 1989c).

Figure 13.1 shows the mean number of solutions, during standard administration, by age and problem. The standard administration group had a mean age of 57.61 years, range 23–89. In this sample, the young respondents created the largest number of solutions, especially in the Cake and BR problems. Table 13.12 shows the mean age of persons formally passing 0 to 6 of the 6 problems, standard administration. Respondents who formally passed most often were younger, $t_{0,1}$ versus $_{5,6}(54) = 2.30$, p .05. Table 13.13 shows the significant correlations between age and elements of problem solving during thinking aloud (group mean age = 54.15 years, range 25–82) and standard administrations.

A difference was apparent, which might be interpreted nomothetically as a decline. However, in what specific mechanisms during problem solving did the differences become noticeable? Were they related to a style difference that might be adaptive overall? We looked at the thinking aloud processes linearly related

Table 13.10

Significant Correlations among Some "Noncognitive" and Problem-Solving Variables, by Problem, Thinking Aloud Data

General Description of Use of "Noncognitive" Processes

50% to 75% incorporated mindwandering into solutions
38% to 63% used personal history
16% to 63% used emotional responses
42% to 84% used evaluative judgments
Respondents used both verbal and visual representation systems
Problems judged "interesting" led to fewer self-referential statements
"Emotional" and "attention-getting" problems were not solved with formal operations

	Pass						#Methods						#Goals					
	ABC	CAMP	VITC	WK	POW	BR	ABC	CAMP	VITC	WK	POW	BR	ABC	CAMP	VITC	WK	POW	BR
EMOTION																		
ABC	-.32						-.40											
CAMP		-.32				.34								.34				
VITC					.35	.63					.42			.62		.32		
WK														.51				
POW					.36												.33	
BR	.37					.54					.47	.54		.43		.44		
MINDWANDERING																		
ABC							-.33											
CAMP																		
VITC			-.32												-.39			
WK						.53	.34				.38					-.33		
POW																	-.32	
BR							-.42											
PERSONAL HISTORY																		
ABC	-.34	-.34															.61	.40
CAMP	-.49	-.41																
VITC																		
WK				-.36														
POW					-.33							.43						

190

BR						.36			.43						
EXPERIENCE WITH PROBLEM														
ABC	-.48													
CAMP		.34					.46	-.35	.55		.55		.33		
VITC							-.45								
WK	-.38			-.43	-.41		-.37	-.33							
POW							-.37	-.33			-.33				
SELF EVALUATION														
ABC			.49		.37	.49		.34				.37	.40		
CAMP					.40	.78		.34					.44		
VITC															
WK				.35		.56									
POW			.47			.54									
BR			.41		.49	.43		.34					.41		
REPRESENTATIONAL STYLE														
VISUAL														
ABC	.38	-.47					-.33						.33		
CAMP													.44		
VITC								.56	.37	.37					
WK										.35					
POW													.41		.36
BR									.51	.37				.47	
VERBAL														
ABC	.39	.38								.35					
CAMP															
VITC							-.43	.32				.33	-.39		
WK				.42					.37				.34		
POW															
BR	.33								.37	.36					
KINESTHETIC														
ABC		.44					.41		-.34			.38			
CAMP	-.67							-.40							
VITC	-.67							-.40							
WK	-.67														
POW	-.41							-.40							
BR	-.53							-.39	-.34				.34		

191

Table 13.11
Summary of Significant and Marginal ANCOVAs after Manipulation of Mood, Productivity, and Mindwandering (age covaried)

Significant Variables		Means			
		Mood	Control	Productivity	Mindwandering
Number of methods-BR	$F_{(3,34)}=3.822$, p .01	1.78	1.27	1.11	1.20
First solution logical? BR (1=no 2=yes)	$F_{(3,29)}=3.862$, p .01	1.29	1.00	1.63	1.56
Number of goals-VC	$F_{(3,35)}=2.886$, p .04	1.56	1.45	1.00	1.10
Refer to personal history-ABC	$F_{(3,34)}=2.740$, p .05	1.11	0.45	1.33	0.20
Marginal Variables					
Pass formally-WK	$F_{(3,34)}=2.529$, p .07	1.56	1.27	1.00	1.40
Pass formally-POW	$F_{(3,34)}=2.616$, p .06	1.50	1.36	1.00	1.40
Number of goals-WK	$F_{(3,35)}=2.342$, p .09	1.00	1.45	1.10	1.10
Number of methods-POW	$F_{(3,34)}=2.246$, p .10	1.22	0.82	0.44	1.00
Self-referential thoughts-POW	$F_{(3,35)}=2.325$, p .09	0.11	0.00	0.20	0.50
Emotional expressions-POW	$F_{(3,34)}=2.426$, p .08	0.67	1.73	0.67	0.30

Figure 13.1
Mean Number of Solutions by Problem and Age

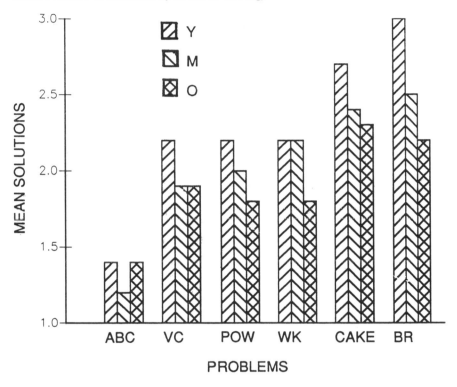

to age to help address that question. The older the respondent was, the more goals he or she had for the most naturalistic BR problem and the less likely he or she was to pass formally. The older the respondent, the more likely he or she usually was to speak in a "nonspecific" representational style rather than using concretized predicates that were verbal, visual, or kinesthetic. Older respondents were more likely to use personal history in solving the very abstract ABC problem and very *unlikely* to look to prior personal experience to solve VC, a slightly more naturalistic problem. There were also significant negative age correlations for self-referential thought instances for ABC, CAMP, BR, and WK. Mindwandering on POW was positively related to age.

We next looked at the standard administration processes linearly related to age. Significant correlations were smaller in magnitude. Older respondents rated WK "less important" and BR and POW as "more important," and also formally passed BR, POW, and VC less frequently. They created significantly fewer solutions for three problems this time: WK, BR, and POW. They finished solving WK and POW more quickly than the young respondents.

These nomethetic age-related results present a confusing picture but do seem

Table 13.12
Mean Age of Respondents Formally Passing Various Numbers of Problems, Standard Administration

	Mean Age
Fail all 6	60.40 years
Pass 1	63.22
Pass 2	57.89
Pass 3	57.18
Pass 4	56.23
Pass 5	54.62
Pass 6	50.00
Mean of sample	**57.61**

consistent with one interpretation. On less abstract problems, despite wide individual variability, older respondents more often tended to focus on: (a) finding one general, working solution path that could be used to compromise (i.e., somewhat fill all the problem demands even if not completely filling any); (b) finishing fast; and (c) ignoring detail, after making action (but not verbal) decisions about the gist of the problem. Expansiveness of thought was more often occasioned by the more naturalistic problems (BR and POW). This pattern would not fit all persons who are chronologically older, but certainly did fit the older respondent in the in-depth ideographic analyses presented at the 1985 Harvard Conference (Sinnott, 1985). That respondent's main goal was to identify a *good process*, after which he left that problem to hurry on to the next.

The basic strategy identified here could represent both decline and adaptive coping. Decline could be manifest in a husbanding of "resources" such as memory, time, effort, and words, due to dwindling "capacities." The meaning of these terms has never been made clear, however (Salthouse, 1988). On the other hand, the entire style could represent an adaptive choice, given that many mature adults in this study and as well as others have said that it is hard to be more concrete about a solution until specific feedback is received as the process is put into effect. For example, the answer (the "solution") that I would give you right now, without real feedback, would depend on the view I, the problem solver, chose to take about what will happen next to the system as a whole. A number of results could flow from the system's response. I know too much to

Table 13.13
Significant Correlations between Age and Problem Solving

Think Aloud Administration

Pass BR formally	-.29
Number of goals-BR	.32
Use of verbal representation	
POW	.28
BR	-.27
Use of kinesthetic representation	
WK	-.29
CAMP	-.44
Use of personal history	
ABC	.37
Prior experience with this problem	
VC	-.25
Mindwandering POW	.33
Self-referential thought	
ABC	-.31
CAMP	-.25
BR	-.29
WK	-.40

Standard Administration

Number of solutions to POW	-.14
Number of solutions to BR	-.15
Number of solutions to WK	-.12
Pass BR formally	.16
Pass POW formally	-.14
Pass VC formally	-.11
Importance of BR	.17
Importance of POW	.22
Importance of WK	-.11
Time to finish WK	-.13
Time to finish POW	-.19

suppose only one feedback outcome, so I can only give you with certainty the process that *should* lead to a useful place of one kind or another. Beyond that, I am just guessing and arbitrarily choosing the parameters of the problem.

It may make more sense to hypothesize an adaptive move, using mechanisms based on complex thought, to explain this age difference in style than to hypothesize a decline in unspecified "resources" in otherwise healthy persons. It would be fair to hypothesize that decline causes these differences only if the respondent, followed over the time course of a real problem episode and given feedback in real terms, failed to integrate it into the problem's solution. Data from Arenberg's (1982) "poisoned food" problems can be seen in this way.

The purpose of this chapter was to describe several analytic attempts to understand the nature of postformal thought, viewed within Sinnott's model. This brief discussion will be used to summarize the results of the five studies, to relate them to earlier work and theory in several domains, and to suggest the future directions this work might take. Results will be related to Sinnott's model, to ill-structured problem solving, to postformal studies, to adult life-span development, and to basic research of other sorts.

SUMMARY OF RESULTS

Is there evidence for Sinnott's postformal self-referential operations? Earlier studies as well as the current studies have reliably demonstrated that the operations can be found in the thinking aloud texts or inferred from the products of standard administration testing sessions. Up to 85% of adult respondents gave evidence of any one operation. Adult thinkers apparently do go beyond formal thought to a constructionist view of truth, at least within the limits of this operationalization.

Do physical functioning variables or other cognitive variables such as memory relate to self-referential thought? When physical functioning was operationalized in terms of blood pressure level or blood pressure change, and age was controlled, there was little or no relationship. This does not rule out effects for general health or for other specific physical-functioning variables. As for cognitive variables, whether memory was measured with naturalistic items or with laboratory tests, relations with problem solving were found. The many significant results in Table 13.5 could be the source of intriguing hypotheses. Complex webs of motivation, judgment, speed, adaptive naturalistic skills, and adaptive laboratory skills seemed to be interwoven with problem solving and self-referential thought.

How do goal clarity and heuristic availability relate to problem-solving performance? Operationalizing goal clarity and heuristic availability as either-or phenomena to simplify the situation may have led to our own undoing in the two initial hypotheses tested. There was only minimal support for the hypotheses in their original form, but there was a suggestion of support for an expanded form of the hypotheses. The original hypotheses (Table 13.6) were written from the experimenter's point of view, whereas they *should* have been written from the respondent's point of view. (The author, in this case, was displaying a situation-specific lack of self-referential cognitive operations.) From these data it appears that, whether the experimenter considered a problem ill-structured or not, if a respondent experienced the goal as clear and had a heuristic to use, future problems in that set were handled the same way; that is, goals seen as the same type of goal as problem number 1, with the problem amenable to the use of the same heuristic, as predicted in Table 13.6, situation 1. Apparently, probes are needed to adequately test the Table 13.6, situation 4, hypothesis.

Does manipulation of problem context matter? It does, to a great extent, in that respondents were more likely to show self-referential thought on ill-structured problems with naturalistic contexts. Context also influenced use of processes like emotion and mindwandering.

Did probe questions uncover additional evidence of postformal self-referential thought? They did, possibly because respondents did not think to vocalize these truth decisions without a request, since they were so automatic. Probes did not seem to elicit postformal thought in all respondents, though; even when shown solutions as they might be handled by a postformal thinker, some respondents maintained that such solutions were simply wrong.

Did minimal priming experiences influence performance? Yes, they did. Improving mood and relaxing demands helped, while focusing attention hurt self-referential thought. Coupled with the results related to memory, it seems there may be two styles available: (a) relaxed, upbeat, open attention; or (b) goal-oriented, focused attention, with reliance on memory. It remains to be seen if solutions created by the two groups are qualitatively different.

Are there age differences in performance? Differences were found in the performance of formal and postformal operations. There also were differences on the parameters related to problem solving. Differences suggest that postformal operations may be part of an adaptive coping style in which the older person wisely limits efforts on a hypothetical problem when denied feedback concerning the next state of the system. August de la Pena (personal communication, June, 1988) also discussed such a mechanism, in this case a sensory one, which filters out irrelevant data in old age.

RELATION TO EARLIER WORK

Only a limited number of points will be made in this chapter due to space considerations. These will focus briefly on Sinnott's postformal theory, problem solving, information processing, and life span cognitive development within a General Systems Theory framework.

Regarding postformal self-referential thought, we see support for the model. We do not see support for a stage of postformal operations as in Piagetian theory; or, rather, we see no more support for a postformal stage than for a formal stage. A different set of processes—self-referential truth decisions and ordering of formal operations—do occur. A key difference is in the use of logic: What *is* logical is a matter for *logical* decision. This key difference is not found at other Piagetian stages or described by other postformal theories but is intrinsic to the logic of modern physics and is compatible with the ideas of General Systems Theory.

The utility of postformal skills is shown in the solution of ill-structured, naturalistic problems. Daily life is full of such problems; the postformal thinker seems eminently equipped to tackle them. Work on postformal problem solving fits the philosophical literature on inquiring systems (Churchman, 1971), the concept problem-solving literature, and selected artificial intelligence approaches (Newell & Simon, 1972). The postformal thinker seems to enlarge the problem space by using operations not strictly considered "cognitive" or "information-processing" by all writers, operations such as emotional reactions. This enlarged problem space enlarges the concept description and the permissible systems of logic available to the solver. Postformal thought is the mechanism for "satisf-icing" (Howard, 1983), choosing a "good enough" solution where no perfect solution is available. Since no perfect solution is available for many real-life problems, postformal skills would seem to prevent endless futile attempts at the solution of pressing problems. Therefore, these skills allow the mature adult to be practical and to take care of the tasks of family and work.

This means that the intelligent human is seen within Sinnott's model as an orchestrated living system that interacts with other systems and operates in interaction with them by General Systems Theory rules. In such a human living system, the emotions, cognitions, and intentions are not separate entities but rather feed information back and forth to each other. The other living human systems in the sphere of influence of the first also coordinate within themselves and between one another. They are social. It makes sense, then, for the problem-solving process to be influenced by many other personal, emotional, cognitive, and experiential factors. It also makes sense that the nature of truth should have some room for the impact of these other elements and the feedback from other thinkers, co-constructing truth together. In this study we intentionally established a situation where the person operates alone as a problem solver. He or she, when faced with an ill-structured problem, must decide alone about the nature of the problem space, and other factors. However, as Meacham and Emont (1989) have pointed out, in the real world other thinkers would be present to help the solver construct the nature of the problem and the goal. Testing a group—while more complicated—would point out even more clearly the use of self-referential operations in problem solving as several views of the nature of the task would be apparent. A systems approach—intrapersonally or interpersonally—would certainly enrich future studies.

FUTURE DIRECTIONS

Besides continuing the sort of analytical tasks begun in this chapter, future researchers need to address a basic question. Does having complex "postformal" skills matter in life? How do the tasks and skills we think of as complex adult thought, positive development in adulthood/aging, and postformal thought relate to traditional laboratory measures of cognition, to coping, to personality, and to physical functioning? What relation do complex adult thought, positive development during adulthood/aging, and postformal thought have to solution of real problems by real people? This means collecting data concerning real behavior used to validate postformal tasks. Applications to aging, education, the workplace, clinical work, marketing, and family life need to be made. Moreover, we need to understand more deeply the relations between postformal thought and emotion and overall cognitive competence.

Our mission now is to *refine* our ideas and *communicate* them to others. We need to:

1. Perfect the fine points of coding, task taxonomies, validation, and reliability of measures;
2. Demonstrate what the concepts we discuss are "good for"; this means that we need to outline the *limits* and *central features* of the concepts we use, and to understand *functioning* and all that it entails;
3. Work with teams who are willing to create (*and* obtain funding for) a research *program* focused on this area;
4. Bring in new investigators and fund them with start-up money; and
5. Address the valid and legitimate concerns of those coming from many areas in cognitive psychology and development by: relating our measures and concepts to standard or laboratory tasks of known characteristics; formulating problems that focus on current scientific or health concerns; collaborating with those who come from more traditional disciplines within psychology; and contrasting our ideas or methods with those that come from "wisdom," "information processing," and other areas within psychology.

NOTES

This research was supported in part by an NIA grant and by a faculty research grant from Towson State University. Thanks to David Arenberg, Ph.D., and to Donna Baumgartner, Debbi Johnson, Lena Phillips, Judith Plotz, June Sacktor, and Lisa Shanahan for their help.

REFERENCES

Arenberg, D. (1982). Changes with age in problem solving. In F. I. M. Craik & S. Trehub (Eds.), *Aging and cognitive processes* (pp. 221–235). New York: Plenum.

Bateson, G. (1979). *Mind and nature.* New York: Bantam.

Benton, A. L. (1963). *The Revised Visual Retention Test: Clinical and experimental applications* (3rd edition). New York: Psychological Corporation.

Churchman, C. (1971). *The design of inquiring systems: Basic concepts of systems and organizations.* New York: Basic Books.

Commons, M., Armon, C., Kohlberg, L., Richards, F., Grotzer, T., & Sinnott, J. D.

(Eds.). (1989). *Beyond formal operations III: Models and methods in the study of adult and adolescent thought*. New York: Praeger.

Commons, M., Richards, F., & Armon, C. (Eds.). (1984). *Beyond formal operations*. New York: Praeger.

Commons, M., Sinnott, J. D., Richards, F., & Armon, C. (Eds.). (1989). *Beyond formal operations II: Comparisons and applications of adolescent and adult developmental models*. New York: Praeger.

Hofstadter, D. (1979). *Godel, Escher, Bach: An eternal golden braid*. New York: Random House.

Howard, D. (1983). *Cognitive psychology*. New York: Macmillan.

Inhelder, B., & Piaget, J. (1958). *The growth of logical thinking from childhood to adolescence*. New York: Basic Books.

Isen, A., & Shalker, T. (1982). The effect of feeling state on evaluation of positive, neutral and negative stimuli: When you "accentuate the positive" do you "eliminate the negative"? *Social Psychology Quarterly, 45*, 58–63.

Kramer, D. (1983). Postformal operations? A need for further conceptualization. *Human Development, 26*, 91–105.

Lee, D. M. (1987, June). *Relativistic operations: A framework for conceptualizing teachers' everyday problem solving*. Paper presented at the Third Beyond Formal Operations Symposium at Harvard University: Positive Adult Development. Cambridge, MA.

Meacham, J., & Emont, N. C. (1989). The interpersonal basis of everyday problem solving. In J. D. Sinnott (Ed.), *Everyday problem solving: Theory and application* (pp. 7–23). New York: Praeger.

Newell, A., & Simon, H. (1972). *Human problem solving*. Englewood Cliffs, NJ: Prentice-Hall.

Salthouse, T. (1988). Paper presented at the Second Cognitive Aging Conference, Atlanta.

Shock, N. W., Andres, R. A., Arenberg, D., Costa, P. T., Jr., Greulich, R. C., Lakatta, E. W., & Tobin, J. (1985). *Normal human aging: The Baltimore Longitudinal Study of Aging*. Washington, DC: National Institutes of Health.

Sinnott, J. D. (1981). The theory of relativity: A metatheory for development? *Human Development, 24*, 293–311.

Sinnott, J. D. (Nov., 1983). *Individual strategies on Piagetian problems: A thinking aloud approach*. Paper presented at the Gerontological Society Conference, Boston, MA.

Sinnott, J. D. (1984). Postformal reasoning: The relativistic stage. In M. L. Commons, F. Richards, and C. Armon (Eds.), *Beyond formal operations: Late adolescent and adult cognitive development*. (pp. 298–325). New York: Praeger.

Sinnott, J. D. (1985). *The expression of postformal relativistic self-referential operations in everyday problem solving performance: Adult life span data*. Paper presented at the Second Beyond Formal Operations Symposium at Harvard University, Cambridge, MA.

Sinnott, J. D. (1986). Prospective/intentional everyday memory: Effects of age and passage of time. *Psychology and Aging, 1*, 110–116.

Sinnott, J. D. (Ed.). (1989a). *Everyday problem solving: Theory and applications*. New York: Praeger.

Sinnott, J. D. (1989b). General systems theory: A rationale for the study of everyday memory. In L. Poon, D. Rubin, & B. Wilson (Eds.), *Everyday cognition in adulthood and old age* (pp. 59–70). New York: Cambridge University Press.

Sinnott, J. D. (1989c). Lifespan relativistic postformal thought: Methodology and data from everyday problem solving studies. In M. Commons, J. Sinnott, F. Richards, & C. Armon (Eds.), *Beyond formal operations II: Comparision and applications of adolescent and adult developmental models* (pp. 239–278). New York: Praeger.

Sweller, J. (1983). Control mechanisms in problem solving. *Memory and Cognition, 11,* 32–40.

Sweller, J., & Levine, M. (1982). The effect of goal specificity on means-end analysis and learning. *Journal of Experimental Psychology: Learning, Memory and Cognition, 8,* 463–474.

Wechsler, D. (1955). *WAIS Manual. Wechsler Adult Intelligence Scale.* New York: Psychological Corporation.

Wolf, F. A. (1981). *Taking the quantum leap.* New York: Harper & Row.

14

What Do We Do to Help John? A Case Study of Postformal Problem Solving in a Family Making Decisions about an Acutely Psychotic Member

JAN D. SINNOTT

Postformal self-referential thought has been studied in a number of contexts (Commons, Richard, & Armon, 1984; Commons, Sinnott, Richards, & Armon, 1989; Sinnott, 1984, 1989a; 1989b; 1989c) but has not been examined frequently in clinical or mental health domains (Kramer & Bopp, 1989). This chapter applies ideas about the nature and parameters of postformal thought discussed elsewhere (Sinnott, 1989b, c) to the thinking process of an individual. This individual is part of a family faced with the very difficult real-life problem of what to do about a close relative experiencing a first-time acute paranoid episode. After presenting the case, the chapter is meant to do three things (very briefly, due to space limits): to illustrate the complex problem-solving process described by Sinnott in an emotion-laden ill-structured interpersonal domain; to capture and illustrate the interpersonal and emotional factors, described in more abstract problems by Sinnott in Chapter 13 (this volume), in a real, volatile family situation; and to illustrate how the presence or absence of postformal skills is associated with family members' views of the problem and themselves, as well as with the outcome for the identified patient and others. This chapter is not meant to be an analysis of the patient's or family's functioning except as it relates to cognitive processes.

The case described here is a real one. The names and identifying features related to this event have been altered sufficiently to preserve the anonymity of the individuals involved. Events have been described by a key participant who has given the author permission to retell the story here. The story was obtained through extensive interviews in person or by telephone and from notes and diary entries, both during and just after the event. Sample notes and entries are in the Appendix. The informant reviewed and approved this chapter.

The hypotheses proposed elsewhere (Commons et al., 1984; Sinnott, 1989 b, c; this volume) that postformal thought is personally and socially adaptive, that it can be modeled, that it includes many "noncognitive" elements, and that it can develop during middle adulthood are supported by this case study. Events associated with this case also suggest hypotheses about clinical ramifications of postformal thought, which can be tested empirically.

SUMMARY OF SOME CONCRETE FACTS ABOUT THE CASE

One peaceful afternoon, the main informant ("Jane") received a telephone call from her father, who lived hundreds of miles away. According to her father, her brother ("John"), who lived in the father's city, had been behaving very strangely. John was accusing family members of trying to get rid of him, making him sick, and plotting against him. Others were against him too, trying to control him, John said. The situation was at a crisis point.

This was very upsetting news for Jane for more than one reason. It was the first she had heard of this problem, as communication was not a strong skill for her family. Two weeks ago, for the first time, it had appeared that John was taking responsibility for his life. Only the previous week John had been examining familial relationships and trying to piece together family motives. John wanted to see Jane very much. Also, Jane and John had always been very close, although she was nearly a decade older than he. They were each others' emotionally closest relatives. For the better part of 30 years, John had experienced problems with drugs, alcohol, and dependence on his father, but had never experienced a psychotic break.

John's life seemed always to get worse. As a teen, John had been intensely hurt by his parents' destructive divorce, and he later had been a troubled participant in his father's second marriage, whereas Jane and an older brother had distanced themselves. Over and over again, John would be involved in some problem and his father would try to "handle" the situation, while his mother complained about them both and his stepmother complained about John. Jane felt very lucky to have escaped the family situation, but she felt helpless. She grieved over her brother's and family's pain.

Jane had planned a short visit with her father in a few days to keep family ties intact and to bring her children to see their grandfather. She had hoped for a peaceful visit, but that hope was rapidly fading with the phone call. Instead of feeling peaceful, she was going into the eye of the hurricane. However, Jane had always known she was the "invulnerable child" (Garmezy, 1976) who could cope and love, and that now it was time to take that role again. With children in tow, she headed for the plane, unsure of the reality of the situation or her brother's state.

Upon her arrival, she found that her father had already hospitalized John and was in a state of great anxiety himself. John's behavior had frightened their father seriously when John had sought refuge at the father's house, although John had not threatened others or himself. Since John refused the medication prescribed by a "well-reknowned" psychiatrist, the father, acting on the psychiatrist's advice, was certain that commitment was the only solution. John valued his freedom and was angry at his father's unilateral decision to hospitalize him and to commit him involuntarily. Even worse, John would be under control of a private psychiatrist whom John felt was not listening to him or sympathetic with him. John had seen the psychiatrist several years before but had refused treatment from him at that time and had felt antagonistic toward him. John's stepmother was glad he was out of the house. John's mother was distancing herself from the problems. The father pleaded with Jane to avoid John, the hospital, and the whole problem, and to pretend to her children that nothing was happening, so they could "have a good time." Jane was too upset about her brother to pretend that everything was normal, and intended to communicate with him unless the doctors disapproved. When they told her they had no objection, she drove at once to the hospital to visit and to find out some facts, determined to offer love and support to John.

When she arrived, she found that John was refusing to take the prescribed antipsychotic medication because he "needed to keep his mind clear." Clarity was needed, John said, because their father (with the private psychiatrist chosen by their father) had decided to try to involuntarily commit him. As a prelude to that action, the police were due to arrive momentarily to transfer John to a locked ward at a private hospital. His agitation was increasing. No one paid attention to what he said! Why wouldn't anyone listen to him? Even his family seemed to be plotting against him! Jane listened and talked, and tried to describe John's options to him. She told him she loved him and that he could count on her support. They discussed their "crazy family," and John became more calm and rational. Hours passed, and the police, whom they had feared would arrive, did not appear.

When night came, the staff made it known that a family member needed to stay overnight with John to insure that he would not leave the psychiatric ward. Jane said she would stay (she saw no other options); she drove the 40 minutes to her father's house, comforted her children and her father, argued against involuntarily commitment with her father, and drove back to the hospital. She urged John to take his medication to avoid commitment. John agreed to do so, but was concerned that he would not have a "clear" head to defend himself at the court hearing in the morning. Jane talked to him about the pros and cons of taking the medication, and they jointly decided that he should wait until after the hearing. That night she explored within herself many of her own terrifying issues about her childhood, as she tried to sleep, waited with John at the hospital and wondered how and in what ways she might be able to affect the commitment hearing in the morning.

In the morning she prompted her brother to tell the judge he would take the medication, and immediately before the hearing she negotiated with her father to delay the commitment proceedings. At the hearing, however, neither of these things occurred, and John was involuntarily committed for a week.

Jane spent the next 3 days trying to understand when (and if) a second commitment hearing was to be held (which would extend the commitment to a possible 90 days), trying to find a new psychiatrist, talking with John's current and prospective psychiatrist and therapists, and talking with John. She was unsure which of John's stories were true or the extent of his paranoia. She feared that involuntary commitment would destroy John's remaining threads of trust and self-esteem, but also feared that her father could not cope with John's release. She was looking for an ethical and practical solution to John's situation within continually shifting demands and expectations from both her brother and her father. She was concerned for her children—for their anxiety in the middle of this chaos and the lack of time she was spending with them. During this time she sustained herself through journal writing, meditation, and the support of a couple of close friends. John took the medication, established a relationship with a therapist, and seemed better, but no one would call off the second commitment hearing. Everyone else in the family seemed worse—more changeable, angry, and confused. The father and stepmother were frightened by the idea that if John were released he would want to stay with them. John lapsed into paranoia as the commitment hearing was on, then off, and then on again, regardless of how he behaved as a patient. It appeared that Jane was unable to comfort John, find another doctor acceptable to her father, penetrate the legal system, or shift her father's perspective from involuntary commitment to voluntary commitment. She grew depressed. Everyone grew more confused and less able to cope. In this highly charged emotional atmosphere, it became hard to say whose reality was "real" and whose goals merited attention.

Finally, the second hearing took place, and John was voluntarily committed. John's father now opposed the psychiatrist he had originally picked, and John then chose this psychiatrist, the very person he had once vehemently rejected. No one in the family really accepted the commitment as necessary or useful, although they seemed to think there was no other alternative.

John continued contact with Jane, with whom he had a good relationship, and broke contact with their father. He soon was able to discontinue medication and enter a halfway house. Jane, exhausted, returned home with her children and a new awareness of the dynamics in her family of origin. The mother and stepmother seemed unchanged, but the father shed some illusions and began to communicate with Jane in a new way. However, John remained convinced he was fine, the father decided to blame the psychiatrist for the chaos, and, as things calmed down and they needed her less, no one kept in touch with Jane.

THE PROBLEM-SOLVING PROCESS: AN ILL-STRUCTURED, EMOTIONAL, INTERPERSONAL PROBLEM

Sinnott (1989a, 1989b, 1989c) described steps in the solution of ill-structured problems based on solutions of old and young adults to Piaget's formal operational problems in various contexts. When adults thought aloud, the strategies they used became evident, and hypotheses about their process of solving could be tested. A model of advanced problem-solving strategies was created, demonstrating important postformal and information-processing subcomponents in the process.

Sinnott's earlier studies used audiotaped thinking aloud material from problem-solving sessions as basic data. In this current study based on the case above, the process description does not rest on thinking aloud material but rather on notes and journal entries made by the major informant before talking with the author. It also rests on interview material in which the author sought to clarify points in the informant's notes. Samples of the informant's notes and journal entries are in the Appendix.

In the earlier thinking aloud studies, it was possible to use verbatim transcripts of the entire process of solving the problem. In this current case study, which covered several days and several persons' input, a verbatim record could not be obtained. The author, in this chapter, is imposing the 1985 model on new data that are in hand, trying to test whether the same processes that were found before (Sinnott, 1989, b,c) are found in this case. If the original processes fail to appear, the model may have limited generalizability. If new processes appear, they will be categorized and hypothesized to be context-specific, a hypothesis that can be tested in laboratory situations.

In the original model, several basic processes were named, and categorized either as *operations that are part of postformal thought* (Piagetian developmental view) or as *components of complex, ill-structured, logical problem solving* (information-processing view). The nine operations are in Table 14.1 (from Sinnott, 1984). The five components (from Sinnott, 1989) include: processes to construct problem space, processes to generate and choose solutions, monitors, memories, and noncognitive elements.

Postformal Self-Referential Thought: Sinnott's Model

What is this complex thought that is hypothesized to be of use to this family as they address the problem of John? Postformal thought is a complex way of solving problems which develops with social experience, usually in midlife or old age. It allows a person to solve problems even in situations where many conflicted belief systems and priorities overlap. In postformal thought in Sinnott's model the solver faces multiple conflicting ideas about "what is true." She or he realizes that it is not possible to "get outside the mind" to find out which

Table 14.1
Operations in Piagetian Postformal Self-Referential Thought

1. Metatheory shift: shift in beliefs about reality or a prioris underlying the problem.
2. Problem definition: naming what the problem is, within underlying a prioris or any reality.
3. Process/product shift: looking at a problem as both "finding a good answer" and "finding a good general way to get answers to problems of this type."
4. Parameter setting: deciding on the key variables in this problem.
5. Pragmatism: evaluating the comparative worth of several good solutions.
6. Multiple solutions: generating several solutions to a defined problem within a certain metatheory and parameters.
7. Multiple causality: evaluation of the several causal paths leading to a goal.
8. Paradox: awareness of inherent conflicts in reality within a problem.
9. Self-referential thought: realization that Truth is a commitment to one of several versions of reality that seem equally correct and that we construct with other individuals in societies or relationships on an ongoing basis.

Source: Sinnott, 1984.

"truth" is "True," but that a solution must be found to the problem anyhow. She or he then realizes that the truth system that she or he picks as true will *become* true, especially in relation to other people, as she or he lives it to a conclusion.

The main characteristics of relativistic postformal operations (Sinnott, 1984) are: (a) self-reference; and (b) the ordering of formal operations. Self-reference is my general term for the ideas inherent in the new physics (Wolf, 1981) and alluded to by Hofstadter (1979) using the terms "self-referential games," "jumping out of the system," and "strange loops." The essential notions are that we can never be completely free of the built-in limits of our system of knowing, and that we come to know that this very fact is true. This means that we take into account, in all our decisions about truth, the fact that all knowledge has a subjective component and therefore is, of necessity, incomplete. Consequently, any logic we use is self-referential logic. Nonetheless, we must *act*; we do so by making a lower-level decision about the higher-level "rules of the game" (nature of truth), and then play the game by those rules. Sooner or later we come to *realize* that this is what we are doing. We then can *consciously* use self-referential thought.

The second characteristic of postformal operations is the ordering of Piagetian formal operations. The higher level postformal system of self-referential truth decisions gives order to lower level formal truth systems and logic systems, one of which is somewhat subjectively chosen and imposed on data.

Together these two characteristics form the basis of the logic of the "new" physics (relativity theory and quantum mechanics, Sinnott, 1981). New physics is, oddly enough, the next step beyond Newtonian physics, and is built on the logic of self-reference. It is reasonable that the development of logical processes themselves would follow that same progression to increasing complexity. Some characteristics that separate new physics thinking from earlier forms can be found in Sinnott (1984).

Another kind of coordination of perspectives also seems to happen on an *emotional* level, over developmental time (Labouvie-Vief, 1987). This coordination may parallel the cognitive one, or may be in a circular interaction with it. It is expected that postformal thought will be adaptive in a social situation with emotional components (Sinnott, 1984) because it is hypothesized to ease communication, reduce information overload, and permit greater flexibility and creativity of thought. The postformal thinker knows she or he is helping create the eventual Truth of a social interaction by being a participant in it and electing to hold a certain view of the truth of it. This choice "creates" situations and ultimately "creates" one's own identity as one acts in situations.

Problem-Solving Processes Used by Key Informant: Data from Informant's Notes

In Figure 14.1 is a summary of the processes that appeared to be used by the key informant, taken directly from the notes in the Appendix. Figure 14.1 includes symbols denoting the use of certain problem-solving elements and certain postformal operations from Table 14.1. The figure indicates that the elements and operations were present. The decision process was a complex, multistage one, and operations of Sinnott's postformal thought were present.

From the descriptive information drawn from one informant and summarized in the figure, several relations can be hypothesized and tested in later nomothetic data from experiments or multiple cases. First, the solution of real, ill-structured interpersonal problems can be modeled in terms of postformal operations. Second, the procedure of solving them can be modeled using key problem-solving processes drawn from an information-processing tradition, described above. Third, postformal thought is essentially a subroutine that can prevent an infinite cognitive loop from stopping the problem-solving process. Finally, the situation in which many thinkers cocreate a problem is the kind most likely to either lead to infinite loops or to be solved using postformal thought. In such a conflict there are separate realities for each thinker that can only truly be resolved using postformal skills.

SOCIAL FACTORS IN THE SOLUTION OF THIS PROBLEM

Sources of social factors encountered in this case problem include: role-related factors, current interpersonal relationship factors, belief systems, and factors based on the past history of interpersonal relations. These factors are like those

Figure 14.1
Summary of Processes Used by Key Informant Based on Her Notes Alone

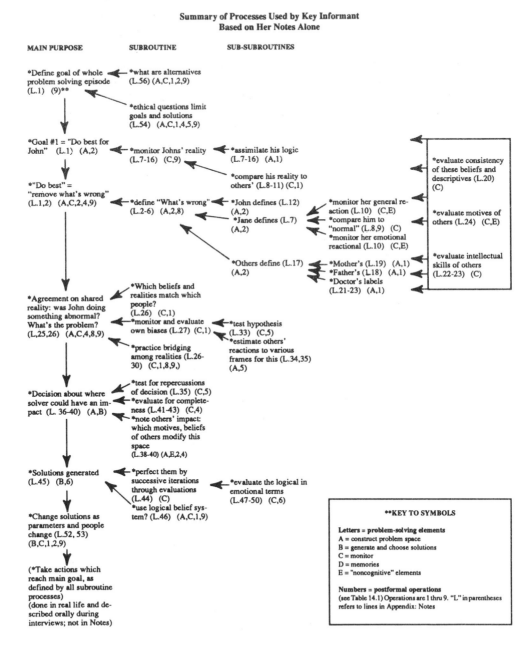

**Summary of Processes Used by Key Informant
Based on Her Notes Alone**

MAIN PURPOSE **SUBROUTINE** **SUB-SUBROUTINES**

*Define goal of whole problem solving episode (L.1) (9)**

*what are alternatives (L.56) (A,C,1,2,9)

*ethical questions limit goals and solutions (L.54) (A,C,1,4,5,9)

*Goal #1 = "Do best for John" (L.1) (A,2)

*monitor Johns' reality (L.7-16) (C,9)

*assimilate his logic (L.7-16) (A,1)

*compare his reality to others' (L.8-11) (C,1)

*evaluate consistency of these beliefs and descriptives (L.20) (C)

*"Do best" = "remove what's wrong" (L.1,2) (A,C,2,4,9)

*define "What's wrong" (L.2-6) (A,2,8)

*John defines (L.12) (A,2)
*Jane defines (L.7) (A,2)

*monitor her general reaction (L.10) (C,E)
*compare him to "normal" (L.8,9) (C)
*monitor her emotional reactional (L.10) (C,E)

*evaluate motives of others (L.24) (C,E)

*Others define (L.17) (A,2)

*Mother's (L.19) (A,1)
*Father's (L18) (A,1)
*Doctor's labels (L.21-23) (A,1)

*evaluate intellectual skills of others (L.22-23) (C)

*Agreement on shared reality: was John doing something abnormal? What's the problem? (L,25,26) (A,C,4,8,9)

*Which beliefs and realities match which people? (L.26) (C,1)

*monitor and evaluate own biases (L.27) (C,1)

*test hypothesis (L.33) (C,5)
*estimate others' reactions to various frames for this (L.34,35) (A,5)

*practice bridging among realities (L.26-30) (C,1,8,9,)

*Decision about where solver could have an impact (L. 36-40) (A,B)

*test for repercussions of decision (L.35) (C,5)
*evaluate for completeness (L.41-43) (C,4)
*note others' impact: which motives, beliefs of others modify this space (L.38-40) (A,E,2,4)

*Solutions generated (L.45) (B,6)

*perfect them by successive iterations through evaluations (L.44) (C)

*evaluate the logical in emotional terms (L.47-50) (C,6)

*use logical belief system? (L.46) (A,C,1,9)

*Change solutions as parameters and people change (L.52, 53) (B,C,1,2,9)

(*Take actions which reach main goal, as defined by all subroutine processes) (done in real life and described orally during interviews; not in Notes)

KEY TO SYMBOLS

Letters = problem-solving elements
A = construct problem space
B = generate and choose solutions
C = monitor
D = memories
E = "noncognitive" elements

Numbers = postformal operations
(see Table 14.1) Operations are 1 thru 9. "L" in parentheses refers to lines in Appendix: Notes

found in the test problem solutions described in Sinnott (ch. 13, this volume). Each of these sources delivers information to the key informant. Each is a product of—and a creator of—perceptual filters. In the last two relationship factors, each acts to alter the path or trajectory of the key informant's decisions by adding a kind of "gravitational field" from others' decisions to the sum total of forces operating (see Sinnott 1981, 1989a). The role-related factors seem to change the flow of problem solving via mechanisms of social learning; the interpersonal-relations factors seem to change the flow of the problem solving of the key informant by setting up a dialogue between others' processes and hers; and the belief systems seem to use both mechanisms. In any case, elements are introduced into her problem-solving process that have no well-defined counterparts in traditional artificial-intelligence literature, problem-solving literature, information-processing literature, or Piagetian theory. These elements only appear in clinical models, General Systems Theory models (Johnson, 1989; Sinnott, 1989a), post-formal models (e.g., Commons, Richards, & Armon, 1984; Sinnott, 1984), or new physics models (Sinnott, 1981).

What are some of the social factors seen in the informant's notes? At what point did they seem to have an impact in the problem-solving process? A summary of the answers to these questions is in Table 14.2. Table 14.2 is not an exhaustive listing, however.

The social factors in this case were more often expressed as interactions in present time or as belief systems, but role factors and history-of-interactions factors were also frequently present in the report. Social factors seemed to be connected with all the nine operations and with all the information-processing factors described above, and the informant verbally expressed their influence on her thought. This suggests that our measures of problem-solving performance are frequently interlaced with social elements of which investigators do not seem conscious and that they do not measure or analyze directly as part of the process.

The informant's awareness of the social factors, however, lets her shift among levels of reality while making her decisions. The impact of these "social" shifts during problem solving was evident at many points, but was especially important for the outcome early in the process. At that early point, the key informant left for her family hometown with her own definitions of the problem, which would have led to her fighting her father and the doctor to "save" her brother who was being "railroaded" into a pathological role. Upon entering her brother's, father's, and the doctors' definitions of the reality of the problem through dialogue with them, she could see several new things. Her brother was frightened, confused, and truly unable to live alone; her father had run out of emotional resources and was nearly incompetent from stress at this time; and the doctors were more flexible than they first appeared, and possibly were just as eager as she was for her brother to be released. This led to her shifting her problem-solving heuristic from a battle for rights (Informant and Brother versus Father and Doctors) to a balancing across many needs of many persons (Brother, Father, Doctors). (In an ethical sense, she moved in this case from a Kohlberg stance reflecting rights

Table 14.2
Social Factors in Problem Solving of Key Informant, and Examples of Their Point of Impact in Her Process

FROM INFORMANT NOTES

Factor

1. Goal is in service of other (line 1)
2. Value system of others defining; "What's wrong with John?" (line 5)
3. Others' criteria for definition of what's wrong (lines 12, 17)
4. Reaction of informant to John—object relations (line 10)
5. Accessing John's framework of logic (line 15)
6. Father as codefiner of problem (line 18)
7. Mother as codefiner (line 19)
8. Comparison of realities of several persons (lines 19, 20)
9. Doctor as definer of reality (line 21)
10. Doctor/Mother as subject to distortion of reality due to own motives (lines 19, 24)
11. Ownership of realities (lines 26, 27)
12. Information gathering to fit others' frame of reference (lines 29, 31)
13. Reactions of others that could influence quality of solution (lines 34, 35)
14. Worth of heuristic dependent on others' cognition and decision processes (lines 37–40)
15. Feedback from others to determine value of solution (line 44)
16. Fitting solutions to continuously changing input of others (line 51)
17. Overall ethics of personal freedom (line 53)

POINT OF IMPACT

1. Goal setting; increase size of problem space
2. Set size of problem space; define goal, solution, metatheory, heuristics; parameter setting
3. Same as 2
4. Problem definition; problem space
5. Problem definition; parameter setting
6. Problem definition; parameter setting
7. Problem definition; parameter setting
8. Metatheory shift; monitor; self-referential thought
9. Metatheory shift; monitor; self-referential thought
10. Problem definition, problem space
11. Metatheory shift; self-referential thought
12. Monitor
13. Multiple causality; processes to choose solutions

Table 14.2 (continued)

14. Processes to choose solutions
15. Processes to choose solutions
16. Self-referential thought
17. Monitor; self-referential thought

to a Gilligan stance reflecting consideration of the needs of all participants [Gilligan, 1982].) The new heuristic resulting from the shift in reality seemed to lead to more positive results and new strategies to help her brother. However, it also fueled her sense of heavy responsibility.

Social factors, as stimuli for a shift in realities, took up the majority of the key informant's decision-making process. Determining how she logically solved the problem while ignoring the interpersonal factors would leave us with very impoverished data, which would fail to reflect her real decision process. Keeping *all* the information displayed in her problem-solving process allows us to begin an analysis of her various "logics" and to begin to see her postformal self-referential use of those elements to solve the problem, as well as her use of them as data, feedback, or content. We can only sketch the very beginning of this analysis here. The descriptive ideographic analysis suggests several hypotheses for future experimental research. First, we could hypothesize from this case that knowing that a person with whom one is emotionally close holds a disparate belief (from one's own) about the reality of a situation leads to a large problem space, hypothesis testing, and postformal thought. Second, being in close relationship to others over time is more likely to lead to postformal, self-referential thought during problem solving than is *not* being in close relationships with others. Third, the individual who is able to resolve family crises and emerge as a leader is most likely a postformal thinker. Fourth, the more emotional and realistic the problem-solving scenario, the more social and interpersonal factors will be present in the problem-solving process.

ADAPTIVITY OF POSTFORMAL THOUGHT IN THIS CASE

The third goal of this chapter is to reflect briefly on the utility of postformal aspects of problem solving for these family members in crisis, and, conversely, on what difficulties arise from lack of postformal elements in their thought. While the chapter has stressed the thinking processes of the key informant, this section of the chapter contrasts the problem-solving styles of three persons in the case: Jane, John, and the father. Postformal thought appears to be available in this context to Jane, and unavailable to John and the father. Postformal thought seems adaptive to Jane in several ways, since it lets her effectively operate in any one of several realities (those of her brother, her father, or the doctor), lets her avoid being caught up in arguments over what "really" happened or who is "right" about the situation, and lets her keep communication channels open among the participants, who do not share a common reality. On a concrete level, it allows her to get the best treatment for her brother and to keep family bonds intact. Lack of postformal thought, in turn, hampers John and the father. John seems to express a problem of family dynamics in a maladaptive, paranoid way because he cannot move into the reality of his family or that of the larger society to attribute more benevolent motives to people. For John, only *his* reality is "True." This is not to say that the lack of postformal thought leads to psychosis, but the lack of such thought may change the form of psychotic symptoms or make it harder to avoid being trapped in them. The father struggles and expends considerable energy to maintain personal control over what he sees as chaos in the family because he cannot enlarge his set of realities to include (in a meaningful way) the separate realities of other family members such as Jane or John. If someone's actions appear to have no meaning, chaos appears to result, and must be controlled. Both John and the father limited the overstimulation coming from others to a bearable level, but only by sacrificing information and seeing everything in black-and-white terms, thereby controlling stimulation as suggested by Sinnott (1984). Jane made overstimulation more bearable by jumping out of her own reality system (Hofstadtler, 1979) to a larger system of which her reality as well as the reality of John and her father were a part, viewing all their contradictory realities as equally true and choosing one reality at a given time in which to operate. Jane could handle more stimulation and information, and could potentially reach a solution of greater utility. She also could respond in a more complex way to the differences, difficulties, and anger around her, seeing those things as reasonable responses within a different reality system, rather than as attacks. As seen in the second section of this chapter, Jane enlarged the "space" in which the problem was defined so that more strategies could be used to work out the family crisis to everyone's advantage. We might assume that a therapist working effectively with this sort of family would be a postformal thinker. He or she could have the basic thinking tools to intervene cognitively at any or all of the process steps in Figure 14.1 or bring the whole process with its emotional components to awareness. The figure could also be used to teach conflict resolution skills by using it to show how alternate views of reality operate to influence decision paths. Even the theraputic modalities that seem to *narrow* views of reality seem (from the writings of their founders) to have been started by persons who did have postformal concepts. (Communication and social change are discussed further by Johnson in chapter 6, this volume. Transformation in clinical settings is addressed by Kramer and Bopp, 1989.)

It is possible to theorize that postformal problem-solving ability lets one enlarge one's identity and make it more flexible, and by doing so makes it easier for one to avoid some of the cognitive or behavioral pitfalls that show up as pathology. (Of course, incomplete postformal development could bring its own type of pathology, and a complex thinker can *be* pathological in different ways than a simplistic thinker. This will be discussed in future work.) The idea of a concrete, unchanging identity, acting in defensive opposition to other concrete identities, might give way with further development to the idea of a flexible identity that is a sum total of one's (not necessarily consistent) ways of interacting with others and the world, and one's ways of transforming the self. The challenge of other persons—the social factors—may open the window to multiple views of truth *and* multiple views of a self, held together by consistent relational processes. The complex thinker is freer, then, to live out more of his or her potential selves. When a potentially pathological response threatens such a thinker's adaptivity, he or she has a wider range of alternative reactions to bring to life. However, the utility of this complex thought is limited by the context in which the thinker operates.

To summarize, the following advantages of postformal thought appeared to be present in this case and can be hypothesized in further experimental research:

—ability to "speak" in "others' languages" or belief systems; better communication (for more discussion of communication and postformal thought, see Johnson, this volume);

—ability to argue within others' logics; better communication;

—a flexible view of what is possible for a family;

—more effective interventions, based on others' psychological realities;

—awareness of one's own biases and filtered worldviews;

—ability to limit overstimulation without limiting information flow;

—more creative problem solving;

—more flexible interpersonal relations;

—ability to get perspective on family problems;

—ability to be more effective in emotion-laden interpersonal situations;

—a flexible view of who the other "is";

—ability to reach the best solution in view of all realities;

—lessened need for control and defenses—lower anxiety level; and

—ability to interact with all the other group members at their level.

CONCLUSIONS

The purpose of this chapter was to illustrate Sinnott's model of complex problem solving in the real case of an emotion laden, ill structured interpersonal problem; to describe the interpersonal and social factors that impinge on problem solving; and to illustrate the adaptivity of postformal skills for the family in the case. This necessarily brief discussion has offered support for these relationships from a real case history. Hypotheses for future experimental studies are offered, and can be used to test further for support for the presence, form, parameters, and utility of self-referential, postformal, complex thought.

NOTE

The assistance of Janis Carlos, Kathleen Henderson, and Barbara Skinner in the preparation of this chapter is gratefully acknowledged.

APPENDIX A: NOTES OF MAJOR INFORMANT

Line

1   Goal—to do the best thing for John
2   1. Define What is wrong with John
3   immediate
4   long term
5   Who is defining—value system
6   Criteria for defining
7   a. I define
8   I spent time with John watch his behavior judge how it
9   varies from *his* "normal" behavior and "normal" behavior
10   I pay attention to gut reaction, my emotions, how I react to
11   him and what I am feeling
12   b. John defines
13   How to distinguish whether what he says happened or not.
14   Work from known facts, gray area, obviously false
15   What causes him to say these things—his logical leap
16   within his framework
17   c. Others define
18   Father—his behavior, words
19   Mother—motivation, ability to be objectively defined
20   Are descriptions consistent
21   Doctor—labels—analysis (question basis—dependent upon
22   amount of information available, reliability, his ability
23   to distinguish what happened from imagined)
24   Motivation involved
25   What has happened
26   What is whose reality
27   Motivation and biases involved
28   (including my own)
29   How can questions be presented to obtain answers
30   (verbally rehearse)
31   Need understanding of emotional involvement
32   of each player and myself.
33   Test hypotheses

34	Test for probable reaction
35	Weighing possible repercussions could result from decision
36	Analysis of what I could probably, possibly affect—focus
37	there
38	dependent on others' decision strategies
39	emotional involvement
40	motivation
41	Scan for missing elements
42	missing repercussions
43	unexpected consequences
44	Talking, feedback—testing
45	helps formulate solutions until they feel good
46	Logic weighed against emotional
47	Even if most logical solution monitor against emotions if
48	uncomfortable
49	try to examine why.
50	understand
51	re-evaluate
52	Continually changing solutions as actions, people,
53	emotions, circumstances change
54	Larger ethical question—under what circumstance is
55	it ethical to commit a person
56	What are the alternatives (ideally and realistically)

Journal Entries

Sample Entry I

Committed, such a strange term
    Devoted, focused, determined
    looked away
    My heart aches
    As he struggles
The butterfly with glistening wet wings
    newly formed
    Beats them frantically
    Against walled cocoon
    Desperate to break through
    one hole
    Glimmer of light
    Knowing deep down

There must be a world out there
. Beat harder
Torn wings
beat and frayed
drop off
wild eyed staring
Entombed
As I fly and soar
together
in love and peace and joy
Will John make it?

Sample Entry II

Tightrope juggling act
Two children lost in feelings of anxiety, worry, guilt, despair
confusion, fear
Father balanced between control and total loss of all even self
Stepmother removed, defensive but there
Doctor of power, eye trip
And is he to be trusted with my brother's life
When any other alternative may break my father
Superwomen
All things to all people
John, how to reach him through his reality while being honest and
maintaining trust
Mother—what does she think now
Already blaming John for my honesty
Video of kids
An intimacy of love and sharing
That once existed
Now gone

REFERENCES

Commons, M. L., Richards, F. A. and Armon, C. (Eds.). (1984). *Beyond formal operations: Late adolescent and adult cognitive development*. New York: Praeger.

Commons, M. L., Sinnott, J. D., Richards, F. A., & Armon, C. (Eds.). (1989). *Adult development: Comparisons and applications of developmental models*. New York: Praeger.

Garmezy, N. (1976). Vulnerable and invulnerable children: Theory, research, and intervention. *Master Lectures in Developmental Psychology*. APA.

Gilligan, C. (1982). *In a different voice: Psychological theory and women's development*. Cambridge, MA: Harvard University Press.

Hofstadter, D. R. (1979). *Godel, Escher, Bach: An eternal golden braid*. New York: Basic Books.

Johnson, J. G. (1989). On the implications of the relativity/quantum revolution for psychology. In D. Kramer & M. Bopp (Eds.), *Transformation in clinical and developmental psychology.* (pp. 25–50). New York: Springer-Verlag.

Kramer, D., & Bopp, M. (Eds.). (1989). *Transformation in clinical and developmental psychology.* New York: Springer-Verlag.

Labouvie-Vief, G. (1987). *Speaking about feelings: Symbolization and self-regulation through the lifespan.* Paper presented at the Third Beyond Formal Operations Symposium at Harvard University, Cambridge, MA.

Sinnott, J. D. (1981). The theory of relativity: A metatheory for development? *Human Development, 24,* 293–311.

Sinnott, J. D. (1984). Postformal reasoning: The relativistic stage. In M. L. Commons, F. Richards, & C. Armon (Eds.), *Beyond formal operations: Late adolescent and adult cognitive development* (pp. 298–325). New York: Praeger.

Sinnott, J. D. (1989a). Changing the known, knowing the changing: The general systems theory metatheory as a conceptual framework to study complex change and complex thought. In D. Kramer & M. Bopp (Eds.), *Transformation in clinical and developmental psychology.* (pp. 51–69). New York: Springer-Verlag.

Sinnott, J. D. (Ed.). (1989b). *Everyday problem solving: Theory and applications.* New York: Praeger.

Sinnott, J. D. (1989c). Life-span relativistic postformal thought: Methodology and data from everyday problem solving studies. In M. L. Commons, J. D. Sinnott, F. A. Richards, & C. Armon (Eds.), *Adult development: Comparisons and applications of developmental models* (pp. 239–278). New York: Praeger.

Wolf, F. A. (1981). *Taking the quantum leap.* New York: Harper & Row.

15

The Influences of Formal versus Informal Education on Planning Skills: A Cultural Perspective

FABIENNE TANON

Over the past several years there has been a flourishing current in adult development research stemming from Piaget's theory on formal operations. Questions about postformal thought have brought researchers to widen their scope of inquiry to include not only pure logical thinking (the hard structural approach), but also the psychosocial dimension of adult reality (the soft structural approach; Kohlberg & Armon, 1984).

A more recent trend has emerged considering adult cognitive functioning from a completely different point of view; that is, the study of adult intelligence within a contextual and practical perspective (Sternberg & Wagner, 1986). Studies focusing on the contrast between academic and practical intelligence indicate that these two modes of functioning are relatively independent of each other (Ceci & Liker, 1986). Hence, the objective of this study is to examine the influence of specific educational experiences on cognitive development. The focus will be on comparing the influence of formal education (with schooling) with that of informal education (with weaving) on the development of planning strategies. This research addresses two main questions:

1. How do complex daily activities such as weaving foster the development of cognitive processes?
2. How can we evaluate and contrast the influences of formal versus informal education on planning skills?

Formal education, as referred to in this research, is a highly institutionalized education with a prescribed curriculum that students must follow, in specified settings, with specific teachers. Informal education, by contrast, is defined as a spontaneous and ongoing process embedded in daily activities. The teacher is often a family member, and learners never lose sight of the practical goal of their training (Childs & Greenfield, 1980; Dasen, 1987; Greenfield & Lave, 1982; Scribner & Cole, 1973).

Most learning transmitted through informal training is usually tied to the practice of a craft or a trade. In addition, as Dasen (1988) has mentioned, this informally learned knowledge is often rejected or undervalued by formal schooling, thus creating a schism between individuals formally and informally educated in many developing countries.

Lengthy and numerous studies in psychology have detailed the influence of schooling on cognition (Rogoff, 1981; Scribner & Cole, 1973). In contrast, we find only a few cross-cultural studies dealing with informal education, not in its social, but in its cognitive aspects (Dasen, 1987; Greenfield & Lave, 1982). To compare these two modes of education and to analyze their separate and joint effects, it is necessary to find these two forms of education co-occurring within the same sociocultural setting. However, in Western societies, it is very difficult to contrast these two types of education due to the emphasis, availability, and values placed on schooling. This explains why an African country, the Ivory Coast, was chosen for this research. There, cultural and educational diversity on one hand, and a great weaving tradition on the other, presented an ideal setting to isolate or combine these two educational experiences for the study.

This chapter will comprise four parts: After a brief introduction on the weaving practiced in the northern Ivory Coast and a quick overview of the theoretical aspects framing this research, the research design will be described along with a presentation of the main results. A final discussion will conclude this chapter.

BACKGROUND OF DYULA WEAVERS IN THE IVORY COAST

The Setting

The study took place in a weavers' village located in the north of the country: Waraniene, which has about 3,000 inhabitants. The village is divided between Dyula and Senoufo people. The Dyula, mostly traders and itinerants, are Muslim. For their part, the Senoufo, mainly agricultural and sedentary, are animist and belong to a secret society called *Poro*. The nearest town, Korhogo, is within 5 kilometers and represents an important tourist center. Weaving constitutes a prominent traditional activity in this area and is performed only by Dyula men. There are around 210 weavers in this village.

The school of Waraniene opened in 1975 and admitted boys and girls, from both ethnic groups, providing the six grades of elementary education. The school curriculum is based on the French system.

Informal Education: Training in Dyula Weaving

Weaving is done outside, in the open air, on very simple looms, producing narrow bands 10 to 15 centimeters wide that will be sewn selvage to selvage to make up the final cloth. A cloth is composed of 9, 11, or more bands, and usually presents an overall design that the weaver keeps in mind while weaving every single band. Thus, it is important to make sure that all the designs woven on each band are placed at correct intervals so that they all fit together well when the final cloth is prepared.

Children are in daily contact with the weavers, since weaving is done outdoors. Thus, when young adolescents start their training, they are already familiar with the different aspects of this activity.

Usually the father is in charge of the training, although sometimes it may be an uncle, an older brother, or even the teacher in the Quranic school. The average age when children start their training is around 12 or 13 years old. However, there is no age limit to learning to weave; it can vary from age 10 to 20. The training usually lasts 2 to 3 years, and sometimes even 4 years.

Several additional aspects of weaver training should be noted:

1. Preparing the warp is a complex and difficult task taught after the apprentice knows how to weave. Because the warp must be prepared based on the design of the final cloth, novices are considered too inexperienced to handle this task. In this type of weaving, the bands are made consecutively, without any interruption. Therefore, a weaver must evaluate the total length of the warp threads depending on the number and the length of all the bands necessary to produce the desired cloth. In addition, the quality of the warp threads and their number are essential in determining the texture of the final product. Thus, preparation of the warp requires advanced planning activities and skills.

2. Mistakes in the weft are easy to correct when seen immediately (the apprentice undoes the work and starts again), whereas mistakes in the warp are much more difficult or even impossible to correct without wasting threads once the band is started. In their study among Zinacantecan weavers, Childs and Greenfield (1980) showed that training by scaffolding leads to a work without errors and is observed in communities where material resources are limited. Scaffolding is also used by Dyula weavers when mistakes are not allowed (e.g., in the warp preparation), but training by trial and error is used when mistakes are easy to correct (e.g., when the novice learns his first designs).

3. The intervals between designs and the length of each design within each band have to be carefully controlled in the weaving process to ensure an overall correct pattern once all the bands are sewn together. It is at the last moment, when all the bands are cut to be sewn, that the weaver sees his work as a whole and is able to control its final assembly.

This short description of Dyula weaving, as practiced in the northern Ivory Coast, shows how crucial it is for the master to guide the apprentice and to teach him how to organize and control his work until the very last step.

THEORETICAL ASPECTS

Since strip weaving entails meticulous planning to be executed well, and since knowing that planning is considered a major cognitive ability (Chi, Glaser, & Rees, 1983; Kirby, 1984; Miller, Galanter, & Pribram, 1960), it is worth studying weaving from a cognitive point of view, more specifically, in its link with planning. Previous research in planning has shown differences between good and bad planners, between novices and experts, and between younger and older children (Chi & Greeno, 1987; Chi, Glaser, & Rees, 1983; Gauvain & Rogoff, 1988; Goldin & Hayes-Roth, 1980; Hayes-Roth & Hayes-Roth, 1979). These studies have demonstrated that planning is a developmental process. Indeed, people learn to build successful plans as they integrate preexisting knowledge with new and relevant information, coordinate different levels of the plan, adjust appropriate strategies to the demands of the situation, and elaborate complex control procedures (Boder, 1978; Chi & Greeno, 1987 Kirby, 1984; Rogoff, Gauvain, & Gardner, 1985). However, no study has focused on the influence of complex daily activities on planful behaviors. Accordingly, one major goal of this study was to ascertain how a "know-how," or the practice of a craft such as strip weaving that requires extensive planning, influences planning activities in different contexts.

Because weaving is learned through informal education, one can compare the cognitive skills acquired in this manner with those acquired through formal education. Thus, a second goal was to determine whether these two modes of learning are antagonistic or complementary.

The present research differs from Childs and Greenfield's (1980) and Rogoff and Gauvain's (1984) work. Although these previous investigators also focused on weaving and contrasted this experience with formal schooling, their main question addressed the generalizability of cognitive skills in gradually differing situations, but not planning abilities. Their results stressed the importance of the context in which a task is embedded and the major role of familiarity in problem solving. According to these authors, knowledge is tied to the specific experience that generated it and does not transfer from one domain to another or from one context to another. Consequently, these previous authors concluded that schooling has a rather limited influence on tasks (such as weaving) that are not directly related to it.

The present study, examining planning activities associated with weaving and schooling, is based on two hypotheses. The first one focuses on weaving. The practice of band weaving implies two levels of interconnected organization: a figural level related to the design and the composition of the bands, and a global level concerning the planning of the weaving activity itself. Thus, the first hypothesis predicts that weavers, as opposed to nonweavers, should have good performances on planning problems related to pattern decompositions and recompositions. Furthermore, weavers should obtain better performances on more familiar items. The second hypothesis is more related to formal education.

Schooling fosters general planning strategies through its curriculum and daily activities (e.g., preparing all books and material needed for the day, organizing one's work for the week, solving different types of problems, ordering and ranking sets of items, reversing that order, categorizing, clustering, and so forth). Consequently, schooled subjects should achieve better performances than non-schooled ones on a task using simple planning activities.

In order to test these hypotheses, two planning tasks were prepared: The first was related to weaving—and a better performance by the weavers was expected. The second task was close to an everyday activity calling for simple planning activities similar to those learned at school, and schooled subjects were expected to perform better than nonschooled ones.

The next section provides a description of the research design, along with the presentation of the tasks and their results.

RESEARCH DESIGN AND RESULTS

Sample Composition

The sample consisted of 110 male subjects, 56 weavers and 54 nonweavers, between 13 and 58 years old. Among the weavers, 25 were schooled and 31 non-schooled. Regarding the nonweavers, 28 were schooled and 26 nonschooled. The age range of the schooled subjects was 13 to 30 years; the nonschooled subjects were between 13 to 58. The ages of the weavers and nonweavers have been matched in order to control for this variable.

In addition, nonweavers were involved in agricultural work, small-scale trading, or unskilled labor, all activities normally carried out by people living in the village.

The schooled subjects had between 5 and 10 years of schooling, and all had received their primary education at the village school. Those who went on to secondary education had to obtain it from a nearby city.

The Method

This design was established after long observation of the weavers at work and real training in weaving received by the researcher. This preparatory work was done in order to become familiar with the real life of the subjects. In this approach, three main points were carefully considered: (a) the familiarity with the material used; (b) the adaptation of the language to the local culture, as recommended in cross-cultural studies (Dasen & Heron, 1981; Frijda & Johoda, 1966; Nyiti, 1982). The tasks were presented by two Ivorian assistants who were school teachers. They gave the instructions in the subjects' native language. A lengthy preparation and translation of the instructions was previously developed with the assistants until a consensus on word meaning was obtained for each task. Also considered was (c) the tasks' format: they were nonverbal and the performances were evaluated based on the subjects' actions.

First Task: The Cloths

Description. This task, close to weaving, included two series of three cloths made up of several bands sewn together. The first three cloths were handwoven in the country (Woven 1–3), and the other three were made of industrial fabrics found at the local market, cut into bands, and then sewn back together (Commercial 4–6). In addition, small squares of fabric were sewn onto the bands in order to make an overall pattern on top of the simple alternance of the band. These last three cloths, although akin to the structure of the woven cloths, were quite unfamiliar to all the subjects in the sample, as they were specifically made up by the researcher.

The degree of familiarity with the cloths decreased from Woven 1 to Commercial 6, as determined during the pretesting:

Familiar: woven cloths: 1: woven in the village, 9 bands
                         2: woven in the region, 9 bands
                         3: woven in another region, 12 bands
               Commercial cloths: 4: fairly simple, 5 bands
                         5: intermediate, 7 bands
                         6: difficult, the most unfamiliar, 12 bands

In addition to these cloths, the subjects had at their disposal:

- A large set of loose bands, most of them identical to the bands of the cloths, plus a few more that were different to be used as a distractor.
- A set of squares of fabrics, corresponding to those of the three commercial cloths but in a larger number.

The task objective was to reconstruct the cloths presented by means of the bands (and the squares when necessary) put at the subjects' disposal. Each cloth was defined by a certain number of features that subjects must notice to successfully organize their reconstruction: number of bands, the repetition of some bands, the presence of symmetry, the designs of the woven bands, the number and position of the squares for the commercial cloths, and so on. The procedure was the following: subjects first observed the cloth in an unlimited time frame, and then went to the pile of bands in a corner of the room and started to recompose the cloth. This was the first trial. If necessary, subjects could go back to the cloth, which had been laid outside the room, and observe it again. Then they came back to finish their recomposition; this was the second trial, also called "second chance." The instructions mentioned that there was no "third chance." Each subject was free to take his "second chance" at any time—and so on, until the last cloth. The order of the cloths' presentation was constant: first the three woven, then the three commercial, ordered according to their difficulty

Table 15.1
Proportion of Subjects in Each Group Achieving Correct Recompositions, for the Six Cloths Respectively

	Weavers		Non-weavers	
	Schooled n=25	Non-Schooled n=31	Schooled n=28	Non-Schooled n=26
Woven				
I	96.00%	96.77%	89.28%	57.69%
II	76.00%	74.19%	53.57%	19.23%
III	44.00%	61.30%	10.71%	7.69%
Comm				
I	76.00%	54.83%	57.14%	26.92%
II	84.00%	58.06%	67.85%	42.30%
III	72.00%	51.61%	60.71%	26.92%

and degree of familiarity. Although the order could have been varied to prevent any order effect, it was preferable to allow all the subjects to proceed from simple to complex items due to the difficulty of the task.

The Results

The results are based on the subjects' performances: They received one point each time the reconstructed cloths exactly corresponded to the models presented. The points were then summed up for the three woven cloths (Woven), for the three commercial cloths (Comm.), and for all six cloths (Total).

Table 15.1 presents the scores as percentage of correct reconstructions of cloths, and conveys the following information:

1. The schooled weavers had better performances than the other groups for five out of six cloths.
2. As the degree of familiarity decreased and the difficulty of the presented cloths increased, the percentage of success dropped. This is particularly true for the woven cloths 1 to 3, for all groups of subjects.
3. Though the weavers as a whole achieved better scores for the three woven cloths, the schooled subjects (weavers and nonweavers) obtained better scores for the commercial cloths.

To test the statistical significance of any differences, a series of simple regressions were first performed on woven and commercial scores. The independent variables in this analysis were Age, Education, Weaver (yes/no), and the intelli-

Table 15.2
Multiple Regressions on the Three Scores, Woven, Commercial, and Total, for the Entire Sample (* = p < .05; ** = p < .01)

N=110	Woven		Comm		Total	
	F Adj. R²		F Adj. R²		F Adj. R²	
Variables						
AGE	1.904	0.008	1.411	0.004	0.000	0.000
EDUC1	0.913	0.000	12.158**	0.093	6.916**	0.051
WEAVER	42.070**	0.274	5.663*	0.041	22.675**	0.166
PM47	21.060**	0.155	32.957**	0.227	28.376**	0.255
Equations						
AGE, EDUC1	2.032	0.019	6.041**	0.085	3.779*	0.049
AGE, EDUC1, PM47	7.975**	0.161	13.067**	0.249	13.369**	0.254
AGE, EDUC1, PM47, WEAVER	19.481**	0.404	12.103**	0.289	19.576**	0.405

AGE = Subject's age; EDUC1 = Schooled or Non-schooled;

WEAVER = Weaver or Non-weaver; PM47 = Score on Raven's

Progressive Matrices 47

gence score at the Raven's Progressive Matrices 47 (PM47). The purpose of this test is to evaluate all subjects on a general intelligence scale. These variables were then entered in a sequence of multiple regression equations to obtain the contribution of each independent variable to the overall variance (see Table 15.2). By adding variables to the multiple regression equation in a hierarchical model, we see exactly how much additional variance is explained by being a weaver, once the other variables are controlled for. This statistical analysis was done on the three scores separately (Woven, Comm., and Total), but since the total score is a combination of the two other scores, only results for woven and commercial cloths will be discussed.

For the woven cloths, Table 15.2 shows that the variable Weaver was the most important predictor when standing alone, explaining 27% of the variance with a F value = 42.07, significant at $p < .01$. This same variable dropped for the commercial cloths, explaining only 4% of the variance (F value = 5.663, $p < .05$), whereas the intelligence test PM47 increases in statistical significance (F value = 32.95, $p < .01$), explaining 22.7% of the variance.

The variable Educ1 (schooled or not) was not significant for the woven cloths, and it explained only 9.3% of the variance for the commercial cloths (F =

12.158, $p < .01$). The variable Age had no effect at all, no matter which cloth was being presented.

When age and schooling were combined, they explained 1.9% of the variance in Woven and 8.5% of the variance in Commercial, leaving much variance available to potentially be explained by intelligence and weaving. When PM47 score was added to these two variables, the total equation explained 16.1% of the variance ($F = 7.975$, $p < .01$) for the woven cloths and 24.9% of the variance for the commercial cloths ($F = 13.067$, $p < .01$). Finally, when the variable Weaver was entered into the equation, the explained variance jumped to 40.4% for the woven cloths. It also added an extra 4% to the overall variance for the commercial cloths.

To conclude, this survey of the results confirmed the expected difference regarding the familiarity criterion between woven and commercial cloths. Because the woven cloths were more familiar to the weavers, these subjects achieved better performances on this type of cloth. In contrast, the commercial cloths were new for all the subjects, thus putting the weavers on an even keel with the nonweavers. This might explain why the variable Weaver had a weaker influence on the three commercial cloths.

On the other hand, the score PM47 seemed to be the best predictor for the performances on commercial items. This may be due to the fact that a similar process for solving both tasks was required. For example, when confronted with nonfamiliar fabrics, the subject must first analyze their main characteristics and then combine these elements together in order to reconstruct the cloths. With the Progressive Matrices 47, the subject must proceed in a similar way, examining the displayed drawings in order to find the piece that completes the design perfectly. Thus, the analogy between both tasks suggests that the PM47 score may predict the success with commercial cloths.

Second Task: The Taxi Van

Description. This task was designed to investigate the second hypothesis stated above, namely, that schooled subjects should achieve better performances than nonschooled ones on a task calling for simple planning activities such as those taught in school. The task consisted of loading and unloading a taxi van going to five different villages. This task was related to an everyday situation in that this means of transportation is widely used in the country. The materials included:

- A model of a taxi van with 22 seats, made of wire,
- 14 passengers, with 2 pieces of luggage each (total 28 pieces), and
- A road, made of paper, on which the five villages were symbolized by flags of different colors.

In order to avoid lengthy explanations and to make it easier, the passengers' clothing and their luggage were matched to the flag of the village to which they were going. Passengers were distributed as follows, in the order of the villages:

Table 15.3
Percentages of Subjects within Each Group Achieving Correct Performances on Perf 1C, Perf 2C, and Exit 2C

	Weavers		Non-weavers	
	Schooled n=25	Non-Schooled n=31	Schooled n=28	Non-Schooled n=26
Perf 1C	80.00%	61.29%	67.85%	38.46%
Perf 2C	80.00%	54.84%	57.14%	30.76%
Exit 2C	80.00%	58.06%	50.00%	30.76%

1 violet, 3 greens, 2 pinks, 5 blues, and 3 browns. The loading phase was done in two steps:

Step 1: The taxi was at the departure point. The subject was the driver, and he had to organize the loading of 10 passengers in the van and of their luggage on the roof. The instructions for the task specified that all passengers: (a) went out by the back door, (b) without disturbing anybody, and (c) in proper order, one at a time. The same was true for unloading the luggage at the rear end of the roof.

Step 2: At the first village, the violet got off while 4 late passengers were waiting to be loaded in the taxi with the others, following the same constraints. This constituted the second loading.

The unloading phase included passengers and luggage at their respective villages. This phase was the final control of the plan, meaning that generally, if the loading had been well organized, the unloading should be smooth.

Performances were noted separately for steps 1 and 2, plus a score for the unloading of passengers and luggage. If subjects followed the instructions, without errors, they received a perfect score for step 1, step 2, and the unloading. A reliability check was done for each score, and the agreement between the two examiners was 97%, 100%, and 100% respectively.

The results. The results are based on subjects' performances for the three variables:

Perf 1C: performance for the first loading

Perf 2C: performance for the second loading

Exit 2C: performance for the unloading

Table 15.3 displays the following points:

1. The weavers in general maintained good performances throughout the task (from Perf 1C to Exit 2C), especially the schooled weavers.

Table 15.4
Two X² Tables for the Three Scores, Perf 1C, Perf 2C, and Exit 2C

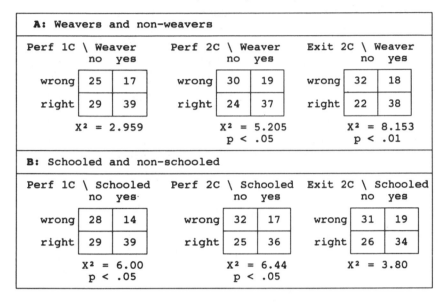

Perf 1C = Score on First Loading

Perf 2C = Score on Second Loading

Exit 2C = Score on Unloading

2. The schooled nonweavers showed more variability in their performances, which were poorer as the task unfolded (from Perf 1C to Exit 2C).

3. Finally, the unschooled nonweavers obtained the lower performances on the three scores.

To see whether these differences were significant, separate chi-square tests were performed on each score, first for weavers versus nonweavers, and then for schooled versus nonschooled subjects. Keeping the two groups distinct allowed us to see how the significance in the chi square varied within each group.

Table 15.4 shows that although the weavers did not differ significantly from the nonweavers for the first loading (Perf 1C), for the second loading (with the four late passengers), the difference between the two groups became significant at p < .05, and for the unloading, the weavers' best performances are significant at $p < .01$.

Looking at the same three scores, but this time for schooled versus nonschooled subjects, we see instead the reverse pattern of significance. At the first and second loading (Perf 1C and 2C), the differences between the two groups of subjects were significant at $p < .05$, but they were no longer significant at the unloading (Exit 2C).

In short, these results demonstrate that the weavers as a whole appeared more consistent throughout the task. They monitored the activity as it unfolded until the very end, as observed at the unloading (e.g., forgetting neither passengers nor luggage in the taxi van). We have seen earlier how strip weaving requires the weaver to plan and monitor his work until the very last step when the bands are sewn to make up the final cloth. In like fashion, a correct unloading of all the passengers, with two bags each, constitutes the final step of the experimental task. Hence, these two activities, although asking for a different type of work, share similar procedures that allowed the weavers to plan their two loadings without losing sight of the unloading. On the contrary, schooling, which seems to have helped the schooled subjects plan their loadings, did not necessarily enable them to monitor and control the task to its final step. Some of the questions raised by this study will be addressed in the next section.

GENERAL CONCLUSION AND DISCUSSION

With respect to the hypotheses stated at the beginning of the study, the first hypothesis predicting a better performance by the weavers in a planning task close to weaving practice was for the most part supported by these data. Weaving experience was observed to have a strong influence on the woven cloths and a lesser effect on the commercial ones.

However, the second hypothesis predicting a better performance by the schooled students in a planning task calling for simple planning activities was only partially confirmed by the results. Indeed, at the point of unloading of the passengers and their luggage from the taxi van, the schooled subjects' advantage disappeared. In fact, the weavers succeeded better at the unloading that concluded the correct unfolding of the task.

In neither of the planning tasks analyzed here did schooling demonstrate the amount of influence it was expected to show. When it did contribute to predicting performances, its effect remained rather limited. This demonstrates that schooling, at least in the Ivory Coast, does not promote general skills that are usable in any situation. On the contrary, it seems to promote the growth of a specific knowledge utilized only in situations closely similar to school. This leads us to consider once more the importance of the context in which a task is performed, whether familiar or not; the task's significance for the subjects; and the role of the procedural knowledge used to solve it.

This research confirms previous work done by researchers examining behaviors and cognitive processes in their real-life context in order to better understand their relevant mechanisms (Rogoff & Lave, 1984; Scribner, 1984; Sternberg & Wagner, 1986).

In addition, these findings show how weaving influences and fosters planning activities in familiar situations. We also see that control procedures involved in strip weaving, so important in this activity and stressed throughout the apprentice's training, could be transferred to a less familiar task. Despite the different work to be performed, the needs for monitoring the task and controlling the work remain similar. This last point calls into question the studies pointing to a nontransfer of knowledge out of its usual context (Childs & Greenfield, 1980; Rogoff, 1981; Rogoff & Gauvain, 1984). The results we obtained here permit us to reactivate the debate about the meaning of transfer, the conditions for its occurrence, and its limitations. It seems that a distinction should be made between transfer of skills (e.g., when skills are applied from one task to another, but both tasks are similar and remain related to the same activity), and generalization of skills or knowledge (e.g., when knowledge or skills related to one task can be used in another, very different activity). However, more rigorous research is needed to evaluate which factors may enhance or limit this complex phenomenon of generalization (Chi & Greeno, 1987; Dasen, 1987; Kirby, 1984; Tanon, 1989).

As a last point, these data show how formal and informal education influence the planning involved in two different tasks. These influences vary according to the task and its demands. The practical context in which planning skills are embedded in strip weaving is certainly determinant of the weavers' planful behaviors (Tanon, 1989). It nonetheless remains true that the schooled weavers who have had both modes of education achieved greater success in both tasks. One can conclude that these people made the best use of both types of education. Moreover, for countries where informal education remains the only source of training for a large part of the population, it would be wise to reevaluate and combine it with basic schooling. This would lead to the creation of some alternative schools as a possible solution to the educational dilemma in developing countries (Simmons, 1982).

In conclusion, this research shows how planning abilities are related to specific contexts, in accordance with Sternberg's definition of intelligence (Ford, 1986; Sternberg & Wagner, 1986). This study is one example of the numerous avenues open to investigate planning skills among adults in a non-Western culture. Whether these abilities remain the same in varying contexts is an important question still open to further research, and one that will contribute to a better understanding of how planning develops through the life span.

NOTE

Among the many people who contributed to the success of this project I owe a special debt to Mary Gauvain and Brian Sutton-Smith. I would also like to thank Marguerite Lavallee, who encouraged me throughout my research and helped me with her comments on a previous draft of this chapter. I am also grateful to Gary Klein for his statistical assistance.

REFERENCES

Boder, A. (1978). Etude de la composition d'un ordre inverse: Hypothèse sur la coordination de deux sources de controle du raisonnement. (Study of the composition of a reverse order: Hypothesis on the coordination of two sources of control on reasoning). *Archives de psychologie, 46*(178), 87–113.

Ceci, S. J., & Liker, J. (1986). Academic and nonacademic intelligence: An experimental separation. In R. J. Sternberg & R. K. Wagner (Eds.), *Practical intelligence: Nature and origins of competence in the everyday world* (pp. 119–142). Cambridge, MA: Cambridge University Press.

Chi, M. T. H., Glaser, R., & Rees, E. (1983). Expertise in problem solving. In R. J. Sternberg (Ed.), *Advances in the psychology of human intelligence* (Vol. 1, pp. 7–75). Hillsdale, NJ: Erlbaum.

Chi, M.T.H., & Greeno, J. G. (1987). Cognitive research relevant to education. In J. A. Sechzer & S. M. Pfafflin (Ed.), *Psychology and educational policy, Annals of the New York Academy of Sciences*, New York, *517*, 39–57.

Childs, C. P., & Greenfield, P. M. (1980). Informal modes of learning and teaching: The case of Zinacanteco weaving. In N. Warren (Ed.), *Studies in cross-cultural psychology* (Vol. 2, pp. 269–316). New York: Academic.

Dasen, P. R. (1987). Savoirs quotidiens et éducation informelle (Everyday knowledge and informal education). Document de travail DPSF N 22. Université de Genève.

Dasen, P. R. (1988). Cultures et développement cognitif: La recherche et ses applications (Cultures and cognitive development: Fundamental research and its application). In R. Bureau & D. de Saivre (Eds.), *Apprentissages et cultures* (pp. 123–142). Paris: Karthala.

Dasen, P. R., & Heron, A. (1981). Cross-cultural tests of Piaget's theory. In H. C. Triandis & A. Heron (Eds.). *Handbook of cross-cultural psychology* (Vol. 4, pp. 295–341). Boston: Allyn & Bacon.

Ford, M. E. (1986). For all practical purposes: Criteria for defining and evaluating practical intelligence. In R. J. Sternberg & R. K. Wagner (Eds.), *Practical intelligence: Nature and origins of competence in the everyday world* (pp. 183–200). Cambridge, MA: Cambridge University Press.

Frijda, N., & Johoda, G. (1966). On the scope and methods of cross-cultural research. *Journal International de Psychologie, 7*(2), 109–127.

Gauvain, M., & Rogoff, B. (1988). Collaborative problem solving and children's planning skills. *Developmental Psychology, 24*(6), 1–13.

Goldin, S. E., & Hayes-Roth, B. (1980). *Individual differences in planning processes* (Document prepared for the Office of Naval Research). Santa Monica, CA: Rand Project.

Greenfield, P. M., & Lave, J. (1982). Cognitive aspects of informal education. In D. A. Wagner & H. W. Stevenson (Eds.), *Cultural perspectives on child development* (pp. 181–207). San Francisco: W. H. Freeman.

Hayes-Roth, B., & Hayes-Roth, F. (1979). A cognitive model of planning. *Cognitive Science, 3*, 275–310.

Kirby, J. R. (1984). Educational roles of cognitive plans and strategies. In J. R. Kirby (Ed.), *Cognitive strategies and educational performances* (pp. 51–88). New York: Academic.

Kohlberg, L., & Armon, C. (1984). Three types of stage models used in the study of adult development. In M. Commons, F. Richards, & C. Armon (Eds.), *Beyond formal operations* (pp. 383–394). New York: Praeger.

Miller, G., Galanter, E., & Pribram, K. (1960). *Plans and the structure of behaviors.* New York: Holt & Co.

Nyiti, R. M. (1982). The validity of "cultural differences explanations" for cross-cultural variation in the rate of Piagetian cognitive development. In D. H. Wagner & H. W. Stevenson (Eds.), *Cultural perspectives on child development* (pp. 146–165). New York: Freeman.

Rogoff, B. (1981). Schooling and the development of cognitive skills. In H. Triandis & A. Heron (Eds.), *Handbook of cross-cultural psychology* (Vol. 4, pp. 233–294). Boston: Allyn & Bacon.

Rogoff, B., & Gauvain, M. (1984). The cognitive consequences of specific experiences: Weaving versus schooling among the Navajo. *Journal of Cross-Cultural Psychology, 15*, 453–475.

Rogoff, G., Gauvain, M., & Gardner, W. (1985). The development of children's skills in adjusting plans to circumstances. In S. L. Friedman, E. K. Scholnick, & R. R. Cocking (Eds.), *Blueprints for thinking: The role of planning in psychological development.* Cambridge, MA: Cambridge University Press.

Rogoff, B., & Lave, J. (1984). *Everyday cognition: Its development in social context.* Cambridge, MA: Harvard University Press.

Scribner, S. (1984). Studying working intelligence. In B. Rogoff & J. Lave (Eds.), *Everyday cognition: Its development in social context* (pp. 9–40). Cambridge, MA: Harvard University Press.

Scribner, S., & Cole, M. (1973). The cognitive consequences of formal and informal education. *Science, 182*, 553–559.

Simmons, J. (1982). *The education dilemma.* New York: Pergamon.

Sternberg, R. J., & Wagner, R. (1986). *Practical intelligence: Nature and origins of competence in the everyday world.* Cambridge: Cambridge University Press.

Tanon, F. (1989). *A comparative study of formal versus informal education on planning abilities: Schooling versus weaving in the Ivory Coast.* Unpublished doctoral dissertation, University of Pennsylvania, Philadelphia.

16

Expert Systems in Nature: Spoken Language Processing and Adult Aging

ARTHUR WINGFIELD AND ELIZABETH A. L. STINE

There is a general principle of human information processing which, to paraphrase Norman and Bobrow (1975), we might call the Principle of Graceful Overload. In a variety of perceptual and processing tasks, performance is often better than one might have otherwise predicted given the load under which the system is operating. As information loads increase to a point that should severely challenge one's capacity for effective processing (i.e., "overload" conditions), performance does not usually drop off in a sudden or precipitous manner. Rather, although performance will decline as processing loads are increased, such declines tend to be gradual. The form of such performance curves, in other words, usually reflects more a "graceful degradation" than an abrupt failure (Norman & Bobrow, 1975; Schneider & Detweiler, 1987).

The literature on cognitive aging reports age-related losses in a number of sensory and cognitive domains. Most notable are complaints of deficiencies in rapid organization of, and memory for, recent events, as contrasted with early, or tertiary, memories (e.g., Pozard, 1980). Among the abilities classically maintained across the life span are those characterized by Barr (1988) as more "natural" tasks. These typically arise from rich stimulus environmments that allow large sets of knowledge structures to be accessed and brought to bear on the task. We can put our position quite simply: To understand information processing across the life span, we need to account for why it is that such natural skills show so little decline with normal aging.

To illustrate this position we have chosen a particularly intriguing and powerful example of a natural task, that of spoken language processing, and the ability to remember accurately what has been heard. Among the reasons for choosing this task are first, its clear importance to so much of everyday life, and second, its many implications for other sensory and cognitive processes as they operate in especially rich stimulus environments.

ELEMENTS OF SPOKEN LANGUAGE PROCESSING

Although language comprehension may be a natural process, it is certainly not a simple one. One feature of spoken language is the very rapid rate at which it arrives. Ordinary conversational speech typically arrives at between 140 and 180 words per minute (wpm), with much of this time occupied by hesitations and pauses as the speaker thinks of what it is he or she wants to say next. A radio or television newsreader speaking from a prepared script can easily exceed 210 wpm. Unlike reading, where the reader can control the input rate or backtrack for review, spoken language must be held in memory for such review, and the bulk of processing is conducted "on-line" as the speech is being heard (Marslen-Wilson, 1984; Marslen-Wilson & Welsh, 1978; Wingfield & Butterworth, 1984).

Neither is even the concept of a word in natural speech a simple one. When we analyze the speech waveform, we see that the speech signal comes in a continuous stream without regular breaks between words, phonemes, or other linguistic elements. Correctly segmenting this continuous stream into perceived "words" is a mental process one step removed from the acoustic properties of the input signal. For example, a particular sound pattern can be perceived as either "a nice bucket" or "an ice bucket," depending on the sentence context, and distinguishing "a lighthouse keeper" from "a light housekeeper" requires context plus the rapid use of timing and stress. Indeed, the speech signal is actually far less clear than it sounds to the human listener. Excerpting a single word from a recording of fluent speech and presenting it in isolation can make this point dramatically (Hunnicutt, 1985; Pollack & Pickett, 1964). Less accessible to introspection, but following the same general principles, are context effects on speech recognition at the level of phonemes and syllables (Cole & Jakimik, 1980; Liberman, Cooper, Shankweiler, & Studdert-Kennedy, 1967).

One reason speech at the sentence and discourse level can be processed so rapidly is our ability to supplement the product of perceptual *bottom-up* analysis of the acoustic signal with *top-down* support from linguistic and real-world context. Although the interaction between the two is rapid, and is inaccessible to conscious awareness, a sense of this top-down input is experienced whenever we hear people (sometimes annoyingly) finish sentences for other people in the belief that they know what it is the person is about to say. Although we are stressing the role of context in language processing here, we should note that real-world survival may well necessitate a bottom-up priority. In times of danger we must be able to detect what is being heard rather than what is expected to be heard (Marslen-Wilson, 1987).

The interactive process, as we describe it here, could not be accomplished through performance of a series of discrete, linear-stage operations. (A linear-stage model assumes a sequence of operations in which one operation is not begun until the prior one has been completed.) Rather, we believe that the system must be a parallel interactive one, in which perceptual operations at multiple levels are conducted in concurrent or overlapping fashion. Our position is thus consistent with a number of parallel-network formulations both for speech input processing (Marslen-Wilson, 1984, 1987; Salasoo & Pisoni, 1985) and for word and sentence production (Dell, 1986; Ellis, 1985; Stemberger, 1985).

Full speech analysis, of course, also requires resolution of the linguistic structure of the text and the organization of the propositions (*idea units*) of the speech into a higher-order coherence structure of the message at the discourse level (Kintsch, 1988; van Dijk & Kintsch, 1983). To complete what is already a complex picture, most writers stress the need for an effective memory store to hold temporarily the products of preliminary analyses for integration with what has yet to be heard, and to make possible delayed analysis when on-line processing cannot keep pace with the input. This would also be true for a *garden path* sentence in which a preliminary parsing turns out to have been incorrect. There is still some disagreement, however, on the nature or number of such memory systems (Caplan, Vanier & Baker, 1986; Martin, 1987; Monsell, 1984).

Consider now that elderly adults are often claimed to have limitations in processing resources and working memory capacity (Craik & Rabinowitz, 1984; Morris, Gick, & Craik, 1988; Wingfield, Stine, Lahar, & Aberdeen, 1988), a significant incidence of auditory-processing deficits (Corso, 1984), difficulty with rapidly organizing stimuli for memory (Smith, 1980), and a general reduction in processing speed (Salthouse, 1982). Like the engineer who studied the weight and aerodynamic shapes of insects and concluded that bumble bees cannot fly, one might be tempted to the erroneous conclusion that elderly adults should have inordinate difficulty with spoken language comprehension and recall. However, this clearly is not the case. (One can make a formal distinction between comprehension and memory, in the sense that one can memorize nonsense words without knowing their meaning or comprehend a message but later remember little of it. In general, however, when natural language is involved, comprehension is an integral part of the memory task [Bartlett, 1932; Clark & Clark, 1977; Wingfield & Byrnes, 1981, pp. 93–107]. Indeed, in regard to constructing a meaningful semantic representation of discourse, Klatzky [1988] has commented that in memory tasks, "comprehension is essentially a form of elaborative rehearsal" [p. 10].)

There are age decrements when speech contains complex syntax (Kemper, 1987), when distant inferential processes are required (Cohen, 1981; Zacks & Hasher, 1988), or when the processing load is otherwise especially high (Stine & Wingfield, 1990). Nevertheless, linguistic knowledge and memory for linguistic materials can be well preserved in normal aging (Meyer & Rice, 1981; Wingfield, Lahar, & Stine, 1989). More to the point, we will show that, even under difficult listening conditions where elderly adults show significant hardship with unstructured speech, these same listeners have little difficulty with spoken natural language. As illustrative of our earlier point, we shall see that the effects of overload for such materials are more graceful than they are abrupt.

AN ILLUSTRATION OF GRACEFUL OVERLOAD

To get a feeling for what we mean by graceful overload, consider data taken from an earlier study using *time-compressed* speech as a way of exploring effects of processing overloads on young and elderly adults (Wingfield, Poon, Lombardi, & Lowe, 1985). In this experiment, young and elderly adults heard three kinds of sentence-length verbal materials. The first of these consisted of normal English sentences (N). These were ordinary meaningful sentences, representing a variety of common syntactic forms. They were recorded by a female speaker of American English at a comfortable speaking rate and in normal intonation.

The second type of speech materials were referred to as syntactic strings (S). These were composed by taking the words of the normal sentences and rearranging them to form additional sets of same-length word strings without meaning, but that followed the general constraints of normal English grammar. That is, the nouns, verbs, adjectives, and grammatical endings were all there, but the "sentences" themselves did not make sense. Such materials have a long history in psycholinguistics research (e.g., Marks & Miller, 1964), and take the form of strings such as "Colorless green ideas sleep furiously," or "Frisky water drank clear dogs."

Our final type of speech materials, random strings (R), represented our attempt to examine "pure" processing ability for verbal materials, devoid of any linguistic or semantic constraints. These word strings were composed by again rearranging the words from the original normal sentences, but this time they were shuffled into a random order to produce totally meaningless and unstructured word strings. These were recorded by the same speaker in a carefully controlled monotone. (Because the words for the S and R strings were taken from the original normal sentences, the three sets of materials were automatically equated for such features as word length and word- and form-class frequency. This is an important control for such work.)

Although we will only talk here about the fastest and slowest speech rates we tested, four rates ranging from 275 to 425 wpm were used in the full experiment. These speech rates were varied by using the *sampling* method of speech compression on a Lexicon Varispeech II compressor/expander. In this method, small (20-millisecond) segments of the speech signal are electronically deleted at regular intervals with the remaining segments then abutted in time. When played back at normal speed, the result is speech reproduced in less than normal time, but without the distortions in pitch or quality that would, for example, accompany tape-recorder playback at faster than normal speed (Foulke, 1971). Note, by the way, that while 275 wpm was the slowest speech rate we used in this experiment, it is still far faster than ordinary speech rates.

Our elderly participants in this study were all active, community-dwelling men and women (mean age = 69.1 years), in good health and with good educational backgrounds and high vocabulary scores. Our young group were university undergraduates matched with the elderly group for education and Wechsler Adult Intelligence Scale vocabulary score (WAIS-V). All participants heard samples of the three types of speech materials presented at the speech rates used in the study. The participants' task was simply to listen to each speech segment as it was presented, and when it was finished, to recall as much of it as they could, as accurately as possible. (See Wingfield et al., 1985, for additional detail on procedures and participant selection.)

The left panel of Figure 16.1 shows recall performance for the three types of speech materials when heard at 275 wpm, and the right panel shows the same types of materials heard at 425 wpm. It is clear in both cases that there was a significant age effect for random word strings (R), and that this effect was more marked at the faster speech rate. The same pattern is seen for the syntactic strings (S), except that the age differences are much smaller. Equally notable, however, we see that for normal sentences (N), the differences are even smaller at the very rapid rate of 425 wpm, and nonexistent at 275 wpm: Both young and elderly subjects are virtually at a ceiling of 100% accuracy. Thus, the loss of structure hurt the elderly participants differentially more than it did the young ones, particularly at the high speech rates. (Across all the speech rates tested there was a significant Age × Speech Rate × Type of Material interaction, $p < .001$.)

Implications of Compression

Had we tested just the normal sentences, we would have erroneously concluded that the elderly participants had virtually no processing deficits for spoken language, even at very rapid rates. By contrast, had we tested only the "pure" speech materials of the random word strings, we would have come to just the opposite conclusion. Both statements are in their own way true, although the latter focus on deficit may better typify the early focus of much of the cognitive aging literature than does the former.

It is thus clear that one can find significant age-related deficits for speech recall, but that, in spite of such deficits, most elderly adults, like those in our study, do handle spoken language well. The answer to this apparent paradox is that natural language processing is not only a highly practiced skill. Normal language contains highly structured internal organization that is as well appreciated by the elderly as it is by the young. Although elderly adults may lose

Figure 16.1
**Percentage of Words Correctly Recalled by Young and Elderly Adults for Normal
Sentences (N), Syntactic Strings (S), and Random Word Strings (R), Heard at
Either 275 or 425 Words per Minute**

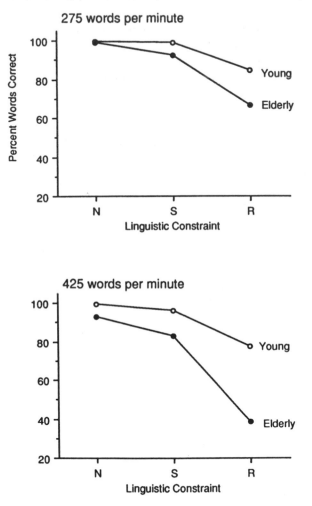

some degree of processing speed, they do not lose the procedural knowledge
about how to use the rules or the structure of their language. Their detection of
syntactic boundaries and the propositional structure of the language remains
strong (Stine, Wingfield & Poon, 1986; Wingfield et al., 1989), as does their
ability to use other cues to detect linguistic structure such as word stress and the
prosodic contour of speech (Cohen & Faulkner, 1986; Stine & Wingfield, 1987;
Wingfield et al., 1989). In terms of vocabulary size, the elderly can often have
a distinct edge (Birren & Morrison, 1961).

EXPERTISE, PROCESSING INTERACTIONS, AND THE
PRINCIPLE OF GRACEFUL OVERLOAD

The notion that acquired knowledge or expertise can compensate for reduced processing resources is well represented in the aging literature (cf. Denney, 1984; Rybash, Hoyer, & Roodin, 1986). A good example of this principle comes from Salthouse (1984), who showed that older, experienced typists can maintain good typing speed in spite of a general decline in sensorimotor speed. Typing from a script or dictation is, of course, another example of a linguistically oriented task. It has long been known, for example, that typing speed increases as the passages being typed are made to more closely approximate the normal structure of English text (Attneave, 1959, pp. 76–77).

If a person, due to age or illness, were to become less efficient in processing bottom-up sensory information, one might expect the system to be easily overloaded. However, as we have seen, this does not always appear to be the case. To see why this is true, let us look first at the general principle of top-down contributions to task performance.

Top-Down Contributions to Task Performance

Figure 16.2 represents a schematic illustration of how top-down information can contribute to observed performance so as to compensate for declining levels of bottom-up processing capability. The level of observed performance is labeled Curve O, and it shows the sort of gradual and small decline that might be found in a skilled task across the age span. The more steeply sloping lower curve is drawn to represent a declining level of efficiency in bottom-up processing of sensory information. We have labeled this Curve IP to represent Input-Processing capacity. (We have not put values on the "age" dimension on the abscissa, nor do not want to make any specific claims about presumed biological declines or their shape. Curve IP should rather be seen as an abstract, or generic, curve showing a range of levels of processing capability.)

There are many reasons why the height and shape of curve IP must be a generic one in this illustration. For example, even in a processing domain generally thought to be age sensitive, the height and shape of Curve IP would be expected to vary greatly from one individual to another. No less important, the capability level represented by Curve IP will also vary from task to task and for different components of an input processing task. As a case in point, speech recognition at the level of the phoneme might have one function of decline, while the ability to detect pitch, timing, or intensity changes that give rise to recognition of prosodic contour might have another rate of decline, or perhaps no decline at all.

The shaded area in Figure 16.2, labeled TDC, illustrates the relative amounts of top-down contribution that would be necessary for performance to reach the level of observed performance as indicated by Curve O, given the different levels

Figure 16.2
Schematic Illustration of Possible Top-Down (linguistic context, language knowledge) Contribution to Observed Performance Level Given Various Levels of Bottom-Up (input-processing) Capacity

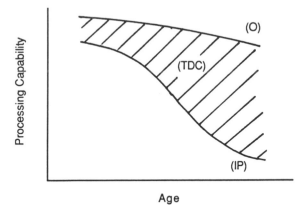

Curve *IP* represents input-processing capacity, Curve *O* represents the level of observed performance, and Area *TDC* represents the amount of the top-down contribution necessary to achieve this level.

of bottom-up processing capability. The size of Area *TDC* will depend on the knowledge or expertise available to compensate for a bottom-up deficiency. If language knowledge is good, and if the task is such that knowledge can beneficially interact with the product of bottom-up processes, we would expect a relatively high level of performance.

In the speech study just described, the random word strings were intended to get us close to mirroring the actual level of processing capability for receipt and recall of very rapid speech. The level of performance for natural language, as exemplified by our normal sentences, and to some extent even the syntactic strings, showed how linguistic knowledge (top-down information) could be used by the elderly (and by the young) to compensate for bottom-up processing deficiencies. Note that we are using *deficiency* as a relative term that reflects the degree of shortfall between task demands and processing capacity. As such, the twin notions of input-processing deficiences, and the need to compensate for them, would be incomplete—and misleading—if applied to the elderly alone.

The Concept of Overload

The Principle of Graceful Overload rests directly on the level of top-down, knowledge-driven components of the task that will interact with bottom-up deficiences that may exist in order to keep the level of observed performance high. As the input begins to overload the system, so top-down sources increase their contribution to keep the system from drastic decline.

In general, overload conditions can be said to occur whenever a particular task puts more demand on the system than there is available capacity. *Overload* is thus a very general term. For example, overload could be caused by increasing the information content of the stimulus to be processed, by changing its rate of presentation, or by holding the information content of the stimulus constant but increasing the complexity of the task or tasks to be performed using that input. Alternatively, overload could occur with otherwise simple stimulus or task situations if, for example, input clarity were degraded through sensory impairment, or if the product of this input processing had to be fed to a seriously limited working memory. (The richness of naturalistic stimuli do not always support top-down processes, as for example, in the overload conditions that can sometimes occur in TV news presentations; Stine, Wingfield, & Myers, 1990.)

The formula for overload conditions is thus a relative one: A processing task that might represent overload conditions for one person, with one level of processing capability, may not represent overload for another. By the same token, there will always be some conditions of task demands that will overload any system, regardless of its otherwise strong capability. Our main point, however, is that even under conditions that should represent overload in a processing domain for a particular person, a dynamic interplay between bottom-up processes and knowledge-based, top-down sources operates to prevent anything like zero-level performance. Although observed performance may decline with increasing levels of processing demands, relative to the capability of the particular processing system, only rarely does the system "crash." This is also true even though moment-to-moment performance levels will fluctuate with transient changes in motivation and effort. (See Kahneman, 1973, for a good discussion of attention and effort, and their implications for performance on simple and complex tasks.)

It is certainly the case that in on-line language processing, one does not make conscious decisions to exploit one's linguistic knowledge or to consciously supplement fragile bottom-up input with the richness of human linguistic expertise. The process of compensation in spoken language processing is, in Barr's terms, a natural process, and one that comes automatically to the human listener. Indeed, we can demonstrate such top-down/bottom-up interactions in speech processing even at the level of individual word recognition.

ON-LINE SPEECH PROCESSING AND LINGUISTIC CONTEXT

As we have seen, although ordinary conversational speech typically arrives at between 140 to 180 wpm, our speech study showed excellent performance for short sentences arriving at 275 wpm, and adequate performance at even faster rates. The rate at which speech can be processed and its meaningful elements organized for comprehension is thus very impressive. This is especially so in the case of elderly adults where presumed differences in speed of processing and effective organization of incoming information should create special challenges.

As we have seen, part of the answer to the rapid and effective processing of spoken language lies in listeners' use of linguistic context, and the way in which context-driven, top-down information interacts with the bottom-up information extracted from the sensory input. Although most demonstrations of this inter-action have necessarily used off-line tasks, the processes they are intended to model are presumed to occur on-line, in real time, as the speech is being heard (e.g., Marslen-Wilson, 1984; Marslen-Wilson & Welsh, 1978; but see also, Tyler & Wessels, 1985). Numerous studies have certainly shown that words presented within a linguistic context are more easily and rapidly recognized than words presented out of context, and this is true whether the words are presented visually (Morton, 1964) or auditorally (Tyler, 1984). As we have noted, just as the perception of individual sounds at the phoneme and syllable level are known to be context-dependent (Liberman et al., 1967), many words spoken in ordinary fluent discourse can be totally unintelligible if heard in isolation without their surrounding context (Hunnicutt, 1985; Pollack & Pickett, 1964).

Prior studies with young adults have shown that words heard in context can often be recognized within 200 milliseconds (msecs) of their onset, or when less than half their acoustic signal has been heard (Grosjean, 1980; Marslen-Wilson, 1984; Tyler, 1984). Even though this figure assumes optimal pronunciation (Grosjean, 1985; Nooteboom & Doodeman, 1984), it is close to the duration of just an average word-initial consonant-vowel combination in English. Words out of context require, on average, only 130 msecs more (e.g., Tyler, 1984). This is presumed to be the case because of the rapid decrease in potential word candidates that occurs with increasing amounts of word onset information (Mar-slen-Wilson, 1984; Marslen-Wilson & Zwitserlood, 1989; Tyler, 1984; Wayland, Wingfield, & Goodglass, 1989; Wingfield & Wayland, 1988).

CONTEXT, SPEECH, AND AGING

Not so many years ago, the literature on linguistic context, age, and speech recognition was sufficiently sparse that one could have entertained either of two expectations: (a) The successful use of context must require some temporary storage of prior linguistic information for it to be brought to bear on subsequent elements that have yet to be heard. Claims of age-sensitive reductions in working memory or resource capacity might thus predict an increased difficulty for elderly adults attempting to use linguistic context for speech processing. That is, elderly adults might make less effective use of linguistic context than the young. (b) On the other hand, given that verbal ability in late adulthood is typically well maintained, this could be seen as a form of natural expertise ripe for exploitation. Under these terms, there should be no reason to expect necessary age-related declines in the ability to use contextual cues to facilitate word recognition. We have already seen a positive answer to this question at the level of sentence processing.

An early report of within-word contextual constraints was given by Kinsbourne (1973) who tested young and elderly adults' immediate recall of spoken letter sequences that varied in their order of approximation to English words (random letters versus letters following digram and tetragram frequencies for English words). Kinsbourne's findings showed a similar rate of gain in performance for both age groups as the letter sequences more closely approximated English.

Ten years later, Cohen and Faulkner (1983) looked at the effects of a sentence context on lexical decisions for visually presented words, and on recognition accuracy for noise-masked spoken words heard either in isolation or preceded by a sentence context. In both cases, the elderly appeared to make even better use of context to facilitate their performance than did the young. (Analogous results have been reported by Madden, 1988, for degraded written words.) As we have already seen from our time-compression experiment previously described, our elderly participants made differentially greater use of context than the young in speech memory at the sentence level (Wingfield et al., 1985).

We have characterized such context studies as showing that the elderly make excellent use of top-down information to compensate for, presumably, decreased richness in the products of bottom-up processing. (Logically, if the elderly were better than the young in utilizing top-down information in a task that had no bottom-up deficiency, they would be superior to the young in that task.)

To return to our theme, we could thus contemplate cases in which young and elderly adults might differ in the relative contributions of top-down and bottom-up information in language processing, but where the two sources combine in such a way as to yield apparent equivalence in their observed levels of performance. In a recent experiment we came across just such a case. Our focus of interest was on the time-course of rapid word recognition and in the ways in which linguistic context and word onset information might interact at this level of input processing. Our goal was not merely to compare word recognition ability for young and elderly participants. We wished also to look at the kinds of errors participants made in relation to the target words. Our intent was to explore in even greater detail how context might be used interactively with sensory input (Wingfield, Aberdeen, & Stine, in press). The results of this study can be taken as a second illustration of our thesis about age and interactive processes.

AGE, SENTENCE CONTEXT, AND THE GATING PARADIGM

One way to study linguistic context effects on word recognition is to use a technique known as *gating* (Cotton & Grosjean, 1984; Grosjean, 1980). In our application of this technique, subjects heard recorded words that were computer-edited so that only the first 50 msecs of the word was heard, then only the first 100 msecs, and so on, with increasing amounts of word onset information presented until the word could be correctly identified. As previously indicated, correct target word identification in the absence of the complete acoustic signal in such cases is presumed to be made possible by a rapid decrease in the number of possible word candidates that share the same initial sounds as the target word as more and more of the word onset information is heard. Beginning with a relatively large set of word candidates based solely on initial sensory input (the *word-initial cohort*), candidates are progressively eliminated by accumulating sensory information and, if present, linguistic context, until a single word candidate remains (Marslen-Wilson & Welsh, 1978; Tyler, 1984; Wayland et al., 1989). Although the details of the interaction remain under active contest, contextual constraints can be said to increase the rate at which potential word candidates can be eliminated from the cohort set (cf. Marslen-Wilson, 1987; Salasoo & Pisoni, 1985).

Experimental Procedures

Our stimuli consisted of 18 spoken target words, each of which was recorded as the final word in three different sentence contexts that differed in the extent to which they predicted the likelihood of the target word. In all cases the contexts were incomplete sentences that could be completed by the addition of a single word. The sentences were taken from Morton (1964) and were chosen to represent *High Context* (probabilities of response selection from .16 to .89) or *Low Context* sentences (probability of response from .02 to .14). Morton determined these probabilities using a standard *cloze* procedure: One hundred young adults were given each of the sentences, with the final word missing, and were asked to complete the sentence with what to them would be the most likely final word. The percentage of people giving the target word was expressed as the transitional probability of the target word in that sentence context. For example, for the sentence, "Coming in he took off his _____," 32 of the 100 people gave *coat* (i.e., $p = .32$; High Context for *coat*), and 14 out of the 100 gave *shoes* (i.e., $p = .14$; Low Context for *shoes*). Sentences were constructed in which each of the 18 words was preceded by a High Context sentence in one case and by a Low Context sentence in another (e.g., for *shoes* the High Context sentence was, "She cleaned the dirt from her _____," which had a response probability of $p = .44$ for *shoes*. This same sentence was used as the Low Context sentence for *dress*, $p = .06$).

In a final *No Context* condition, each of the 18 words was preceded by the carrier sentence, "The word is _____." Thus, a total of 54 sentences plus target word combinations (18 words $\times$ 3 conditions) were available for the experiment.

The sentences and their target words were recorded in normal intonation by a female speaker of American English and were then digitized at a sampling rate of 22 kilohertz (kHz) and edited using the *Soundcap* speech editing system on a MacPlus microcomputer to produce a sequence of sentence presentations in which the gate size of the target word from word onset began at 50 msecs and then was increased by 50 msec increments until the *gate* included the full duration of the word. This was accomplished by selecting the desired gate sizes on a computer-generated visual display of the speech waveform of the sentence plus target word. Accuracy of selection of the target word onset for start of the gate duration was determined visually on the waveform and then verified by auditory monitoring. As the preparation of each presentation in the gating sequence was completed, it was transferred to standard cassette tape for preparation of individual participant tapes.

Each participant heard all 18 target words once only, 6 preceded by their High Context sentences, 6 preceded by their Low Context sentences, and 6 preceded by their No Context sentences. The sentence plus target combinations were counterbalanced across participants such that, by the end of the experiment, each target word was presented in each of its context conditions an equal number of times. The order of target words within conditions was varied between subjects. The stimuli were heard over good-quality binaural earphones at a comfortable listening level. Each word plus sentence frame was presented in successive presentations with word onset duration of the target word increased by 50 msec increments on each presentation. Presentations continued until the target word was correctly identified without the participant changing his or her answer on the next two successive presentations. After each presentation, participants were asked to say what they thought the gated word might be, and to rate their confidence on a 1 ("guess") to 5 ("absolutely certain") scale.

Our elderly participants were 18 volunteers from the community, 3 males and 15 females, with ages ranging from 61 to 82 ($M = 69.1$). The elderly group had a mean of 14.4 years of education ($SD = 2.1$), and a mean WAIS vocabulary score of 64.0 ($SD = 9.8$). The young participants were 18 university undergraduates, 7 males and 11 females, with ages ranging from 17 to 23 years ($M = 18.6$). The young group had a mean of 12.9 years of education ($SD = 1.5$), and a mean WAIS vocabulary score of 52.6 ($SD = 11.7$). Thus, as a group, the elderly participants had an average of one and a half more years of education, $t(34) = 2.54$, $p < .05$, and were superior to the young on WAIS vocabulary, $t(34) = 3.17$, $p < .01$.

Results of the Gating Study

Figure 16.3 shows the mean word-onset gate size (in msecs) at which words were correctly recognized by the young and the elderly participants in the three context conditions. Recognition was taken as the first presentation on which the person gave the correct target word and did not change that answer for the next two successive presentations. (Other measures of recognition thresholds or *isolation points* produce similar results at this level of analysis. For a discussion, see Cotton & Grosjean, 1984; Grosjean, 1980; Tyler, 1984.)

Consistent with prior literature, our words heard in context were, on average,

Figure 16.3
Mean Recognition Times (in milliseconds) for Young and Elderly Adults Hearing Gated Words Presented under No Context, Low Context, or High Context Conditions

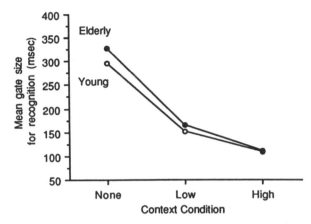

recognized well within the first 200 msecs of their onset, or when less than half their total word onset information was heard. Indeed, even out of context, the target words were on average recognized well within 60% of their onset (an average of 300 to 350 msecs of onset duration). These figures are numerically consistent with data from a variety of prior studies with young adults (e.g., Grosjean, 1980; 1985; Tyler, 1984; Wayland et al., 1989).

Our special focus in this study was, of course, on age effects that might appear on various aspects of this task. In our case, the effect of context was significant, $F(2,34) = 20.62$, $p < .001$, and these effects were similar for both young and elderly participants. As Figure 16.3 shows, the mean recognition points for the young and the elderly participants were very close. The effect of age was significant, $F(1,17) = 4.39$, $p < .05$, but we can see it was a very small one in absolute terms. Indeed, the mean difference in recognition times between the young and elderly participants across all data points was only on the order of 16 msecs. Although Figure 16.3 might appear to suggest the hint of an age difference increasing with decreasing context, there was no significant Age × Context interaction, $F(2,34) = 1.27$, $n.s.$

We thus have the sort of case we described earlier, one in which young and elderly adults appear roughly equivalent on surface performance: in this case, word recognition with varying degrees of context. Were one to consider these data alone, one might reasonably conclude that there are no qualitative (and virtually no quantitative) differences in young and elderly participants' performance for the recognition of gated words under these conditions. The only noticeable difference at this level of analysis was that the young participants tended to be more confident of their correct recognition judgments than were the elderly in the High Context condition ($p < .01$). The two age groups did not differ in their confidence ratings at either the Low Context or No Context conditions.

In an attempt to get below the surface of simply counting correct word responses, we examined participants' responses over the first four gated presentations in terms of whether the responses matched the first sound of the target word, regardless of whether the full word was correct or not. In the No Context condition, the elderly participants were far poorer than the young in identifying the words' initial phonemes over the first 50 to 150 msecs of word onset. For example, at the first gate, an average of approximately 90% of the young participants' responses matched the first sound of the target word, as contrasted with just over 65% for the elderly. Although the elderly in the No Context condition could not get the first phoneme as quickly as the young, they did "catch up," albeit with the necessity of a larger temporal gate than needed by the young. By the fourth gate, the level of first phoneme identifications for the elderly was very close to that of the young.

Note that in these cases there were no sentence contexts to hint at the potential identity of the target words. The increase in first phoneme identification over gate size in the No Context condition for both the young and the elderly participants thus had to be due to participants taking advantage of increasing amounts of within-word acoustic/phonetic context, such as information about first phoneme identity being carried by the acoustic coloring of following sounds (i.e., coarticulation), and sound juxtaposition frequencies in common English words. The point we wish to make is that to say that participants use linguistic context should not imply conscious knowledge of this use, nor the ability to articulate the nature of what is being used. Coarticulation, for example, operates at a very low automatic level of speech recognition, well beyond control by conscious intervention (see Liberman & Mattingly, 1989, for a discussion).

When the linguistic context of the sentence frames preceded the target words, however, these underlying differences in processing capability at the phonological level became almost totally obscured. In the case of the Low Context condition, the age difference in the accuracy of first sound matches at the early gates was smaller than in the No Context condition, and there was virtually no age effect at all at High Context. Thus, even though the young and the elderly participants showed very similar levels of performance in whole word identifications, this similarity on surface-level performance arose from use of a very different ratio of bottom-up versus top-down information sources in input processing (Wingfield et al., in press).

How much of the context effect of the sentence frames was due to linguistic-semantic constraints at the lexical level, and how much to potential differences in coarticulation cues imposed by word-final endings of the sentence frames as they preceded the target words? (For example, the No Context sentence frames always ended with the word "is".) Both would represent top-down information sources, albeit at different levels of context. The differences noted between the

Low Context and High Context conditions occurred in the presence of a variety of frame endings, and hence, word-final sounds preceding the target words. The general literature on context effects in word recognition at the sentence level would also support the presumption that coarticulation cues played a subsidiary role to linguistic context under the experimental conditions we were investigating in this study (Grosjean, 1980, 1985; Marslen-Wilson & Zwitserlood, 1989; Morton, 1964; Pollack & Pickett, 1964; Tyler, 1984).

Implications of Gating

For both young and elderly adults, most of the information necessary for word recognition is available when only the first half of the word has been heard. In the study we have just described, even with no sentence context to constrain the possibilities, participants were able to recognize words after hearing only 50 to 60% of word onset information. With low and high levels of sentence context, participants required only 20 to 30% of word onset information for correct recognition.

Our analysis of participants' prerecognition responses, especially in the No Context condition, did suggest that less bottom-up information was available to the elderly listeners in the gating task. Because word recognition in meaningful sentence contexts reflects the combined activity of both top-down and bottom-up sources, such age-related processing differences can be obscured by gross performance measures. No less important, we have been able to demonstrate the use of top-down sources to compensate for fragility in bottom-up information to occur spontaneously at multiple levels of language processing in an equally natural and automatic way.

NATURAL LANGUAGE PROCESSING AS AN EXPERT SYSTEM: CONCLUSIONS

What began as one question has now turned into two. Our first question was how both young and elderly adults handle so well the extraordinary demands of natural-language processing, even under conditions that should stress the processing system beyond its capability. We described such performance as reflecting a Principle of Graceful Overload, accounting for minimal declines under high load conditions by showing how bottom-up processing can be supplemented by top-down, knowledge-driven sources derived from linguistic context. We showed this to be true for sentence recall at rapid speech rates, and for recognition of individual words before their full acoustic duration had been completed.

This brings us to the second question. Why were our participants, both young and elderly, so adept at using linguistic context to enhance their performance? Was this a skill that was learned, and if so, were the elderly adults better at using context in speech processing because they had been doing this longer than the young? To set the stage for the argument, one can reject the notion that there is some point at which auditory processing passes some threshold of difficulty and linguistic context becomes useful. On the contrary, contextual interaction with bottom-up processing is fundamental to on-line spoken-language analysis. It is, to put it bluntly, the way the system works. Let us cite several examples to illustrate this position.

Our first hint that this must be so comes from early arguments that there are severe limits to the temporal resolving power of the ear. Such limits would, in fact, make it impossible to listen to speech on a phoneme-by-phoneme basis (Liberman et al., 1967). Liberman and his colleagues began by considering a speech rate of 400 wpm which, as we know, can be followed by listeners, albeit with some difficulty. A speech rate of 400 wpm, with an average of 4 to 5 phonemes per English word, would correspond to an input rate of 30 phonemes per second. However, data from research in auditory psychophysics would suggest that 30 phonemes per second would far over-reach the temporal resolving power of the ear. Not only would discrete acoustic events at this rate merge into "an unanalyzable buzz," but even a rate of 15 phonemes per second (a fast-normal rate of 200 wpm) would tax the temporal resolving power of the auditory mechanism beyond any hope of adequate function. To Liberman and his colleagues, this was clear evidence that phonemes cannot be heard as a string of discrete acoustic events.

If each and every phoneme cannot be perceived in running speech, it follows that the acoustic and linguistic surround must be used to correct or insert misheard or totally missed segments. The principle here is one of perceptual redintegration, the reconstruction of missing elements from context.

Our second example of inherent context-dependency in speech comes from the fact that there are few acoustic invariants of the sort that would make completely veridical bottom-up processing useful, even if it were possible. For example, spectral analyses of speech sounds show that the same sound (e.g., /du/) will show wide variability in how it is uttered from one time to the next in different words within a single conversation. This is true even though perceptually the sound remains /du/ each time it is heard. The other side of this coin is that a single sound will be perceived quite differently depending on its phonemic environment. For example, the same 15-msec noise burst at 1,440 hertz (Hz) preceding different sounds through the vowel range can be heard as /p/ before /i/, /k/ before /a/, and again as /p/ before /u/. That is, even at the level of phoneme recognition, speech perception is heavily context-dependent (Liberman et al., 1967).

This use of context is clearly not a conscious process. It requires no volition and no conscious attention; moreover we do not even have the ability to refrain from doing it, even if one wanted to. Liberman and Mattingly (1989) refer to the use of context at this level as *precognitive*, in the sense that context plays its part without cognitive mediation. By contrast, we also recognize that context can be utilized consciously, as when one is confronted by a noisy telephone line and consciously asks oneself what a particular static-masked word might have been (or much as one uses volitional inference to reconstruct missing words from a telegraphic message such as "AIRPORT CLOSED SNOW. TAKING TRAIN.").

Whatever the level of analysis or degree of conscious control, our examples suggest that top-down interaction with sensory input is an integral part of normal-language processing. It thus seems reasonable to propose that as one gets older and the richness of bottom-up information decreases, one need not do anything that one has not been doing all one's life. The basic principles of the interactive process remain the same. What gradually changes is the ratio of top-down to bottom-up information that has to be integrated in the perceptual-cognitive mix.

We have followed Liberman and Mattingly (1989) in referring to context at the phoneme level as precognitive. At what levels do cognitive operations come into play? Is syntactic parsing, like phonetic analysis, part of a distinct precognitive module? What of the detection of semantic propositions, or the construction of coherence hierarchies within a message structure? We recognize that these are serious questions, even though we will resist speculation here about the point or points at which language processing first becomes accessible to cognitive computation, whether conscious or otherwise. Current efforts to use neurophysiological assays such as localized cerebral blood flow to explore attentional demands across tasks might ultimately prove useful (cf. Posner, Sandson, Dhawan, & Shulman, 1989).

Indeed, Liberman and Mattingly (1989) argued that even if a processing module is precognitive, one should not presume that it could not adjust its internal processes and representations to accommodate new acoustic inputs. As such, even such a precognitive module could be said to "learn." In the context of normal aging, such "new" acoustic inputs could be represented by sensory changes through the life course. At some levels, conscious utilization of top-down sources can surely be learned. We have also shown elsewhere that scores in general verbal ability, such as vocabulary scores, can affect performance levels for elderly adults confronted by high-load listening conditions (Stine et al., 1986).

These questions, however, are ones of modulating what we have referred to as an expert system in nature; in this case, that of spoken-language processing. The central position is that as adults age and certain processes become less effective, a naturally evolved processing system is already in place to utilize multiple sources of information. We believe that it is this preexisting system that accounts for the seemingly natural ease with which top-down contributions change, not in kind but in ratio, to produce the skilled performance levels we observe.

REFERENCES

Attneave, F. (1959). *Applications of information theory to psychology*. New York: Holt-Dryden.

Barr, R. A. (1988; August). *Toward naturalism*? Paper presented to the Symposium on New Developments in Cognitive Aging, Annual Meeting of the American Psychological Association, Atlanta.

Bartlett, F. C. (1932). *Remembering: A study in experimental and social psychology.* Cambridge: Cambridge University Press.

Birren, J. E., & Morrison, D. F. (1961). Analysis of the WAIS subtests in relation to age and education. *Journal of Gerontology, 16*, 363–369.

Caplan, D., Vanier, M., & Baker, C. (1986). A case study of reproduction aphasia: II. Sentence comprehension. *Cognitive Neuropsychology, 3*, 129–146.

Clark, H. H., & Clark, E. V. (1977). *The psychology of language.* New York: Harcourt, Brace, Jovanovich.

Cohen, G. (1981). Inferential reasoning in old age. *Cognition, 9*, 59–72.

Cohen, G., & Faulkner, D. (1983). Word recognition: Age differences in contextual facilitation effects. *British Journal of Psychology, 74*, 239–251.

Cohen, G., & Faulkner, D. (1986). Does "elderspeak" work? The effect of intonation and stress on comprehension and recall of spoken discourse in old age. *Language and Communication, 6*, 91–98.

Cole, R. A., & Jakimik, J. (1980). A model of speech perception. In R. A. Cole (Ed.), *Perception and production of fluent speech* (pp. 133–163). Hillsdale, NJ: Erlbaum.

Corso, J. F. (1984). Auditory processing and aging: Significant problems for research. *Experimental Aging Research, 10*, 171–174.

Cotton, S., & Grosjean, F. (1984). The gating paradigm: A comparison of successive and individual presentation formats. *Perception and Psychophysics, 35*, 41–48.

Craik, F. I. M., & Rabinowitz, J. C. (1984). Age differences in the acquisition and use of verbal information. In H. Bouma & D. G. Bouwhuis (Eds.), *Attention and performance X* (pp. 471–499). New York: Academic.

Dell, G. S. (1986). A spreading-activation theory of retrieval in sentence production. *Psychological Review, 93*, 283–321.

Denney, N. W. (1984). A model of cognitive development across the life span. *Developmental Review, 4*, 171–191.

Ellis, A. W. (1985). The production of spoken words: A cognitive neuropsychological perspective. In A. W. Ellis (Ed.) *Progress in the psychology of language* (Vol. 2, pp. 107–145). Hillsdale, NJ: Erlbaum.

Foulke, E. (1971). The perception of time-compressed speech. In D. Horton & J. Jenkins (Eds.), *The perception of language* (pp. 79–107). Columbus, OH: Merrill.

Fozard, J. L. (1980). The time for remembering. In L. W. Poon (Ed.), *Aging in the 1980s* (pp. 273–290). Washington, DC: American Psychological Association

Grosjean, F. (1980). Spoken word recognition processes and the gating paradigm. *Perception and Psychophysics, 28*, 267–283.

Grosjean, F. (1985). The recognition of words after their acoustic offset: Evidence and implications. *Perception and Psychophysics, 38*, 299–310.

Hunnicutt, S. (1985). Intelligibility versus redundancy—Conditions of dependency. *Language and Speech, 28*, 47–56.

Kahneman, D. (1973). *Attention and effort.* Englewood Cliffs, NJ: Prentice-Hall.

Kemper, S. (1987). Syntactic complexity and elderly adults' prose recall. *Experimental Aging Research, 13*, 47–52.

Kinsbourne, M. (1973). Age effects on letter span related to rate and sequential dependency. *Journal of Gerontology, 28*, 317–319.

Kintsch, W. (1988). The role of knowledge in discourse comprehension: A construction-integration model. *Psychological Review*, *95*, 163–182.

Klatzky, R. L. (1988). Theories of information processing and theories of aging. In L. L. Light & D. M. Burke (Eds.), *Language, memory, and aging* (pp. 1–16). New York: Cambridge University Press.

Liberman, A. M., Cooper, F. S., Shankweiler, D. P., & Studdert-Kennedy, M. (1967). Perception of the speech code. *Psychological Review*, *74*, 431–461.

Liberman, A. M., & Mattingly, I. G. (1989). A specialization for speech perception. *Science*, *243*, 489–494.

Madden, D. J. (1988). Adult age differences in the effects of sentence context and stimulus degradation during visual word recognition. *Psychology and Aging*, *3*, 167–172.

Marks, L. E., & Miller, G. A. (1964). The role of semantic and syntactic constraints in the memorization of English sentences. *Journal of Verbal Learning and Verbal Behavior*, *3*, 1–5.

Marslen-Wilson, W. D. (1984). Function and process in spoken word recognition. In H. Bouma & D. G. Bouwhuis (Eds.), *Attention and performance* (Vol. 10, pp. 125–150). Hillsdale, NJ: Erlbaum.

Marslen-Wilson, W. D. (1987). Functional parallelism in spoken word recognition. *Cognition*, *25*, 71–102.

Marslen-Wilson, W. D., & Welsh, A. (1978). Processing interactions and lexical access during word recognition in continuous speech. *Cognitive Psychology*, *10*, 29–63.

Marslen-Wilson, W. D., & Zwitserlood, P. (1989). Accessing spoken words: The importance of word onsets. *Journal of Experimental Psychology: Human Perception and Performance*, *15*, 576–585.

Martin, R. C. (1987). Articulatory and phonological deficits in short-term memory and their relation to syntactic processing. *Brain and Language*, *32*, 159–192.

Meyer, B.J.F., & Rice, G. E. (1981). Information recalled from prose by young, middle, and old adult readers. *Experimental Aging Research*, *7*, 253–268.

Morris, R. G., Gick, M. L., & Craik, F.I.M. (1988). Processing resources and age differences in working memory. *Memory and Cognition*, *16*, 362–366.

Monsell, S. (1984). Components of working memory underlying verbal skills: A "distributed capacities" view. In H. Bouma & D. G. Bouwhuis (Eds.), *Attention and performance* (Vol. 10, pp 327–350). Hillsdale, NJ: Erlbaum.

Morton, J. (1964). The effects of context on visual duration threshold for words. *British Journal of Psychology*, *55*, 165–180.

Nooteboom, S. G., & Doodeman, G.J.N. (1984). Speech quality and the gating paradigm. In M.P.R. van den Broeke & A. Cohen (Eds.), *Proceedings of the Tenth International Congress of Phonetic Sciences* (pp. 481–485). Dordrecht: Foris.

Norman, D. A., & Bobrow, D. G. (1975). On data-limited and resource-limited processes. *Cognitive Psychology*, *7*, 44–64.

Pollack, I., & Pickett, J. M. (1964). Intelligibility of excerpts from fluent speech: Auditory versus structural context. *Journal of Verbal Learning and Verbal Behavior*, *3*, 79–84.

Posner, M. I., Sandson, J., Dhawan, M., & Shulman, G. L. (1989). Is word recognition automatic? A cognitive-anatomical approach. *Journal of Cognitive Neuroscience*, *1*, 50–60.

Rybash, J. M., Hoyer, W. J., & Roodin, P. A. (1986). *Adult cognition and aging:*

Developmental changes in processing, knowing and thinking. New York: Pergamon.

Salasoo, A., & Pisoni, D. (1985). Interaction of knowledge sources in spoken word identification. *Journal of Memory and Language, 24*, 210–231.

Salthouse, T. A. (1982). *Adult cognition: An experimental psychology of aging.* New York: Springer-Verlag.

Salthouse, T. A. (1984). Effects of age and skill in typing. *Journal of Experimental Psychology, 113*, 345–371.

Schneider, W., & Detweiler, M. (1987). A connectionist/control architecture for working memory. In G. H. Bower (Ed.), *The psychology of learning and motivation: Advances in research and theory* (Vol. 21, pp. 53–119). New York: Academic.

Smith, A. D. (1980). Age differences in encoding, storage, and retrieval. In L. W. Poon, J. L. Fozard, L. S. Cermak, D. Arenberg, & L. W. Thompson (Eds.), *New directions in memory and aging: Proceedings of the George A. Talland Memorial Conference* (pp. 23–45). Hillsdale, NJ: Erlbaum.

Stemberger, J. P. (1985). An interactive model of language production. In A. W. Ellis (Ed.), *Progress in the psychology of language* (Vol. 1, pp. 142–186). Hillsdale, NJ: Erlbaum.

Stine, E.A.L., & Wingfield A. (1987). Process and strategy in memory for speech among younger and older adults. *Psychology and Aging, 2*, 272–279.

Stine, E.A.L., & Wingfield, A. (1990). The assessment of qualitative age differences in discourse memory. In T. M. Hess (Ed.), *Aging and cognition: Knowledge organization and utilization* (pp. 33–92). Amsterdam: North Holland.

Stine, E.A.L., Wingfield, A., & Myers, S. (1990). Age differences in processing information from television news: The effects of bisensory augmentation. *Journal of Gerontology: Psychological Sciences, 45*, P1–8.

Stine, E.A.L., Wingfield, A., & Poon, L. W. (1986). How much and how fast: Rapid processing of spoken language in later adulthood. *Psychology and Aging, 1*, 303–311.

Tyler, L. K. (1984). The structure of the initial cohort: Evidence from gating. *Perception and Psychophysics, 36*, 417–427.

Tyler, L. K., & Wessels, J. (1985). Is gating an on-line task? Evidence from naming latency data. *Perception and Psychophysics, 38*, 217–222.

van Dijk, T. A., & Kintsch, W. (1983). *Strategies of discourse comprehension.* New York: Academic.

Wayland, S. C., Wingfield, A., & Goodglass, H. (1989). Recognition of isolated words: The dynamics of cohort reduction. *Applied Psycholinguistics, 10*, 175–187.

Wingfield, A., Aberdeen, J. S., & Stine, E. A. L. (in press). Word onset gating and linguistic context in spoken word recognition by young and elderly adults. *Journal of Gerontology: Psychological Sciences.*

Wingfield, A., & Butterworth, B. (1984). Running memory for sentences and parts of sentences: Syntactic parsing as a control function in working memory. In H. Bouma & D. G. Bouwhuis (Eds.), *Attention and performance* (Vol. 10, pp. 351–363). London: Erlbaum.

Wingfield, A., & Byrnes, D. L. (1981). *The psychology of human memory.* New York: Academic.

Wingfield, A., Lahar, C. J., & Stine, E.A.L. (1989). Age and decision strategies in running memory for speech: Effects of prosody and linguistic structure. *Journal of Gerontology: Psychological Sciences, 44*, P106–113.

Wingfield, A., Poon, L. W., Lombardi, L., & Lowe, D. (1985). Speed of processing in normal aging: Effects of speech rate, linguistic structure, and processing time. *Journal of Gerontology, 40,* 579–585.

Wingfield, A., Stine, E.A.L., Lahar, C. J., & Aberdeen, J. S. (1988). Does the capacity of working memory change with age? *Experimental Aging Research, 14,* 103–107.

Wingfield, A., & Wayland, S. C. (1988). Object-naming in aphasia: Word-initial phonology and response activation. *Aphasiology, 2,* 423–426.

Zacks, R. T., & Hasher, L. (1988). Capacity theory and the processing of inferences. In L. L. Light & D. M. Burke (Eds.), *Language, memory, and aging* (pp. 154–170). New York: Cambridge University Press.

Author Index

Subject Index

About the Editors and Contributors

JAN D. SINNOTT, Professor of Psychology and Director of the Center for Study of Adult Development and Aging at Towson State University at Baltimore, has been doing cognitive aging research in cooperation with the National Institute on Aging (National Institutes of Health) since 1980 and is a practicing clinician. She is the author of some 70 publications, most in the area of problem solving and single- and multiperson cognition. She has been conducting research in this field since 1972 and was one of the first to extend Piaget's theory to everyday problem solving. She is currently doing experimental cognitive research integrating information-processing and artificial intelligence approaches with general systems theory and Piagetian theory.

JOHN C. CAVANAUGH is Professor of Psychology at Bowling Green State University and is Director of the Institute for Psychological Research and Application. He is also the Director for Behavioral Research at the Northwest Ohio Dementia and Memory Center at the Medical College of Ohio in Toledo. His primary research interests are cognitive aging in everyday life, self-evaluations of cognition, cooperative cognition, and stress and coping processes in caregivers of Alzheimer's disease patients. He is the author of *Adult Development and Aging*.

JUDITH L. ALLEN is Assistant Professor of Psychology at Drake University. Her publications include "Attributions and attribution-behavior relations: The effect of level of cognitive development," "Anxiety, cognitive development, and correspondence: Attribution and behavior prescriptions" and "Specificity of empathy-induced helping: Evidence for altruistic motivation." She has also taught at Colgate University.

JUDITH ARMSTRONG is Associate Professor of Psychology at Towson State University. Her research on multiple personality disorder is conducted at the Sheppard and Enoch Pratt Hospital, where she is Director of the Dissociative Disorder Assessment Program and Associate Director of the Dissociative Disorder Treatment Program. She has published in the areas of multiple personality disorder, eating disorder and psychological assessment, and is assistant editor of the *Journal of Nervous and Mental Disease*.

JULIE R. BRANNAN is an Associate in Neurobiology and Neurology at the Mount Sinai Medical School of the City University of New York. She is the editor of *Applications of Parallel Processing in Vision*, part of the *Advances in Psychology* series. Her publications include many articles in the areas of vision, visual development, and reading.

CAMERON J. CAMP's research has focused on cognitive aging in real-world settings. He is currently engaged in memory intervention research in Alzheimer's disease populations.

STANLEY H. COHEN is a Professor and Associate Chairperson in the Department of Psychology at West Virginia University. His research interests include evaluation of human service programs for the elderly, social support networks, and computer methods in psychology. He teaches social psychology, quasi-experimental research design, and multivariate analysis.

JEFFREY W. ELIAS is Professor, Associate Chair, and Director of Experimental Psychology Graduate Programs in the Department of Psychology at Texas Tech University. Publications include *Biological and Health Influences on Aging*; *Cognitive Change in Parkinson's Disease*; and *Cardiovascular Disease, Aging, and Behavior*. He serves as the Associate Editor for the journal *Experimental Aging Research*, and publishes regularly in the areas of cognitive development and psychobiology.

MERRILL F. ELIAS is Professor of Psychology at the University of Maine and Allied Scientist at Eastern Maine Medical Center. He is editor and founder of *Experimental Aging Research* and executive editor and cofounder of *Gerodontology*.

P. K. ELIAS is President of Beech Hill Enterprises Inc. and a Research Associate in the Department of Psychology at the University of Maine. She is managing editor of *Experimental Aging Research*.

RONALD R. IRWIN is a doctoral candidate in the developmental area of the Psychology Department at York University, where he is currently finishing his dissertation on intellectual development and writing skills. He has published a previous chapter in Commons, Sinnott, Richards, and Armon's *Adult Development I* (Praeger, 1989). His research interests include cognitive development, composition and rhetoric, and computer-assisted instruction. He teaches at York University's Computer-Assisted Writing Centre, where he is also conducting his research.

LYNN JOHNSON is Director of the Office of Research Administration at Towson State University and has worked in university research administration for eight years. She has also worked with international development projects for ten years, as in-country field staff, training consultant, and headquarters' management personnel. She has been a television producer/director for fourteen years, for three commercial and two public television stations, two universities, and three development projects.

DIANE M. LEE is Assistant Professor of Educational Psychology at the University of Maryland, Baltimore County. Her current interests include investigation of relativistic operations in the study of teachers' everyday problem posing and problem solving, in the study of collaboration as master teachers responsible for teaching science work with expert scientists, and in the study of expert and novice teachers.

JOHN A. MEACHAM is Professor of Psychology and Associate Vice Provost for Undergraduate Education at State University of New York at Buffalo. He has also been a member of the Center for the Study of Youth Development at Catholic University of America. He was editor of *Human Development* from 1978 to 1987 and is currently on the editorial board of *New Ideas in Psychology* and the president-elect of the Jean Piaget Society: Society for the Study of Knowledge and Development.

DENNIS R. PAPINI is Associate Professor of Psychology and Director of the graduate training program in experimental psychology at Western Illinois University. He is editor of the Society for Research in Adolescence newsletter and the author of numerous journal articles and book chapters dealing with family relations during adolescence.

LESLEE K. POLLINA is a member of the University of Pittsburgh at Johnstown and is conducting doctoral research on the effects of age, working memory, and problem type on problem-solving performance.

JAMES M. PUCKETT, now at West Virginia University, is an active researcher of several aspects of cognitive aging, including working memory, automatic processing, and everyday problem solving. He is the author or co-author of thirty-five presentations and articles on cognitive aging.

JANE L. RANKIN is Associate Professor and Chair of the department of psychology at Drake University and former director of the Human Aging Program there. Her publications include "Adult age differences in memory elaboration" and "Adult age differences in memory: Effects of distinctive and common encodings." She serves on the editorial board of Educational Gerontology and was previously a Visiting Assistant Professor at the University of Missouri—Columbia.

HAYNE W. REESE is editor of the annual publication *Advances in Child Development and Behavior* and of the *Journal of Experimental Child Psychology*, and a member of the editorial boards of five other journals. He is author or coauthor of 32 books and over 90 published articles.

RICKARD A. SEBBY is Associate Professor of Psychology at Southeast Missouri State University. He has also taught at the University of Nebraska—Kearney. His publications include journal articles on adult cognition and family relationships.

ELIZABETH A. L. STINE is Assistant Professor in the Department of Psychology and is affiliated with the Institute of Life-Span Studies at the University of Kansas. Her publications include several journal articles and book chapters considering the effects of aging on memory and language processing. Her research is funded by a FIRST Award from the National Institute on Aging. She has conducted research and taught at Brandeis University and is on the editorial board of *Psychology and Aging*.

FABIENNE TANON is a psychologist specializing in cross-cultural psychology.

ARTHUR WINGFIELD is Professor of Psychology at Brandeis University. He is an affiliate member of the Aphasia Research Center at the Boston V.A. Hospital and an Adjunct Research Professor of Neurology (Neuropsychology) at the Boston University School of Medicine. His research is funded by a MERIT Award from the National Institute on Aging. His publications include two textbooks, *Human Learning and Memory* and *The Psychology of Human Memory* (with D. L. Byrnes), as well as numerous articles on cognitive aging in scholarly journals.